Political Allegory in Late Medieval England

Also by Ann W. Astell—

Chaucer and the Universe of Learning
Job, Boethius, and Epic Truth
The Song of Songs in the Middle Ages

POLITICAL ALLEGORY *in* LATE MEDIEVAL ENGLAND

Ann W. Astell

Cornell University Press

ITHACA AND LONDON

First published 1999 by Cornell University Press

Printed in the United States of America

Cornell University Press strives to use environmentally responsible suppliers and materials to the fullest extent possible in the publishing of its books. Such materials include vegetable-based, low-VOC inks and acid-free papers that are recycled, totally chlorine-free, or partly composed of nonwood fibers.

Library of Congress Cataloging-in-Publication Data

Astell, Ann W.
Political allegory in late medieval England / Ann W. Astell.
p.   cm.
Includes bibliographical references (p.   ) and index.
ISBN 0-8014-3560-9 (cloth : alk. paper)
1. English literature—Middle English, 1100–1500—History and criticism.   2. Political poetry, English (Middle)—History and criticism.   3. Politics and literature—Great Britain—History—To 1500.   4. Great Britain—Politics and government—1154–1399.
5. Great Britain—Politics and government—1399–1485.   6. Invention (Rhetoric)
7. Rhetoric, Medieval.   8. Allegory.   I. Title.
PR275.P64A68   1999
821'.109358—dc21   98-42272

Cloth printing   10   9   8   7   6   5   4   3   2   1

In Memoriam

Jerome Taylor

(1918–1996)

for rhetoric and poetics

and James Berlin

(1942–1994)

for rhetoric, poetics, and politics

Procursus igitur civitatis Dei
ubi pervenit ad regum tempora . . . dedit figuram,
re gesta significans atque praenuntians . . .
de rerum mutatione futurarum.

Saint Augustine

Contents

Preface

In many ways this book has taken me by surprise. It began with a thrill of discovery in the summer of 1996, when I happened to be reading English chronicles alongside *Sir Gawain and the Green Knight* and noticed connections between and among them that I had never imagined possible. In other ways, however, this book is neither surprising nor recent in its origins. Rather, it brings to a certain culmination years of sustained research and reflection on medieval allegory—in particular, on the ways in which biblical hermeneutics and allegorical interpretations of classical authors affected vernacular composition.

Several factors served to inspire me for this work. I recall with gratitude, for instance, a particular session I attended at the 1996 International Medieval Congress in Kalamazoo, Michigan. David Aers, Jim Rhodes, and Frank Grady delivered "historicizing" papers that excited me greatly. Since then I have corresponded occasionally with each of them, and the exchange has been stimulating for me.

In the fall of 1996 I was fortunate to be able to teach a graduate seminar on medieval rhetoric and poetics. During that time I was able to study theories of rhetorical invention in the supportive atmosphere generated by a small group of zealous students: Alison Baker, Margaret Dick, Holly McBee, Margaret Reimer, and Thomas Wright. To them I owe heartfelt gratitude.

For the 1997 International Medieval Congress I organized three sessions on rhetoric and poetics in loving memory of one of my teachers, Jerome Taylor. This book, which is dedicated to him, reflects in part the atmosphere of those sessions. I wish, therefore, to thank all of the participants: Mary J. Carruthers, Tom Clemens, Rita Copeland, Jody Enders, Dolores

Warwick Frese, Robin Hass, Ernst Ralf Hintz, Douglas Kelly, Robert L. Kindrick, Colleen Page, Margaret Reimer, and Marjorie Curry Woods.

As I worked on this book, I benefited greatly from conversations with my colleague Thomas Ohlgren, who also kindly read Chapters 2 and 5. Another friend and colleague, Charles S. Ross, read a version of Chapter 1. Shaun F. D. Hughes, Ingeborg Hinderschiedt, and other faculty members in Medieval Studies at Purdue University responded in helpful and encouraging ways to presentations that I gave as part of the brown-bag lunch series. For their interest, insights, and moral support I am truly grateful.

My particular thanks go also to Robert Blanch, who read and commented on Chapter 5, and who encouraged me greatly at a time when another, anonymous reader deemed the essay "too wild." I also thank Lisa Kiser and the anonymous *Studies in the Age of Chaucer* readers who commented on an early version of Chapter 3. Among readers of this work, however, Anthony Galloway has surely earned the greatest share of my gratitude. His detailed report was a reliable guide for me in the revision process, and the book is undoubtedly vastly improved because of the suggestions he made and the directives he gave.

As always, Bernhard Kendler has been the most wonderful of executive editors. Amanda Heller copyedited and Carol Betsch and other staff members at Cornell University Press helped to guide the book into print with expert care and attentiveness to detail.

On a more personal note, I wish to express my gratitude in a hopelessly inadequate way to the teachers who have guided me; to those close friends and family members whose love sustains me; to the Schoenstatt Sisters of Mary, whose faith and sense of calling uphold mine; and to God, from whom all good things come.

I have dedicated this book to the memory of two dear departed ones, Jerome Taylor and James Berlin. I have read and reread Jerry's translation of Hugh of St. Victor's *Didascalicon*. It was under his tutelage that I first read many of the Middle English works that I discuss in this book. Most of the books in my library were a gift to me from him after he had retired, when it was no longer possible for him to read and write and do the scholarly work that had occupied him for most of his long, rich life. When I open this volume or that, I am often moved to see his minuscule handwriting on a page, making some precise observation with the customary meticulous care of a great scholar.

James Berlin, a beloved colleague of mine at Purdue University, had a much shorter life and no time for gradual leave-taking. He died suddenly, unexpectedly, while he was literally "on the run" and at the height of a pioneering, scholarly career in rhetoric, composition, and cultural studies. From the beginning, Jim supported my teaching of medieval rhetoric within the department, and I like to think that this book would please him.

Jerry and Jim never met each other during their earthly lives, but their names are conjoined in the dedication of this book. May it somehow continue the work that each of them began.

ANN W. ASTELL

West Lafayette, Indiana

Abbreviations

CCSL	Corpus Christianorum, Series Latina
EETS e.s.	Early English Text Society, extra series
EETS o.s.	Early English Text Society, original series
ELH	*English Literary History*
ELN	*English Language Notes*
JEGP	*Journal of English and Germanic Philology*
MLR	*Modern Language Review*
MP	*Modern Philology*
PL	Patrologiae Cursus Completus, Series Latina. Ed. J. P. Migne. 221 vols. Paris, 1844–64.
PMLA	*Publications of the Modern Language Association*
PQ	*Philological Quarterly*
SAB	*South Atlantic Bulletin*
SAC	*Studies in the Age of Chaucer*
SP	*Studies in Philology*
YLS	*The Yearbook of Langland Studies*

Political Allegory in Late Medieval England

Introduction

Only through a process of historical recuperation can we recover some of [poetry's] power to move, persuade, and instruct.

David Wallace, *Chaucerian Polity*

In one of his most provocative critical pronouncements, C. S. Lewis explains why he consciously chose to "neglect entirely [the] political allegory" of Edmund Spenser's *Fairie Queene* in favor of its "moral or philosophical allegory":

> My qualifications as a historian are not such as would encourage me to unravel it; and my critical principles hardly encourage me to make the attempt. By his political allegory Spenser doubtless intended to give to his poem a certain topical attraction. Time never forgives such concessions to "the glittering of this present," and what acted as a bait to unpoetic readers for some decades has become a stumbling-block to poetic readers ever since. The contemporary allusions in *The Fairie Queene* are now of interest to the critic chiefly insofar as they explain how some bad passages came to be bad; but since this does not make them good . . . we shall not lose very much by ignoring the matter.[1]

At the present moment, when "historicizing" modes of criticism predominate in early modern and medieval studies, Lewis's remarks sound quaintly outrageous. They give expression, however, to problems that are still very much with us. Many critics who strongly disagree with Lewis's conclusions about the possibility of deciphering political allegory and the value of doing so nevertheless preserve and reinforce the binary categories he establishes. Lewis's sense that scholars of literature possess limited qualifications as historians is doubtless shared by self-aware "historicizing" critics who nonetheless endeavor to recover the specific political and cultural contexts within which literary works resonate. More important, the basic distinction Lewis makes between "unpoetic" and "poetic" readers defines the continuing polarity between the political and cultural concerns of (New) Historicists, on the one hand, and the aesthetic interests of formalists, on the other—a polarity that renews the age-old rivalry between the disciplines of rhetoric and poetics in an ever-shifting turf fight that is all the more intense because they share so much common ground.

When Lewis sets political allegory in opposition to moral and philosophical allegory, aligning the former with the "unpoetic" and the latter with the "poetic," he apparently does so on the basis of their respective temporal reference either to currently topical matters or to things eternal. He fails to honor their common allegorical status and its implications in theory and practice for the reciprocal processes of invention and composition by the poet and of discovery via decoding by the poet's intended audience. Indeed, in separating the moral and philosophical from the political, Lewis takes apart what the poet carefully joined together when he embedded both sorts of allegory in a single work as related parts of a holistic rhetoric that covertly referred to current topics and simultaneously commented on them from a moral perspective. He dismisses as irrelevant to us, as a latter-day audience, the role that the poet's own contemporary audiences played in co-determining the structure and meaning of his work—not only directly through their actual historical reception of it, but also indirectly through the poet's conscious manipulation of his material in the hope of anticipating and directing their responses.

In recent years medievalists have treated with far greater seriousness the dialogic relationship between the poet and his audiences (implied, intended, actual) in an attempt to situate late medieval writings within the historical circumstances in which they were produced, to which they gave expression, and which they helped to condition. In a much-cited 1978 article, Anne Middleton alluded to J. A. Burrow's 1971 book *Ricardian Poetry*, and noted that its title "implies a willingness to seek broad connections between social and literary history."[2] Since then Middleton herself has actively sought to make such connections, and her work on the "public poetry" of the reign of King Richard II has been of programmatic importance to a whole generation of historicizing critics, many of whose names appear in this book.

Middleton's major thesis entails the notion that practicing poets in late medieval England shared a guiding idea about the proper form and function of public poetry. Imbued with an "essentially high-minded secularism," they regarded the writing of poetry as "a mediating activity." As they saw it, poetry served "its highest function as a peacemaker and as an interpreter of the common world" at a period in English history when a rising middle class could attest to and urge the values of an emergent commonwealth.[3] More like "complaint" than "satire," this kind of "plain style" poetry is supposedly only very "rarely occasional or topical" and never addresses particular audiences to the exclusion of others. Instead it "speaks 'as if' to the entire community," acknowledging the heterogeneity of its makeup while keeping an equal distance from all its parties in order to forge their unity.[4]

According to Middleton, this poetic "common voice" first developed in the last quarter of the fourteenth century, largely through "the complex experiments of Langland and Gower."[5] David Lawton, whose work builds on Middleton's, sees this development as coming to its completion in the fifteenth century, a "dull" period that "authoritatively consolidates the public voice and role of English poetry." In Lawton's view, the "impressively homogeneous public voice of fifteenth-century poetry was engaged in . . . constructing a public sphere parallel to and connected with the structures of power" as a means to "create continuity and unity" and thus to compensate for instability "in the actual center of power."[6]

Whereas Lawton's study suggests that Middleton's thesis applies well to fifteenth-century texts, recent historicizing treatments of fourteenth-century writings have quietly called it into question. Middleton herself, in fact, suggests that she may be dating the advent of "public poetry" too early when she describes it as a fourteenth-century phenomenon. Distinguishing between "political poetry" and "public poetry," she notes, almost in passing, that "from 1400 on," poetry "of social criticism" acquired the generalized features characteristic of "public poetry," "whereas there is *no trace* of such self-conscious and principled restraint in earlier political poems, which tend to be *occasional or topical.*"[7]

Middleton's distinction between "public" and "political" poetry, like that between "public" and "audience," is problematic in itself, as is the denial of topicality. Stephen Justice, for example, uses Middleton's terminology, which distinguishes between the "public" formally addressed by the poet and the "audiences" who actually interpreted his work, frequently in self-interested ways contrary to the poet's presumed intent. Observing, however, that Gower clearly means "some" when he supposedly speaks for "all," Justice acknowledges in a footnote that "the notion of poetic vocation that I trace here looks more desperately and factionally motivated than the literature of public counsel [Middleton] describes."[8] Similarly, Judith Ferster cites Middleton's articles and adapts her terminology, declaring, "I want to define late medieval England as a context for public literature."[9] In doing so, however, she actually argues (against Middleton) that poetry written during the Ricardian period was frequently, albeit covertly, topical, and that the apparent silence on sensitive issues resulted less from an ideal of peacemaking than from a prudential recognition of "the dangers of critical speech" in a realm where "few can speak openly."[10]

Andrew Galloway has taken pains to defend Middleton's thesis of a "public" and "common" voice in *Piers Plowman*, arguing that Langland's evasive strategies "sought not so much to ignore or elide the gaps between different kinds of English intellectual culture as to speak simultaneously in their various tongues." He admits, however, that Langland's work dramatizes "social divisiveness" more than it forges unity, and that the B text in particular exhibits "an elitist or conspiratorial rhetoric of riddling" that is far from "plain" and "common" and that actually resonates with the enigmatic language that served to establish membership within revolutionary communities.[11]

The more enigmatic, indirect, and allegorical Langland and Gower appear to be, the less distant from Chaucer they seem. This critical trend marks another subtle but significant departure from Middleton's model. Although Middleton attributes a "peacemaking" voice to all three poets, she insists on a marked polarity between Langland and Gower, on the one hand, and Chaucer, on the other. In contrast to the plain style poets of complaint, Chaucer is said to have expressed the "common" values of "public poetry . . . only, as it were, in indirect discourse."[12] Following Middleton, Lee Patterson emphasizes the "ostentatious formalism" of Chaucer's writing and insists that his poetry characteristically "declined to engage the real world of late medieval England explicitly."[13] Justice, too, sets the "public," plain, rhetorical voice of Gower and Langland in contrast to the "cryptic cliquishness" and allegorical art of Chaucer, who wrote for a "coterie."[14]

There are, to be sure, real differences between and among the Ricardian poets, but we must not let them blind us to what characterizes them all as late medieval English writers. Langland, Gower, Chaucer, the *Gawain*-poet, and (to a lesser extent) Malory all practiced an allegorical art, partly as a result of their similar educational backgrounds and also because political pressures encouraged and indeed necessitated indirection in writing about matters of public concern. In this book I delineate enormously artful political allegories, many of them hitherto unnoticed, in their works. Common elements in the construction of these allegories point to a shared theory of allegorical composition and suggest a complex model of audience. That theory and model are, moreover, recoverable. Indeed, one may speak of a match between the practice of these writers (as discussed in Chapters 2–6) and the rhetorical theory that I trace later in this Introduction and in Chapter 1.

Because virtually no work has been done on the medieval theory of invention that governed the actual practice of composing allegories, we have thus far been unable to appreciate the rhetorical strategies implicit and effective in this poetry. Only when such a compositional theory becomes explicit do we find ourselves in a position where we can begin to address the questions of "audience" and "public." As I will argue throughout this book, late medieval English poets looked for a sophisticated response from their intended audiences, who were expected to recognize code names and puns, to notice omissions from and additions to familiar stories, to be able to conclude a whole from its parts and a genus from its species, and to re-assemble the material units that the poems presented in artificial order and at multiple narrative levels. They had to "discover" what the poet had "invented." This was a decidedly step-by-step, diachronic process that worked to delight, educate, and move the auditors.

Such high expectations imply that the poet took his intended audience into material account from the beginning of the inventive process. The au-dience was literally part of the "matter" he invented, and "moving" them rhetorically depended in part on the psychological efficacy of the chosen "arrangement" of selected units of narrative materials.

This model of rhetorical movement, process, and surprise is very differ-ent from the static model that Middleton constructs when she describes public poetry as "defined by a constant relation of speaker to audience within an ideally conceived worldly community, a relation which has be-come the poetic subject."[15] It implies instead topicality and occasionality; an almost constant change in the materials at hand, as they are manipulated by poet and audience alike; a variable distance in the rhetorical relation-ship between the poet and his audience as he leads them from one point to another; and ultimately a conversion in the auditor, who is moved to change his attitude, if not his actions.

Middleton is right when she ascribes a "peacemaking" role to late me-dieval English poets. They had, however, different views about what "peace-making" entailed, as a side glance at John Ball makes readily apparent. They also mediate between opposed parties in their poetry in ways very differ-ent from those Middleton describes. They do not hold up a mirror in the marketplace and call everyone equally, publicly, and generally into the commonwealth; rather, they help individuals and groups to see themselves in fictive form and thus to realize the concrete, personal, and communal consequences of taking revenge, showing mercy, or seeking forgiveness and reconciliation.

Middleton argues for a kind of interpellation (to borrow a technical term from Louis Althusser), whereby heterogeneous audiences were systemati-cally hailed in common as a "public" and thus gradually constituted as such.[16] The public poet, she says, speaks to "the entire community—as a whole and all at once, rather than severally. . . . [H]e occupies the whole field of moral vision spanned by the several views of all those who make up the 'commune.'"[17] The rhetorical addresses I hear in late medieval poetry are much more differentiated, particularized, appellant, polyvocal, and polysemous. Middleton imagines, as it were, a public in a single circle, each auditor equidistant from the poet in the middle, who addresses them all on the same level and tries to attach them all to one "common" center. My image is quite different, suggesting a tiered audience, arranged in multiple rings and addressed severally by the poet, who moves among them even as he seeks to move them.

Whereas such an intricate and intimate dialogism between poet and audience seems almost inconceivable to us, we are forced to conclude its operation in fourteenth-century England, both from the evidence of the texts themselves, when they are considered and compared as allegorical compositions, and from what we know and can surmise about the audiences that received them. As Ferster has indicated, the "criticism of . . . powerful governments and the hermeneutics of reading camouflaged texts . . . are closely related," for the rhetorical efficacy of the first depends on the second.[18] Although a wide audience was purposefully barred (at least superficially) from detecting the poet's veiled message, a small audience of intimates (the poet's immediately intended audince) was well equipped and encouraged to discover it. As Middleton herself has argued, even if the poet addressed a "public" at one level, at another level he had to count on his work being read and appropriated (perhaps misappropriated) by a heterogeneous set of small, localized audiences, in at least one of which he himself enjoyed membership. Such smaller audiences were in fact normative in the reception of medieval works, which, as Joyce Coleman has shown, were habitually read aloud to gatherings of listeners who constituted distinct textual and interpretive communities.[19] It was for these audiences that the fourteenth-century poet wrote.

The well-attested medieval practice of the reading aloud of poetry, including allegorical poetry, underscores its rhetorical potential and blurs a host of distinctions familiar to us: the opposition of public to private, of rhetoric to poetics, and, more specifically, of rhetoric to allegory. This and other aspects of poetic practice confirm what Harry Caplan has called the "merging of poetics and rhetoric" in "mediaeval poetical theory,"[20] not just (as is frequently asserted) with respect to arrangement and style, but also with regard to invention, memory, and delivery.[21] Indeed, the "merging of poetics and rhetoric" in late medieval England is so all-encompassing that we may speak not only of "political poetry" and "political allegory" but also (to borrow a phrase from Michael Murrin) of something that sounds like a contradiction in terms, namely, "allegorical rhetoric."[22]

Middleton's notion of "public poetry" rightly asserts a rhetorical poetics. Whereas Lawton finds support for Middleton's thesis in Terry Eagleton and Jürgen Habermas, Middleton herself turns to Cicero's *Republic* (*De re publica*) for an authoritative formulation of the medieval ideal of the commonwealth. Observing that the frequently used Middle English phrase "common profit" is "the usual translation of *res publica*," she first quotes from Cicero's work and then remarks, "The 'commune,' like the 'public' for Cicero, is not a theoretical or logical construct, derived from postulates about human nature; it is an association neither ideal nor fully voluntary, but evolved, historical, and customary, a creature of time, place, event, and language. It is society regarded experientially, an immanent rather than a transcendent notion." Thus "the 'I' of public poetry presents himself as, like his audience, a layman of good will, one worker among others, with a talent to be used for the common good."[23]

I quote from Middleton so extensively because the Ciceronian concept of speaker, audience, and republic on which her description of Ricardian "public poetry" depends is at once so revealing and so problematic. In attributing a "high-minded secularism" to late medieval Christian poets, Middleton implies that they had an unmediated access, and gave a simple acceptance, to a Ciceronian rhetoric and republicanism. I would argue, to the contrary, that while Cicero (106–43 B.C.) does appear anew in this poetry, he does so in a profoundly Augustinian guise. The poets could have known the *Republic* itself only very indirectly, as it was mediated to them through Saint Augustine's *City of God* and, in fragmentary form, through Macrobius' Neoplatonic *Commentary on the Dream of Scipio.* They knew Cicero's *De inventione* or (more probably) the *Rhetorica ad Herennium* that the Middle Ages attributed to him, but they received these works too within a Christian *paideia.* To a degree that is seldom recognized, Saint Augustine (A.D. 354–430) critiqued and revised Ciceronian rhetoric in the direction of poetics, even as he transmitted it to the Middle Ages. We must, therefore, look to an Augustine in dialogue with Cicero, not to Cicero alone, for an initial theoretical understanding of the rhetoric and poetics of late medieval poetry.

In the remainder of this chapter I support this claim by considering two sets of closely related texts by Cicero and Augustine. Cicero wrote his *Republic* in 54 B.C., shortly after his return from an exile that he had endured as a political consequence of the actions he had taken as consul against Catiline and his co-conspirators. Indeed, he alludes to the Catilinian conspiracy, which threatened the destruction of Rome, in the opening pages of the *Republic.* In the *City of God* (*De civitate Dei*), Augustine also refers to the conspiracy and quotes from both Cicero's orations against Catiline and his *Republic* in ways that establish the *City* as an explicit, extended response to Cicero's work. In A.D. 427, the year after Augustine completed the *City of God,* he wrote the fourth and final book of *On Christian Doctrine* (*De doctrina Christiana*), in which he replies directly to Cicero's rhetorical principles. The two works taken together thus represent Augustine's answer to Cicero as a political philosopher and rhetorician.

Contemplating the dangers posed to Rome by the Catilinian conspiracy and the conditions that led to it, Cicero paints in fresh colors the ideal picture at the commonwealth. Defending the church against the charge "that the Christian religion is responsible for all the wars desolating this miserable world and, in particular, for the recent barbarian sack of the City of Rome," Augustine describes the city of God.[24] Grouping the Ciceronian and Augustinian works that develop these themes has the curious anachronistic effect of casting both the Catilinian conspirators and fifth-century Christians in the role of defendants, charged with responsibility for the ruin of Rome, even as it sets Cicero, as Catiline's prosecutor, against Augustine, the Christian apologist and defender. It puts one kind of rhetoric in dramatic conversation with another, one "city" in dialogue with another, even as it tests the politics of allegory in its two most suspect forms: those of violent revolution and religion.

As Jon Whitman explains, *agora*, the Greek word for an "open assembly," "developed at an early stage two quite different meanings": "On the one hand, it referred to an official assembly. . . . On the other hand, the word *agora* also referred to the open market." When the word *allos*, meaning "other," was added to the verb *agoreuein*, meaning "to speak in the assembly," to form the compound from which "allegory" derives, a double inversion resulted, which reflected the opposite senses of *agora*. "Allegory" came to mean either the "guarded speech" of dissidents and conspirators, which expressed covertly what could not be said openly, or the "elite language" that spoke of matters "unworthy of the crowd." These two meanings, moreover, arose in different cultural contexts: "The sense of secretive, guarded language had special significance for political allegory, in which the allegorist spoke, as it were, other than in the official assembly. The sense of elite, superior language had particular point in religious and philosophic contexts, in which the allegorist spoke other than in the common market place."[25]

Given this etymology, it is not surprising that many have regarded allegory—even political allegory—as a kind of anti-rhetoric, the inverse of public speaking. As Michael Murrin remarks, oratory and allegory "differ radically from each other as modes of communication."[26] Whereas the rhetor speaks in the *agora* to found and preserve the city, the allegorist, standing outside it, accomplishes instead what Frank Kermode has called "the genesis of secrecy."[27] Whereas rhetoric unites the scattered people into a whole, allegory serves to undermine that unity and plots against it, either from below (as in political allegory) or from above (as in an elitist, religious allegory).

At first sight Cicero's impassioned prosecution of Catiline appears to set rhetoric against allegory. A close reading of the orations, however, reveals

Cicero's own use of an allegorical rhetoric in the service of the common-wealth. In the *Republic* Cicero continues his rhetorical and allegorical at-tempt to found the Roman state anew. Augustine's treatment of that trial and of Cicero's *Republic* in the *City of God* highlights this Ciceronian alle-gory, exposes its falseness, and notes its rhetorical limitations. He then uses it as a point of departure to defend Christian allegory as a form of persua-sive communication that not only mirrors society as it actually is, but also works to effect a perfect commonwealth, the city of God.

Cicero, Catiline, and Conspiracy

Lucius Sergius Catiline (108–62 B.C.) was the arch-conspirator of classical Rome, and in Cicero's confrontation with him we find a dramatic representation of the politics of allegory. Not only was Catiline the em-bodiment of a dangerous *allegoria* in the form of a treasonous, secret plot against the Senate and Rome itself; not only did he draw many of his lower-class associates from the theater, another realm of pretense and allegory; but also he based his murderous attempt, in part, on an interpretation of an allegorical text, the Sibylline Books.[28] According to testimony given to Cicero, Publius Cornelius Lentulus, Catiline's closest co-conspirator in Rome, had sought assistance from the Gauls:

> Lentulus had assured them that the Sibylline books and soothsayers had promised him that he was that third member of the Cornelian family to whom the rule and sway of this city was fated to come; Cinna and Sulla had preceded him. He also said that this was the year fated for the destruction of the city and the government, the tenth year after the acquittal of the Vestal Virgins, and the twentieth after the burning of the Capitol.[29]

Cicero's response to the multifaceted *allegoria* of Catiline, Lentulus, and their supporters—an *allegoria* that literally and figuratively threatened the dissolution of Rome and spoke "other than" its government—took the form of a complex apposite allegory: "For if Publius Lentulus, convinced by the soothsayers [*inductus a vatibus*], thought that his name was destined by fate [*fatale*] for the destruction of the state, why should not I rejoice that my consulship has been destined almost by fate [*prope fatum*] for the sal-vation of the Roman people?" (IV.i.2, p. 115).

Echoing Lentulus' reference to the fire that had destroyed the Capitol in 83 B.C., Cicero admits that "the immortal gods seemed to foretell the events which are now come to pass" (III.viii.18, p. 101). Lightning had struck many objects at the Capitol; the storm had overturned the images of gods and the statues of heroes, including that of Romulus, the city's legendary founder; and "bronze tablets of the laws were melted" (III.viii.19, p. 101). At that time soothsayers had prophesied the destruction of the whole city and empire unless the gods were suitably placated. They had urged games and ritual offerings and the enlargement and repositioning of the statue of Jupiter. The games took place, and the enlarged statue was commissioned. The making of that statue had, however, been delayed. It was not in fact completed and set on its pedestal until twenty years later, on the very morning when the conspirators came to trial and were led "through the forum to the temple of Concord," their secret plots "made clear and disclosed" in the sight of all (III.ix.21, p. 103).

Through this narration, Cicero answers the double meaning of the conspirators with an allegory of his own. The conspirators' passage "through the forum" images the disclosure of their plot. Like the eye of the god, the watchful eye of Cicero himself, as the chosen instrument of Jupiter, had seen what was hidden, had detected the treasonous *allegoria*. He and the loyal citizenry had, moreover, correctly interpreted the fiery omens as a warning and a call to placate the gods, rather than taking them and the Sibylline oracles (as Lentulus did) as an invitation to rebel, murder, and destroy.

A master of allegoresis, Cicero can see a spiritual struggle, indeed a psychomachia, in the literal conflict between Catiline and himself: "For on this side fights modesty, on that shamelessness; on this chastity, on that wantonness; on this honour, on that fraud; on this righteousness, on that crime; on this steadfastness, on that madness" (II.xi.25, pp. 73, 75).

Confronted with the near-extinction of the city, Cicero takes recourse in its founding myth. Indeed, in his four successive orations denouncing Catiline, he casts himself in the part of the original rhetor, the "great and wise" man whose words have the power to found Rome anew, transforming wild men "into a kind and gentle folk."[30] The statue of Romulus has fallen, but the statesman-orator has arisen in his place. At the beginning of the third speech, Cicero compares himself explicitly to Romulus: "since we have raised to the immortal gods with affection and praise that man who founded this city, he who preserved this same city, then founded and now grown great, ought to be held in honour by you and your posterity" (III.i.2, p. 81). Graciously accepting the people's praise, Cicero notes that "a thanksgiving was decreed to the immortal gods in my honour because of their unique mercy—an honour which I am the first man in a civil capacity to receive since the founding of the city. And the decree was in these words: 'because I had saved the city from fire, the citizens from slaughter, Italy from war'" (III.vi.15, pp. 95, 97).

Cicero's *Republic* and Augustine's *City*

Ironically, the short-term consequences of Cicero's firm stance against patrician conspirators was his own exile from Rome (March 58–August 57 B.C.). When he returned, he authored the *Republic* to celebrate the civic ideals for which he had suffered and to present himself not merely as a philosopher-statesman but also as a kind of martyr for Rome: "I could not hesitate to expose myself to the severest storms and, I might almost say, to thunderbolts, for the sake of my fellow-citizens, and to secure, at the cost of my own personal danger, a quiet life for all the rest."[31] Newly returned from exile, he allows himself to be named in a catalogue of "eminent men" who have suffered "wrongs . . . at the hands of their ungrateful fellow-citizens" (I.iii.4, p. 19).

Bitterly disappointed, Cicero chronicles in the *Republic* the history of Rome to demonstrate the degeneration of the three primary forms of government—regal, oligarchic, and democratic—and to renew the ideal, but now sadly obscured, image of the city in its first age: "[For] though the republic, when it came to us, was like a beautiful painting [*picturam egregiam*], whose colours, however, were already fading with age, our own time not only has neglected to freshen it by renewing the original colours [*coloribus*], but has not even taken the trouble to preserve its configuration and . . . general outlines" (V.1.2, p. 245).

Cicero uses rhetorical "colors" to restore the "painting" of the republic in three different ways. First, he assumes the voice of Scipio, another historical savior of Rome, to trace its ancestral history from the time of Romulus: "Using our own government as my pattern, I will fit to it, if I can, all I have to say about the ideal State" (I.xlvi.70, p. 107). Second, as Scipio he turns from a historical narrative to portray the ideal state through simile. Using a musical analogy to liken the harmonious blending together of "the upper, middle, and lower classes . . . as if they were musical tones," Scipio declares: "What the musicians call harmony in song is concord in a State . . . and such concord can never be brought about without the aid of justice" (II.xlii.69, p. 183). Finally, this musical image recurs in a dream-vision, the *somnium* of Scipio, which concludes the *Republic*. In Scipio's dream he hears the music of the spheres, sees the revolving planets, and, at a great height above the earth, learns of the eternal reward that is reserved for the virtuous, especially those who practice civic virtue: "The best tasks are those undertaken in defence of your native land" (VI.xxvi.29, p. 283).

In his *City of God*, Augustine's reading of Rome's history, and especially of Cicero's rendition of it, is systematically deconstructive of the republic that Cicero "paints" with these "colors" (*picta coloribus*). He calls attention, for instance, to Cicero's use of ambiguous language ("passing," "suddenly disappearing") in his accounts of Romulus' supposed apotheosis during an eclipse in order to suggest that even Cicero must have believed (as Livy records) that Romulus actually died a violent death, perhaps at the hands of political assassins (III.15, 1: pp. 322, 325).[32] Nonetheless, Cicero accords with others in calling him a god, because rhetorically and politically Rome needed to have a deified founder: "It was necessary for posterity to maintain what their ancestors had received, so that the city, along with the superstition which it imbibed with its mother's milk, so to speak, might grow and come to rule a great empire" (XXII.6, 7: p. 197).

Augustine's critical reading of Cicero's history of Rome distances the historical city more and more from the ideal commonwealth to which Cicero's Scipio attempted to "fit" it. Beginning with Cicero's image of the faded "painting" of the ancestral commonwealth, Augustine not only shows that Rome (by Cicero's own admission) had been lost long before the birth of Christ, but also questions whether the ideal state had ever existed: "Its admirers should consider whether, even in the time of ancient ways and men, true justice flourished in it, or whether perhaps even then its justice was not something kept alive by old ways, but some lively painting" (II.21, Vol. 1:225).

In Augustine's treatment the ideal republic thus becomes an ironic allegory of its corrupt historic counterpart. Augustine highlights that gap, which becomes evident in Cicero's own dialogue when, after Scipio has concluded his historical survey, Philus champions at length the thesis that the state cannot be governed without injustice. Philus' argument, which is supported by many examples of inequity in Rome and elsewhere, is in fact so convincing that Laelius can only reply by arguing the benefits of justice. Scipio, too, is nonplussed by Philus and forced to take a deductive, rather than an inductive, approach to the ideal state.

Augustine quotes Cicero's Scipio, who first defines the state as "a multitude bound together by a mutual recognition of rights and a mutual cooperation for the common good" and then declares that the state cannot by definition exist when justice is violated:

Harmony, concordant and exact, may be produced by the regulation even of voices most unlike; so by combining the highest, lowest, and between them the middle class of society, as if they were tones of different pitch, provided they are regulated by due proportion, the state may produce a unison by agreement of elements quite unlike. The agreement that musicians call harmony in singing is known as concord in the body politic. This is the tightest and best rope of safety in every state, and *it cannot exist at all without justice*. (II.21, 1:217, 219; emphasis added)

Augustine approves this definition and Scipio's conclusion, but he goes on to define justice in relation to God and humankind in such a way that Scipio's ideal commonwealth (like Plato's Republic) is shown never to have existed in any earthly city, but only in the city of God. As Augustine shows, the earthly city exists not as a state founded on justice, but rather as "a large gathering of rational beings . . . united in fellowship by common agreement about the objects of its love," some states being "better" and others "worse," depending on the nature of their interests (XIX.24, 6:233). Since justice means giving everyone, including God, his or her due, then by definition "true justice . . . exists only in that republic whose Founder and Ruler is Christ" (II.21, 1:225).

As a prime example of the nonexistence of the ideal state, Augustine turns to Rome at the time of the Catilinian conspiracy. Comparing the situation in Rome to the case of "Troy, or Ilium, from which the Roman people is sprung," he likens the perjury committed by Catiline and his many adherents to the perjury of Priam's father, Laomedon, who had violated his pledge to Poseidon and Apollo (III.2, 1:271). Augustine terms them equally destructive of the city. Rome did not burn as Ilium did, but it was nonetheless destroyed as a moral entity by the corruption of its members. Indeed, Catiline's conspiracy would never have taken place had the city not already been so full of perjurers in the law courts and the Senate that Catiline had an abundant source from which to draw "a supply of men who lived by hand or tongue on perjury and civil slaughter" (III.2, 1:273).

In his first oration against Catiline, Cicero had compared him to Tiberius Gracchus, who had similarly stirred up dangerous revolts (133 B.C.), and who had suffered the death penalty for his treason (I.i.3, p. 17). Augustine therefore applies to Rome during the Catilinian conspiracy Cicero's argument in the *Republic* where Scipio speaks in the dramatic time of the murder of Tiberius Gracchus to express his opinion of the state "when there were already presentiments that it would at any moment perish" by its own corruption. The state was not merely "utterly wicked and profligate," but by Scipio's definition "it was utterly extinct and no republic remained at all" (II.21, 1:217).

Cicero's Scipio, as we have seen, defines the commonwealth in ideal terms that rival those of Plato's Republic, and Cicero, on that basis, denies its actual existence in a corrupt Rome.[33] Similarly, Socrates in Plato's *Gorgias* imagines the possibility of a true or philosophic rhetoric, unlike the rhetoric of flattery, a "beautiful" rhetoric that tries "to make the souls of the citizens as good as possible" and that works "hard in saying what is best, whether it is pleasant or unpleasant to the audience."[34] This kind of rhetoric, Socrates acknowledges, has never yet existed in Athens.[35]

By his own account, Cicero sought to practice a "beautiful" and virtuous rhetoric. As Cicero himself was too sadly to learn, however, he could save Rome from Catiline, but he could not save Rome from itself. Nor could he, through a rhetorical "painting" of Rome as an ideal state, constitute Rome as such. As Augustine understands it, Cicero's ironic allegory of Rome as something "other" in the past than it was in the present only points from one sign to another sign, to a "painting," not a thing. Because the Romulus and the ancient republic to which Cicero refers never existed, his allegorical rhetoric necessarily lacks power because it lacks truth. Augustine, however, can and does affirm the existence of a true rhetoric, a true poetics, and a true commonwealth in the historical person of Jesus Christ and in the city of God founded by him.

He draws a sharp contrast between Christ and Romulus as divine founders: "Although Christ is the founder of a heavenly and eternal city, his city did not believe in him as God because it was founded by him, but rather it is to be founded because it believes" (XXII.6, 7:199). Through a point-by-point comparison, Augustine sets the image of the city of God, its typological history, and its inspired laws and scriptures against the earthly city and its troubled history, its ineffectual laws, the empty allegory of pagan poets, and the anti-Christian oracles compiled by Porphyry.[36] Thus he gradually constructs an allegorical relationship between the two cities: "Both [of these cities] alike in this life either enjoy good things or suffer evils, but with diverse faith, diverse hope, and diverse love" (XVIII.54, 6:93).

Augustine, Allegory, and Audience

To illustrate the ideal of the city of God, Augustine picks up Scipio's image of musical chords and harmonies and turns to the biblical example of David, who was both a musician and a king, and whose rule in the earthly Jerusalem foreshadowed God's rule in the heavenly one. Standing in a proper relationship to the true God and giving him his due, David modeled for his people the justice that was to characterize their mutual relationship: "David was a man skilled in songs, who loved musical harmony not for vulgar pleasure, but as a man of faith, for a purpose whereby he served his God, who is the true God, by the mystic prefiguration of a great matter. For the rational and proportionate symphony of diverse sounds conveys the unity of a well-ordered city, knit together by harmonious variety" (XVII.14, 5:311).

As a type of Christ, the founder of the city of God, David the lyre player answers not only to Scipio's imagined statesman and musician but also to the myths that associated poets and singers with the founding of cities. Augustine himself mentions Amphion, who was said to have charmed and moved stones "by the sweet tones of his lyre" (XVIII.13, 5:409). The most important mention of Amphion, however, occurs in the *Ars poetriae* of Horace (65–8 B.C.). There the stories of Orpheus and Amphion are used to illustrate the rhetorical power of poetry: "Orpheus, the priest and interpreter of the gods, deterred the savage race of men from slaughters and inhuman diet; hence [he was] said to tame tigers and furious lions: Amphion too, the builder of the Theban wall, was said to give the stones motion with the sound of his lyre, and to lead them withersoever he would, by engaging persuasion."[37]

Horace's myth of Amphion places a named, albeit legendary, poet in the place of the unnamed rhetor who famously appears in Cicero's *De inventione*. There Cicero describes a time before civilization "when men wandered at large in the fields like animals and lived on wild fare." They relied "chiefly on physical strength" for survival, until a "great and wise" man, aware of the latent powers of reason and eloquence, gathered together the people who had been "scattered in the fields and hidden sylvan retreats" and transformed them through his speech "into a kind and gentle folk."[38] In the larger context of the *Ars poetriae*, which records the rivalry between lawyers and poets, the substitution of Amphion for this "great and wise" man urges the superiority of poetics over rhetoric as an art of persuasion.

When Augustine introduces the image of David as a founding figure for the city of God, he too subordinates rhetoric to poetics, even as he fuses the two. Not surprisingly, the passage just quoted, which interprets David's lyre playing allegorically, appears shortly after a chapter in which Augustine discusses the literal and allegorical senses of sacred Scripture (XVII.3), including David's own Book of Psalms. Some passages in Scripture refer to the earthly Jerusalem alone (that is, to the secular city and its persons and events); others refer literally to the heavenly Jerusalem in the eternal realm; still others, referring to both at the same time, have a double signification. Augustine himself is reluctant to say that "each separate statement" in the historical books of the Bible "is wrapped in allegorical meaning," but he does not censure those who "carve out a spiritual application for every event recorded there, provided that they first take care to preserve historical veracity" (XVII.3, 5:223).

Augustine clearly connects the proportionality—that is, the fitting correspondence—between and among the various levels of meaning found in Scripture to the intervals between and among harmonic tones, on the one hand, and the justice governing personal and communal relationships in the city of God, on the other. In *De doctrina Christiana* (II.xvi.25–26) Augustine deals explicitly with the figurative significance of number and music in the Bible. More important, however, he places the whole enterprise of reading and interpreting the Scriptures within the larger context of seven spiritual steps (corresponding to the seven gifts of the Holy Spirit) which the individual takes on his or her journey to union with God and others—a union of charity that reaches its highest expression in the Holy Trinity. Augustine associates the third step, that of knowledge, both with learning to read the Bible literally and figuratively and with discovering the two precepts of charity: love of God and neighbor (II.vii.9–11).

As Augustine explains, it is not simply that exercise in one kind of proportionality—that of discovering the hidden *significatio* of a passage—trains one to think and act justly in one's other relationships, and thus to live as a member of the city of God. Rather, the actual subject matter of the sacred Scriptures, whether openly or obscurely expressed, is charity: "Scripture teaches nothing but charity, nor condemns anything except cupidity, and in this way shapes the minds of men."[39] The work of reading the Bible is, moreover, part of a larger work: the working of the Holy Spirit within the soul of the individual and in the Christian community to which he or she belongs. The same Holy Spirit who inspired the biblical writers acts to illumine the mind and heart of individual readers and to effect a communion among them, diverse as they are.

The unique eloquence of the biblical writings consists in the relationship it establishes between what is "put openly in them either as precepts for living or as rules for believing" and what is expressed obscurely: "Among those things which are said openly in Scripture are to be found all those teachings which involve faith, the mores of living, and that hope and charity which we have discussed" (II.ix.14, p. 42). The coexistence of the open and the veiled in the letter of Scripture, and the need to interpret the latter in terms of the former, call for the closely related methodolgies of concordance and historical typology (at the literal level) and allegoresis (at the figurative level).

As a result of practicing these methods, the reader becomes schooled at the same time through the spiritual insights that recognize the open in the obscure, the familiar in the other, and the known in the unknown, and that enable one to love the "neighbor," "stranger," and "enemy" (depending on the degree of difference) as one's "self." The journey into the hidden meaning of Scripture becomes in this way a means of knowing one's own inmost self, the truth about others, and God himself, the *res* to which all *signa* point. What is taught and how it is taught thus coincide: "Scripture teaches nothing but charity, nor condemns anything except cupidity, and in this way shapes the minds of men" (III.x.15, p. 88). Form and content likewise join, making "eloquence" the "inseparable servant" of "wisdom" (IV.vi.10, p. 124).

Charity that is learned in this way builds the city of God, strengthening the bonds between the members. Indeed, the very process of learning it helps to form the city as a living entity. At a very practical level, Augustine envisions a Church united by reflection on the Word of God, each individual examining the Scriptures and discovering meanings in the "divine eloquence" that he or she can share as an insight with the others: "And certainly the Spirit of God, who worked through . . . [a particular biblical] author, undoubtedly foresaw that this meaning would occur to the reader or listener. Rather, He provided that it might occur to him" (III.xxvii.38, p. 102).

Even as the crucified Christ, the Incarnate Word of God, was "to the Jews . . . a stumbling-block and to the Gentiles foolishness" (1 Corinthians 1:23), so too the Scriptures, the inspired Word of God, present certain similar barriers to nonbelievers. As Saint Augustine relates in his *Confessions,* he himself had at first despised the biblical writings because of the simplicity of their style, which was "far unworthy to be compared to the stateliness of the Ciceronian eloquence."[40] Only later, through hearing the allegorical sermons of Saint Ambrose (see *Confessions* VI.v), did he "espy something in them not revealed to the proud, not discovered unto children, humble in style, sublime in operation, and wholly veiled over in mysteries" (*Confessions* III.v, 1:113). Whereas Augustine in his youthful pride had been put off by the plain style of the Bible, others are offended by its prophetic obscurity. This, too, he says, serves a useful purpose "of exercising and sharpening, as it were, the minds of the readers and of destroying fastidiousness and stimulating the desire to learn, concealing their intention in such a way that the minds of the impious are either converted to piety or excluded from the mysteries of the faith" (*De doctrina* IV.viii, p. 132).

According to Augustine, what makes the eloquence of the sacred Scriptures unique is their double meaning. Rejecting the notion that the divinely inspired writers are "wise" but not "eloquent," he insists that they speak with "the kind of eloquence fitting for men most worthy of the highest authority." No "other kind" of eloquence befits them, nor is their unique eloquence "suitable for others." Scriptural eloquence possesses an incomparable truth and "solidity," which is expressed sometimes openly, sometimes figuratively. Thus the "obscurity itself of the divine and wholesome writings was a part of a kind of eloquence through which our understandings should be benefited not only by the discovery of what lies hidden but also by exercise" (*De doctrina* IV.vi.9, p. 123).

Commenting in his sixth-century *Explanation of the Psalms* on Augustine's treatment of figurative language, Cassiodorus refers to our "father Augustine in the third book of *De doctrina Christiana*" to affirm not only that the tropes found in secular literature can be discovered in the Bible, but also (and more important) that the Bible contains "modes of expression" that are "peculiar to divine eloquence": "The main force of eloquence in the scriptures, previously untried and a pointer to salvation, frequently recounts certain things, yet is often explaining matters greatly different from the words heard. This is a simplicity which is at two levels, a guileless form of double-speaking" that is "not adopted in the interests of deception, but to achieve a most useful effect."[41] Scriptural allegory, in short, is rhetorical in its eloquence and effectiveness.

Augustine is often rightly credited with "the retention of ancient rhetoric" in the Christian curriculum, but, as James Murphy observes, Augustine also "postulates the existence of a new type of eloquence" which contrasts with that of nonbelievers.[42] Augustine certainly does admit and demonstrate a considerable overlap between "their" eloquence and "ours"—especially in the biblical use of ornamental language—but, he insists, "those things in that eloquence which our authors have in common with pagan authors and poets do not greatly delight me" (*De doctrina* IV.vi.10, p. 124). What fascinates Augustine instead are the differences between scriptural rhetoric and the Ciceronian rhetoric in which he had been trained, and the important consequences for the Christian preacher of biblical imitation as a means of invention.

Much could be said about this subject. Augustine's understanding of *ethos,* for instance, is revolutionary.[43] For the purposes of this book, however, I wish to focus on questions relating to allegory and audience. Briefly put, Augustine envisions the audience of the Christian preacher as roughly analogous in its constituency to the audience of the Scriptures themselves (including people who hear them proclaimed, without being able to read them). As George Kennedy explains, "Christianity is addressed to all sorts and conditions of men, and the Christian preacher should be able to move the illiterate and unlearned or the sophisticated and erudite."[44]

The breadth of this intended audience requires the speaker to use a relatively plain style, like that of the Gospels, albeit with appropriate stylistic variation. At the same time, the speaker must expect that his message will be understood by the various constituencies within his audience at different levels—literal or historical, moral, dogmatic, mystical—and, at each of those general levels, in a great variety of ways, depending on their receptivity, prior knowledge, experience, and inspiration.[45] Indeed, as Michael Murrin writes, "various divisions [can] be applied to this audience, according to the number of interpretations possible for a given allegory."[46] It is the work of the preacher to discover and to bring into harmony this diversity of elements among his listeners and within the Scriptures themselves. He must (to echo James Murphy) "suit his discourse to the variety among his hearers."[47]

Whereas the classical rhetor addressed fairly homogeneous audiences, segregated mainly by social class, and used different stylistic levels decorously, depending on whom he was addressing, about what subject, and to what end, the early Christian preacher brought a universal message to a heterogeneous audience and needed to vary his style accordingly within a single speech. As Augustine recognized, the consequence for the three traditional levels of style—plain (subdued), middle, and grand—was that they became detached, first of all, from a corresponding array of possible audiences based on social class. Second, they could no longer be associated, respectively, with matters of varying degrees of importance, from least to greatest, because in an ecclesiastical context "everything we say is of great importance," since it concerns the eternal rather than the temporal welfare of the auditors (*De doctrina* IV.xviii.35, p. 143). Finally, the three styles also became detached from their respective identification with teaching, delighting, and moving. Directly contradicting Cicero's stance in *De oratore* (29.101), Augustine explicitly denies that "the subdued style pertains to understanding, the moderate style to willingness, and the grand style to obedience; rather . . . the orator always attends to all three and fulfills them all as much as he can, even when he is using a single style" (IV.xxvi. 56, p. 162).

Unlike Cicero, who, according to Augustine's interpretation of him, associates "moving" and thus "persuading" only with the grand style the quintessential style of the orator—Augustine insists that persuasion takes place at every stylistic level: "For it is the universal office of eloquence, in any of these three styles, to speak in a manner leading to persuasion" (IV.xxiv.55, p. 161). In keeping with this dictum, Augustine expands the definition of "persuasion" and "moving" to include the prompting not only of outward actions but also of interior acts and the effecting of spiritual change within the person.[48] He agrees with Cicero that an orator "persuades in the grand style" if he convinces his auditors "that those things which we know should be done are done" (IV.xxv.55, p. 162). But a teacher who uses the subdued style and awakens belief through his instruction also "persuades his listener that what he says is true" and thus provides a basis for ethical choice and action.

In what sense, however, can speech in the moderate style be persuasive? In agreement with traditional rhetorical lore, Augustine grants that the use of the middle style in the narration of events and in the praise and blame of persons aims at pleasing and delight. The speaker "persuades in the moderate style that he himself speaks beautifully and with ornament," but this end, which is enough for an entertaining recitation of poetry or for a declamatory oration, is insufficient for the Christian orator: "We . . . refer this end to another end, . . . [namely,] that good habits be loved and evil avoided" (IV.xxv.55, p. 162). It is possible, Augustine insists, that those "who are delighted are changed," converted, and interiorly transformed by what they hear, for "when praises and vituperations are eloquently spoken, although they belong to the moderate style, they so affect some that they are not only delighted by the eloquence of praising or blaming, but also desire to live in a praiseworthy way and to avoid living in a way that should be blamed" (IV.xxiv, p. 161).

Augustine's treatment of stylistic expression in Book IV of *De doctrina Christiana* must be seen in conjunction with his discussion of signs and invention in Books I–III. Too often the fourth book is read in isolation, leading people to the superficial conclusion that Augustine held rhetoric to be "largely a matter of style."[49] What Augustine achieves instead is a powerful originary synthesis of rhetoric and poetics, based on the Incarnation and the indwelling presence of the Divine Logos. True Man and True God through the hypostatic union, Christ is God's True Poem and a perfect fusion of wisdom and eloquence. The mysterious joining of his human and divine natures is reflected in the combination of literal and figurative meanings in sacred Scripture and in the diverse membership of the One Church, which is his mystical body and the city of God on earth. The Christ whom the Christian orator discovers therein is the same Christ whom he proclaims through a fitting juxtaposition of the manifest and the hidden, a variety of styles, and an assemblage of many parts.

The Augustinian Legacy

Augustine's *De civitate Dei*, completed in A.D. 426, and his *De doctrina Christiana*, finished the following year, are in many ways far removed from the political allegories of late medieval England that are the main subject of this book. From a theoretical perspective, however, the Augustinian legacy is of incalculable importance. In *De doctrina*, Augustine is the first to connect the method of allegorical interpretation directly to composition, making the "invention" or discovery of hidden meanings in the Bible not merely a hermeneutical activity but a rhetorical one. After him, Christian poets, even more perhaps than preachers, who were schooled both in biblical exegesis and in the allegorical interpretation of pagan authors, imitated in their own writings the elaborate methods of veiling and indirection that they perceived as intentionally constructed in the antique texts, writing as they had learned to read and (as they believed) the ancient authors had been inspired to write.

They did so, moreover, with a view to a complex, multi-tiered audience, the members of which were expected to understand their fictions at one or more levels simultaneously. To the extent that poet and audience alike shared an education in allegorical interpretation, the poet characteristically had very high (but not unreasonable or unwarranted) expectations of his audience. Judging by the practice of allegory that this book delineates, we must conclude that rebels such as John Ball hoped that their cryptic messages would be understood by their collaborators and misunderstood by their enemies, whereas poets such as John Gower, Geoffrey Chaucer, and the *Gawain*-poet probably "hid" topical meanings mainly (but not exclusively) in order to "reveal" their art, that is, to dazzle appreciative audiences with their powers to alter familiar stories, to layer parallel narratives, and to interweave them.

In either case, the allegorical method certainly was self-protective. It enabled the poet to attempt the delicate instruction of difficult and powerful auditors—King Richard II, for example—or to make a covert criticism of them. Even if no one in the audience was actually excluded from discovering the poem's hidden meaning, however, the poem retained its status as allegory by employing an allegorical method that allows for the possibility of such an exclusion. Admitting that possibility, I would argue, served rhetorically to increase the cohesiveness, unity, mutual commitment, and delight of the listeners whom the poet thereby fashioned into an audience of initiates with a secret to share.

Oral performance, by its very nature, tends toward topical allusion and allegory, and medieval aurality, as Joyce Coleman has emphasized, frequently occasioned "the excitement of a shared, enacted, and high-context reading."[50] In late medieval England we find for the first time poets writing and performing their works in the vernacular who are "clerical" in their knowledge of allegorical Latin texts and who share that knowledge with a significant number of their auditors.[51] These poets could count on their lay and clerical auditors to complete their poems, as Murrin puts it, "by supplying the unspoken words necessary to fill in the extended analogy."[52] The result, as we shall see, was an amazing flourishing of political allegory, intricate in its verbal codes, powerful in its social ramifications, dangerous, and difficult to control.

Augustine certainly understood and appreciated the power of an allegorical text and its figurative interpretation to build a diverse body of believers into a community, indeed, into the city of God. For him, as for Saint Thomas Aquinas after him, preaching is (to echo Mark Jordan) "the Christian political activity in the widest sense, since it is a public speaking which constitutes the true community."[53] At the same time Augustine recognized, as Cicero had before him, the potential for allegories and oracles to divide the community into opposed groups and to promote and sustain actual conspiracies against the state. Augustine's powerful theoretical linkage of the allegorical with the political, and his own allegorical practice in opposing the *civitas Dei* to the worldly city, stand (albeit distantly) behind the interweaving of the hagiographic and the historic in the late medieval English works under discussion in this book.

Before we look at those works, however, we need to examine more closely the rhetorical and poetic theory that supported the composition of allegory in the Middle Ages. We need, in particular, to trace the educational background that was common to the poets and their audiences and that shaped their mutual expectations and reciprocal "invention." That subject is the "matter" of Chapter 1.

1

The *Materia* of Allegorical Invention

For Goddes love, demeth nat that I seye
Of yvel entente, but that I moot reherce
Hir tales alle, be they bettre or werse,
Or elles falsen som of my mateere.

Geoffrey Chaucer, *The Canterbury Tales*

Previous studies of medieval allegory have often treated allegore-sis, that is, allegorical interpretation, as an end in itself, to the point of forgetting that Saint Augustine's hermeneutical *inventio* was also and even primarily rhetorical. According to Augustine, God deliberately veiled his message in order to communicate the divine Word. One therefore discovers the hidden meanings of Scripture in order to be able to preach the Gospel, imitating scriptural eloquence in one's own speech. Similarly, students of Virgil and Ovid were taught not only how to read the *Aeneid* and the *Metamorphoses* allegorically, but also that a double meaning was intentional on the part of the great *auctores*. That is to say, Virgil and Ovid had actually *composed* them as allegories with the expectation that (at least some of) their auditors would decode them and be instructed, delighted, and moved through that process. For these students, imitating the classical poets, not unlike imitating the biblical writers, meant not merely the creative retelling of their literal stories via translation, rearrangement, amplification, abridgment, and versification, but also the practice of allegorical composition.

As we shall see, the act of composing an allegory presupposes that the writer and his or her audience share a set of generic expectations, based on their familiarity with authoritative models. It implies the allegorist's knowledge of the cultural memory of his audience(s)—that is to say, their power to recall narratives, to recite ordered lists of things, to recognize icongraphic images and ritual actions, and so on. Depending on the sophistication of the allegory, it further presupposes a common education, whereby the poets and their intended auditors have been schooled in the grammatical, rhetorical, and logical principles that make both coding and decoding possible. Within a culture strongly informed by such traditions, allegorical meaning is much less hidden (because it is easily discoverable) and thus more rhetorical than has hitherto been recognized. Allegory was, in fact, a recognizable form of communication between a poet and his audience; an acknowledged vehicle of delight, instruction, and persuasion; and a powerful means for poets to define their audiences by dividing them.

The last several decades have seen major advances in the study of medieval rhetoric, but historians of rhetoric and poetic alike continue to minimize the theoretical importance of rhetorical invention in medieval poetics. They tend either to posit a wide gap between vernacular poetic practice and the compositional theory of the Latin arts of poetry, or they acknowledge the stylistic influence of the *artes* on vernacular poets while denying that these treatises have anything significant to say about invention and audience.

The essay "Rhetoric and Poetry" in the 1993 *New Princeton Encyclopedia of Poetry and Poetics,* for instance, aligns medieval poetic with the rhetoric of eloquence rather than the eloquence of persuasion, and makes the astonishing claim that "a concern with rhetorical thought, or any intrusion of *inventio* into systematic philosophy, let alone poetics, was altogether neglected." The essay goes on, predictably, to celebrate a revival of interest in rhetorical thought in the Renaissance, owing to the recovery of Quintilian and the publication of Cicero's *De oratore,* a "dialogue [that, unlike the medieval *artes,*] gives critical importance not to arrangement and style, *dispositio* and *elocutio,* but to the strategies of *inventio.*"[1] Similarly, Susan Brown Carlton's essay "Poetics" in the 1996 *Encyclopedia of Rhetoric and Composition* distinguishes sharply between the "grammatical and allegorical poetic," which culminates in the medieval *artes poetriae,* and "Horace's rhetoric-centered poetic."[2]

The implication, according to Robert O. Payne, is that medieval poetic theory, as expressed in the *artes,* ignores rhetorical invention per se and "turns the classical rhetoricians' three-way relationship among speaker / language / audience into a two-way relationship between idea and poem."[3] Paul Zumthor agrees. In *Toward a Medieval Poetics,* he virtually equates *inventio* with amplification, insisting that medieval theorists of poetic composition "were mostly concerned with *amplificatio* and the doctrine of *ornatus,* which they considered to be the essence of writing."[4]

In a much-cited 1969 essay on Geoffrey of Vinsauf's *Poetria Nova,* the most famous of the thirteenth-century *artes,* Douglas Kelly has refuted some of these claims, arguing that the compositional theory articulated in the *artes* exerted an important influence on poets such as Geoffrey Chaucer, and that the treatment of invention in the *Poetria,* while admittedly brief, nonetheless accords it paramount importance as "the first and foremost step in composition." That step requires two processes on the part of the poet: first, "extracting the *materia* to be used in the poem" from a larger body of inherited source material and, second, "deciding what the beginning, middle, and conclusion of his *materia* will be," before proceeding to the next step, that of disposition, which involves the rearrangement, amplification, and abridgment of the invented material.[5] As Geoffrey advises his students, "Let the inner compasses of the mind lay out the entire range of the material. Let a certain order predetermine from what point the pen shall start on its course, and where the outermost limits shall be fixed."[6]

Since invention in the *Poetria* is by definition the discovery of *materia*, we cannot assess the place of invention and audience within medieval poetic theory and practice unless we understand the meaning of that key term. Douglas Kelly and Marjorie Curry Woods have done important work in this area, tracing the use of the word by Matthew of Vendôme, Geoffrey of Vinsauf, and John of Garland.[7] As Kelly indicates, however, we need to look, in addition, to the *accessus ad auctores,* which regularly include technical discussions of the *causa materialis* of poetry, as well as to the use of the word "matter" by vernacular poets.[8] Other important contexts for investigation are discussions of the *materia* proper to rhetoric and poetics, Boethius' treatment of invention itself as a kind of matter, and other metaphorical uses by medieval authors of the Aristotelian distinction between the matter and the form of a thing.

A survey of medieval texts that discuss poetic materiality indicates that Geoffrey of Vinsauf's brief references to "matter" and "invention" point in shorthand, as it were, to an amazingly complex process, inclusive of sophisticated considerations of audience and argument. The "matter" invented by the poet was not only the literal subject matter of his work but also, and at the same time, its intended allegories, that is, the parallel texts—historical, mythic, biblical, hagiographic—that the poet endeavored to evoke in the minds of his auditors in order to lead them to a personal recognition and application of the poem's message. The poem's materiality, in short, was relational and assimilative by definition. It included the poem's literal subject, its intended allegories, and its anticipated audiences—the total discovery of which then directed the poet's decisions concerning arrangement and style.

The "Matters" of Rhetoric and Poetics

The polysemous "matter" of poetry that emerges in allegorical invention represents in each case a practical application of the conjoined theoretical subject matters of rhetoric and poetics, the historical relationship between which is extremely complex. Depending on what matter is deemed proper to rhetoric as an art or science, they are either sharply distinguished, seen to overlap, or viewed as virtually identical.

In his thirteenth-century *Tresor,* Brunetto Latini echoes Cicero's discussion of the issue in *De inventione.*[9] Brunetto's initial definition is deceptively simple and straight forward: "The matter of rhetoric is what the speaker speaks about, just as illnesses [*les maladies*] are the material of the doctor."[10] Like Cicero before him, however, Brunetto goes on to distinguish two basic positions: that of Gorgias, who says that "all things which are appropriate to speak about are the material of this art," and that of Aristotle and Cicero, who limit the subject of rhetoric to "three things alone, that is, demonstration, counsel, and judgment" (pp. 281–82), which correspond respectively to the matters of epideictic, deliberative, and forensic oratory.[11]

As Brunetto notes, Hermagoras' broad definition of the "matter" of rhetoric as consisting of "causes and . . . questions" tends to blur the distinction between the separate subject matters of grammar, rhetoric, and dialectic, leading people to make the mistake of including as rhetorical *materia* either philosophical questions, "such as the size of the sun," which are subjects of dispute, but which have "nothing to do with governing a city," or fictional arguments. "People are mistaken," he observes, "who believe that telling tales or ancient stories or whatever else one might say is material for rhetoric" (pp. 281–82).

Although Brunetto upholds Cicero's authoritative definition of the three-fold matter proper to rhetoric, as an encyclopedic compiler he also marks that Ciceronian definition as rhetorically and socially constructed—that is, as reflecting one position among several conflicting views. Not only does Cicero's view differ from that of his predecessors Gorgias and Hermagoras, but also it varies from that of his successors. Brunetto himself follows Saint Augustine and others in expanding the *materia* of rhetoric to include written as well as spoken discourse: "The master says that the science of rhetoric is of two types, one which is by mouth and another in which one informs people of things by writing, but the instruction is the same for both, for it makes no difference whether one communicates by speech or by writing" (p. 284). Moreover, in addition to the three traditional matters of classical oratory (praise and blame, counsel, judgment), Brunetto alludes to the typically medieval rhetorical matters of preaching (persuasion to belief), letter writing, and scholastic disputation: "What one says with one's mouth or sends in thoughtful letters for the purpose of persuading others to believe, or disputing, praising, condemning, or taking counsel with respect to a given matter, or to something which requires a judgment: all this is material for rhetoric" (p. 282). In direct disagreement with Cicero, Brunetto also allows for the rhetorical treatment of matters "without controversy" (p. 284).

Indeed, Brunetto's own tendency to expand the definition of the *materia* of rhetoric leads him back, via Boethius, to an all-inclusive position that is closer to Gorgias' view than to Cicero's: "What is said or written without controversy does not belong to rhetoric, according to what Aristotle and Cicero say clearly; but Gorgias says that all that the speaker says belongs to rhetoric. Boethius says and is in complete agreement with the idea that whatever is appropriate to say can be the matter for an orator" (p. 284).

Historians of medieval rhetoric, such as Richard McKeon and Michael C. Leff, point to Boethius as the key figure in the medieval subordination of rhetoric to dialectic and the absorption of the former into the latter. As Leff notes, Cicero's understanding of the threefold matter proper to rhetoric derived from, and corresponds to, actual occasions for oratory as it was regularly practiced in Roman society. His theory of topical invention aimed, moreover, at the discovery of matter appropriate to those particular institutional settings, occasions, and audiences. With the end of the republic, the fall of the empire, and "the demise of the Roman courts, the relevance of the matters to which these topics refer [became] increasingly obscure."[12] Separated from their traditional *materia,* the rhetorical topics (as a means of discovery or *inventio*) appeared to Boethius to be "essentially the same" as dialectical topics, except that, as Cicero had replied to Hermagoras, "dialectic deals with the abstract issue or thesis, rhetoric with the concrete issue or hypothesis." The making of a logical appeal in a rhetorical argument thus became for Boethius and his heirs something learned through studying not rhetoric per se but dialectic, because the rhetorical topics were seen as "subordinate, concrete instances of the purer forms of inference contained in dialectical theory."[13]

Cicero had defined a threefold subject matter for rhetoric, that of epideictic, deliberative, and judicial oratory. Each of these matters, moreover, was understood to have five parts: invention, arrangement, expression, memory, and delivery. As parts of the *materia* of rhetoric, these canons all partook of its very substance. Among them, however, invention was said to enjoy a special material status, because, as Boethius notes, "discovery is the basis for all the others, holding the place, as if were, of their *matter.* . . . For without discovery, there can not be definition or partition, since we divide or even define a thing by the discovery of genera or differentiae."[14] By stressing the materiality of invention as a rhetorical (and dialectical) cause, Boethius preserved a subject matter for rhetoric even as it became in effect an art without a distinct field of application.

The loss of the traditional *materia* of rhetoric, as it had been defined by classical theory and practice, resulted in the attachment of its formal lore to new subject matters. As James J. Murphy has emphasized, the Ciceronian tradition continued and found practical application within the medieval arts of writing letters, poems, and sermons.[15] Whereas Murphy sees each of these applications as a pragmatic narrowing and reduction of classical rhetoric, Richard McKeon emphasizes instead the all-pervasive dissemination of rhetorical lore as it literally animated and formed the subject matters of virtually every field of thought and endeavor. During the Middle Ages, rhetoric as an art "with no special subject matter" was "applied to many incommensurate subject matters; it borrow[ed] devices from other arts, and its technical terms and methods [became], without trace of their origin, parts of other arts and sciences." These "shifts of . . . subject matter" in turn precipitated theoretical shifts that "emerge, not merely as philosophic or sophistic disputes, but in concrete application," and which represent "a challenge to the concept of intellectual history as the simple record of the development of a body of knowledge by more or less adequate investigations of a constant subject matter."[16]

To the extent that rhetoric as an art was hidden within the subject matters of other disciplines, it became, as it were, "allegorical" and functioned in a concealed way to configure dialectic and grammar to itself. Both Jody Enders and Mark Jordan have reminded us that when rhetoric became attached to dialectic as one of its parts (via topical invention), dialectic itself became rhetorical, disputatious, and performative, as evidenced in the public quodlibet debates of the scholastic universities.[17] Similarly, when rhetoric became attached to grammar (via the study of style), grammar in turn became increasingly rhetorical. Poetry was interpreted (*enarratio poetarum*) in ethical terms; its figures of speech and thought were analyzed for their power to stir the emotions; and the study of poetry became increasingly inventive, as its *materia* became the basis for creative imitation.[18]

Indeed, because rhetoric maintained its existence as an art attached to the separate subject matters of other disciplines (grammar, dialectic, law, theology, politics) and thus stood as a common ground between and among them, it could function as a superior art that defined the very relationship between the verbal disciplines, held them together, and thus subsumed them. McKeon has argued persuasively that rhetoric experienced a "renaissance" during the twelfth century, because it supplied a "common method" to poetry and philosophy. According to him, it remained the "connecting link" throughout the Middle Ages not only among "such divergent matters" as "the method of resolving differences in canon law, of posing theological and philosophical problems, and of interpreting poetry," but also "between Platonism and the increasing knowledge of Aristotelian logic."[19]

One indication of such a rhetorical wholeness-with-many-parts appears in Dante Alighieri's "Epistle to Can Grande," in which Dante is discussing the twofold form of the *Commedia,* its *forma tractatus* and *forma tractandi.*

What he means by the technical term *forma tractatus* is clear. It refers to the literal division of the whole work into numbered *cantiche,* cantos, and lines—that is, to its structural arrangement. The meaning of the term *forma tractandi* is much more elusive to us: "The form or manner of treatment is poetic, fictive, descriptive, digressive, and figurative; and further, it is definitive, analytical, probative, refutative, and exemplificative."[20] The conjunction "and further" signals the joining of two separate lists of terms. The adjectives in the first list reflect a primarily grammatical lexicon, the language used to discuss the works of the poets and the expressive style (*elocutio*) of orators. The adjectives in the second list reflect the technical lexicon of logicians and rhetoricians.

According to Alastair J. Minnis, Dante's two lists of different modes of treatment bear witness to the tendency among theologians, beginning in the thirteenth century, to distinguish between the affective mode of procedure in which biblical writers, orators, and poets excel (a mode reflected in the first list) and the rational mode that is proper to logical persuasion and human science (reflected in the second).[21] Significantly, however, Dante joins rather than separates the two lists and thus asserts the holistic rhetoric of the *Commedia*. Its *forma tractandi* makes not only ethical and pathetic appeals by stirring affects of attraction (love and hope) and repulsion (fear and hate) but also logical appeals. The modes of grammar and dialectic thus join together to form the composite *modus* of rhetoric. Medieval rhetoric, such as we find operative in Dante's poetry, *is* a whole, but it is discoverable only when its definite and separable parts are brought together.

The Form and Matter of Allegory

Whereas the early Middle Ages conceived of the relationship between the literal text and its allegorical meaning in primarily Platonic terms, as a body-soul relationship, the late Middle Ages employed a more complex model. In keeping with Cicero's *Topics* and Aristotle's hylomorphism, respectively, the letter, the intended allegory, and the audience were all regarded as material causes—indeed, as metaformations of one another—while the precise correspondence between and among them, as the *causa formalis* or *forma tractandi* of the poem, constituted its "soul." Boethius (d. 524) gives an early statement of this theory in his *In Ciceronis Topica:*

One thing to examine is the nature of those things of which the composite is understood to be made up, and another is the conjunction of the parts by means of which the whole is composed. For example, in the case

of a wall, if you examine the stones themselves by which the wall is constructed, you are looking at the "matter" of the wall. On the other hand,
if you observe the arrangement and composition of the junctions of the
stones, you are considering the nature of the "form." (p. 27)

As this passage suggests, Dante's discussion of the *forma tractandi* of his
poem is directly related to his understanding of the *Commedia* as an intentional allegory with a twofold subject matter. A "poetic" and "figurative"
treatment, especially in the typological sense of biblical *figurae*, is "allegorical" by definition. It directly states its "matter" at one level in such a way
as to refer indirectly to *materia* at another level. If we want to specify the
logical relationship between the literal and the unstated parts of the poem,
however—that is, the relationship that makes the poem as a whole an allegory—we must invoke the second list of terms: "definitive, analytical,
probative, refutative, and exemplificative." In an allegorical poem, what
Eugene Vance has called the movement "from topic to tale" is necessarily
two-directional.[22] That is to say, topical invention not only informs and di-
rects the construction of the literal narrative but also mediates between the
literal narrative and the allegorical narrative(s) it veils, defining the logical relationship between them and making possible both the hiding (by
the poet) and the discovery (by the auditor) of the allegory.

One can best illustrate this by returning to Boethius and Cicero. What
Boethius says in his *In Ciceronis Topica* about argument in general can easily be (and, I would argue, regularly was) applied to the composition of
allegorical arguments. By definition, an intentional allegory makes its argument "from the thing at issue," that is, the literal narrative, by establish-
ing comparisons, contrasts, or contiguities between or among persons,
actions, and things.[23] It does so, moreover, through four possible topical
arguments: "from the whole, from the enumeration of parts, from a sign,
and from related things" (p. 42).

An allegory makes its argument "from the whole" when it encompasses
"the whole that is in the question with a definition and [uses] the definition to produce belief for the thing in doubt that is at issue" (p. 42). A def-
initional argument begins with a whole, the "substance" of a thing, and unfolds its necessary properties. Boethius uses the language of materiality to
describe this "whole" and likens the properties of something to its parts:
"What is said in a definition with regard to parts that join together to make
up a substance must be understood also with regard to parts that unite to
make up the bulk of a thing, as for example, a house is constituted by the
conjoining of a foundation, walls, and a roof. For although a house is just
the union of its parts, it is nonetheless one thing and conjoined. A partition of it by its 'members' is division" (p. 40).

Because "every definition unwinds and unfolds what a name designates in an involuted way," definition has an obvious relationship to allegory as *involucrum,* as that which literally wraps up and enfolds a hidden meaning. In his *In Ciceronis Topica,* Boethius gives as an example of a definition "when we say that a man is a mortal, rational animal" (p. 39). This Aristotelian definition is incomplete from a Platonist and Christian perspective because it fails to mention the immortal soul as a human property. In Boethius' *De consolatione Philosophiae,* a personified Lady Philosophy begins her instruction of the prisoner by asking him to recall this definition of who he is. Whereas the prisoner can give only a partial answer, the reader knows the whole. As I have argued elsewhere, the allegorical argument of the *Consolation* depends on the reader's prior knowledge of the whole as it unfolds, part by part, in the three mythological metra that illustrate mortality, rationality, and immortality, respectively, as the prisoner grows in self-knowledge.[24]

The allegorist and the orator reverse this strategy when they proceed "from the enumeration of parts." This argument, by which the whole is concluded from the prior knowledge of its parts, differs from the discovery of a genus through the naming of its species (as often occurs in late medieval uses of exemplification), but, as Boethius notes, the reasoning processes are similar (p. 101). A genus, as a universal, contains its species and exists prior to them, whereas a whole is actually constituted by its parts, and its existence finally depends on them. The logical discoveries of a genus and of a whole, however, both presuppose division and assembly: "For when we make use of the enumerating of parts for an argumentation, we say that the argument in that case is drawn from that very partition— for example, in the following way. If a place has foundations, walls, and a roof, and is intended for habitation, then it is a house. So, by using this very partition, we have proved that it is a house" (p. 113).

In an allegory employing this argument, at least some of the individual parts are readily apparent, whereas the whole is hidden and implied, requiring discovery. An obvious example of this kind of allegory can be found, as I have argued elsewhere, in Fragment VII of Chaucer's *Canterbury Tales,* where the two tales of Chaucer the Pilgrim, which explicitly exemplify delight and instruction as the Horatian final cause of poetry, stand as parts that make possible the discovery of the four Aristotelian causes of books as the veiled subject matter of the fragment as a whole.[25]

An allegorical argument "from a sign" relates the name of someone or something that is literally mentioned to the name of an unstated person, place, or thing. Boethius writes, "An argument is taken from designation when something is inferred from the explanation of a name" (pp. 108–9). An orator or a storyteller (Chaucer, for instance, in "The Second Nun's Tale") may give an etymology of a person's name as an indicator of the spiritual qualities, often vices or virtues, that the person embodies. Such etymologies regularly appear in medieval *accessus* as a key to the character of the author and a guide to his intent. Etymology is not, however, the only means of argument "from a sign." Personification allegory, for instance, always argues through designation. An allegorist may also use paranomasia, direct allusion, acrostics, or a code name in order to evoke a hidden reference by name-dropping.

As a form of treatment (*forma tractandi*), the last of the four kinds of intrinsic topical arguments "is drawn from related things." This topic subsumes a great variety of arguments: "from conjugates, from the genus, from a kind, from similarity, from differentia, from a contrary, from conjoined things, from antecedents and consequents and incompatibles, from the effects of causes, and from comparison of greater, equal, or lesser things" (p. 50). As we shall see, among these arguments, those from similarity and contrariety are fundamental to allegory as a genre, whether we consider its composition by a poet or its decoding by auditors.

Judson Boyce Allen has demonstrated that the modes specified in Dante's second list are not anomalous, but rather appear frequently in commentaries on the *forma tractandi* of allegorical poetry.[26] These modes, moreover—especially "defining, dividing, and exemplifying"—correspond to, and derive from, the topical arguments that I have briefly surveyed here: from a whole, from the enumeration of parts, from designation, and from related things. What I want to emphasize is their functional importance for the formal joining together of different kinds of *materia*, literal and hidden, in allegorical composition and reception.

Whereas Aristotle had delineated four causes of things—efficient, material, formal, and final—Cicero, as Boethius remarks, spoke of only two kinds of causes: "those which produce something and those without which something cannot be produced" (p. 154). The Ciceronian notion of causality thus allows for an efficient cause (that which produces something) and reduces all the other types of causality "to the idea of matter or to the idea of those things which are conjoined with matter and aid the power of an efficient cause" (p. 155). As we shall see, the relative fullness of meaning that Cicero attached to material causality as a topic of invention perdured, even after the Middle Ages recovered Aristotle's *Organon,* and it contributed to the complex medieval understanding of the "matter" of poetry. Indeed, if we understand the brief references to matter and invention in the *Poetria Nova* within this larger philosophical and pedagogical frame, then we have a firm basis for bridging the apparent gap between medieval poetic theory and the actual practice of medieval poets.

What, then, does "matter" mean? In the *Dialogus super auctores* of Conrad of Hirsau (1070?–1150?), the teacher answers his student's question with the following definition: "Matter [*materia*] is that from which everything is made up. Hence it gets its name, as it were, 'the mother of substance' [*mater rei*]. Matter has two meanings: in a building there are pieces of wood and stones; so too in the realm of words there are kinds and classes and other means which achieve the task the author sets out to do."[27]

This brief answer echoes and abridges the longer definition of *materia* found in Bernard of Utrecht's *Commentary on Theodolus* (ca. 1076–99):

> Matter [*materia*] is that from which anything is composed; hence it is called "matter," the "mother of the thing," as it were. Matter is commonly understood in two ways—with reference to things, as, for example, a home is built of wood or stones; with reference to words, as in Porphyry's *Isagogue*, where a genus is made up of species, difference, property, and accident. Others, moreover, distinguish the matter of something thus, saying that one kind of matter is "about which" (as a letter about the accused), another is "in which" (as the city of Pergamum), and another is "through which" (as a quill). And in the case of authors, some regard their *materia* to be acting persons (for example, Pompey, Caesar, and the senate, in Lucan), whereas others regard their matter to be only the actions of persons (in Lucan's case, the civil war), according to which either the sayings collated by Theodolus or the disputants themselves are said to be the *materia* of his book. Alternatively, some note two materials in a work: first, the subject about which it mainly concerns itself, and second, what happens.[28]

Bernard's extended definition of *materia* is noteworthy from at least two perspectives. First of all, it draws an analogy between verbal matter and the material used in the construction of a house. Referring to Porphyry's *Isagogue*, it likens the material of a house—stones or timber—to verbal and logical *materia:* the assembled species that make up the genus.[29] Second, it asks questions about the *circumstantiae* of a thing—who, where, how—and it regards either persons or actions or both persons and actions to be the matter of poetry, a judgment that recalls Cicero's topical axiom in *De inventione* that "all propositions are supported in argument by attributes of persons or of actions."[30]

There is, I would argue, a direct correspondence between the poetic matter that is described in the *accessus* and the matter that the poet originally invents. In a passage famously recalled by Chaucer's scheming go-between, Pandarus, in *Troilus and Criseyde* I.1065–69, Geoffrey of Vinsauf compares the poet in the process of invention to an architect: "If anyone is to lay the foundation of a house, his impetuous hand does not leap into action; the inner design of his heart measures out the work beforehand;

the inner man determines the stages ahead of time in a certain order; and the hand of the heart, rather than the bodily hand, forms the whole in advance, so that the work exists first as a mental model [*archetypus*] rather than as a tangible thing."[31] Douglas Kelly has noted that the "comparison of poetic composition with architectural planning" appears in a variety of other contexts that help us to understand Geoffrey's use of the analogy.[32]

The key contexts for interpreting Geoffrey's house building are topical and exegetical. As we have seen, in his *In Ciceronis Topica,* Boethius uses architectural images to explain the meaning of an argument "from the whole" and "from the enumeration of parts." In Gregory the Great's *Moralia in Job,* to cite a roughly contemporary exegetical example, the literal meaning of sacred Scripture is compared to the foundation (*fundamenta*) of a house (*aedificium*), the upper stories of which are likened to its allegorical meanings.[33] In his twelfth-century *Didascalicon,* Hugh of St. Victor echoes Saint Gregory in answer to the question about the proper order of scriptural study (historical, allegorical, tropological): "And in this question it is not without value to call to mind what we see happen in the construction of buildings, where first the foundation is laid, then the structure is raised upon it, and finally, when the work is all finished, the house is decorated by the laying on of colour."[34]

We have then before us two broad intertextual contexts within which to interpret the inventive process as Geoffrey of Vinsauf describes it: that of Ciceronian topical invention (from persons and actions, from the whole, and from the enumeration of parts); and that of allegorical invention, understood in Augustinian and Victorine terms as the discovery of hidden meanings in the letter of Scripture. What these two contexts have in common is an assumption that the actual *materia* of any given argument— whether oral or written—includes more than its literal subject, which serves as a part of the whole or as a foundation for other layers of meaning that the poet wishes to communicate to his audience.

These two contexts come together explicitly in Dante's "Epistle to Can Grande," where, referring to Aristotle's *Metaphysics,* Dante discusses the very being of a text as relational and therefore incomplete in itself:

> Now of things which exist, some are such as to have absolute being in themselves, while others are such as to have their being dependent upon something else, by virtue of a certain relation, as being in existence at the same time, as in the case of correlatives, such as father and son, master and servant, double and half, the whole and the part, and other similar things, in so far as they are related. Inasmuch, then, as the being of such things depends upon something else, it follows that the truth of these things likewise depends upon something else; for if the half is unknown, its double cannot be known; and so of the rest.[35]

Dante goes on to explicate the "polysemous" nature of his *Commedia,* which, he declares, like sacred Scripture itself, has a twofold subject: "The subject, then, of the whole work, taken in the literal sense only, is the state of souls after death, pure and simple. For on and about that the argument of the whole work turns. If, however, the work be regarded from the allegorical point of view, the subject is man according as by his merits or demerits in the exercise of his free will, he is deserving of reward or punishment by justice."[36]

Echoing Dante himself, subsequent commentators on the *Commedia*— notably Guido da Pisa, Pietro Alighieri, and Boccaccio—all refer to its *materia* as twofold. In Boccaccio's words, "The material cause is, in the work in question, twofold, as is the subject (the subject and the material being one and the same thing); for one subject is that of the literal sense and the other that of the allegorical sense, both of which appear in this book."[37]

Elsewhere, in the *Convivio,* Dante uses alchemical language, referring to the "form" of the poetic work as "gold," which is produced when the literal meaning, which is always "the substance and material of the others," is properly transmuted into its allegory through the poet's careful "preparation" of his literal matter and the synthetic understanding of the auditor.[38] He insists, "In anything whatever, natural or artificial, it is impossible to make progress without first laying the foundation as, for instance, in the case of a house or of knowledge."[39]

In defining his *materia* as both literal and allegorical, Dante explicitly likens the double meaning of his poem to the fourfold meaning of sacred Scripture.[40] Biblical *accessus* regularly include the allegorical content of a book as part of its *materia.* This is especially evident in late medieval commentaries on the Song of Songs, a book universally regarded as an allegory. In the first prologue to his twelfth-century *Expositio in Cantica Canticorum,* for example, Honorius of Autun dwells on the typological nature of the Song's subject matter, stating that the work deals with the nuptials that take place at each of four levels of application: historical, allegorical, tropological, and anagogical. Its *materia* includes all these marriages: "De his nuptiis materia hujus libri contextitur."[41]

For Middle English writers, "matter" had a wide semantic range, as the entry for that word in the *Middle English Dictionary* attests. Six pages in double columns are devoted to it, showing its use in theological, scientific, philosophical, hagiographic, historical, and literary texts.[42] A brief survey of its appearances in the works of Gower, Langland, and Chaucer will confirm its importance in the theory and practice of composition.

In the opening lines of the Prologue to his *Confessio Amantis,* John Gower refers to the instructive books of old and announces his good intention to "wryte of newe som matiere, / Essampled of these olde wyse" (ll. 4–7).[43] His act of poetic creation mirrors that of the Creator God who fashioned everything that is out of a formless, chaotic "matiere universal" (VII.215). As a self-styled compiler, Gower works to put together preexistent materials, even as he hopes to foster unity in a divided state.

Gower's use of the word "matter," however, frequently intimates the material possibility of a return to chaos, both in art and in society. Already in the Prologue he speaks of division as the cause of all evils, finding a reflection of the troubled body politic in the human body, which is composed of many diverse elements (hot, cold, wet, dry) and therefore subject to dissolution. A Latin sidenote at lines 974–78 reads: "Quod ex sue complexionis materia diuisus homo mortalis existat" ("Man is mortal because he is divided in the very stuff [materia] of which he is made"). Only if the human body (and the state) were completely homogeneous in makeup would it escape division: "Mad al togedre of o matiere / Withouten interrupcioun, / Ther scholde no corrupcioun / Engendre upon that unite" (Prologue, kk, 983–87).

In the Confessio, the witch Medea appears as the dark shadow of the poet's creative muse when she murders Jason's uncle Pelias in a marvelous affair ("matiere") that involves a magical concoction of assorted materials in a burning cauldron: "What thing sche wroghte in this matiere, / To make an ende of that sche gan, / Such merveile herde nevere man" (V.4112–14). "Matter" threatens life and unity in another sense for Gower, when he uses it twice in the legal sense of a suit brought to court.[44] During the just reign of the Emperor Conrad, we are told, bribery ceased to be practiced and "non withinne the city / In destorbance of unite / Dorste ones moeven a matiere" (VII.2835–37), because everything was decided in accord with the law rather than favoritism.

At first sight William Langland's use of the word "matter" in Piers Plowman seems much more routine. He consistently uses the word to mean a subject of discussion, and he almost always alliterates it either with the verb "maken" or "meven." The repetitive force of this alliterative pattern, however, and the specific contexts in which it appears sound a significant theme in Langland's work as a whole, namely, the need to practice control of the tongue and the personal and social consequences of speech. When Langland's narrator says, for example, "Of þis matere I myȝte make a long tale" (IX.74), or "Of þis matere I myȝte mamelen [wel] longe" (V.21), or "Of þis matere I myȝte make a long bible" (XV.89), he signals the possibility of amplification and the choice instead to practice an often telling silence.[45]

The sentences that alliterate "matere" with "meven," however, mark the opposite choice: to speak aloud, to broach a topic, to raise an issue. Again, Langland stresses the necessity of conscious choice, of self-examination concerning one's motives, and of considering the effects on others of one's speech. When Langland quotes Saint Gregory to say that it is more beneficial for the soul to know one's own sins than to study natural philosophy, he remarks: "Why I meue þis matere is moost for þe pouere" (XI.232) and goes on to praise the poor and lowly. Elsewhere he complains that the friars have made bad choices in their preaching of speculative material: "Ye moeuen materes vnmesurable to tellen of þe Trinite / That [lome] þe lewed peple of hir bileue doute" (XV.71). He worries, too, that the speech of a personified Scripture may produce not faith but doubt and discouragement: "Ac þe matere þat she meued, if lewed men it knewe, / Þe lasse, as I leue, louyen þei wolde, / [The bileue [of oure] lord þat lettred men techeþ" (XI.108–10).

Langland knows that "moving" a matter by speaking about it openly "moves" people and has real-world consequences. Scripture speaks just after Will has had a heated discussion with a friar and Loyalty about whether or not it is ever right to speak about the sins of others: "Þyng þat al þe world woot, wherfore sholdestow spare / To reden it in Retorik to arate dedly synne?" (XI.101–2). Loyalty acknowledges that it is *licitum* for laypersons to talk about actual misconduct that is generally known, but he forbids Will to speak about the sins of others that he sees but are not public knowledge. When Scripture then "moves" her chosen matter, selecting as "hir teme and hir text" the parable about the banquet to which many are invited but few admitted, Will takes heed, trembles in his heart, and plunges into an inner debate about his own salvation: "Wheiþer I were chosen or noȝt chosen" (XI.117). The combined episodes thus bring together Will's anxiety about the sinful "matters" he has culpably "moved" in speech, the preacher's responsibility for the impact of his sermons, and the poet's own worry about his social critique.

As students of *The Canterbury Tales* know, Chaucer uses the word "mateere" with a wide range of meanings. Most basically, he employs it to refer to physical matter (notably in "The Canon's Yeoman's Tale" VIII.770, 811, 1232) and to a topic of conversation (e.g., II.205: "And, shortly of this matiere for to pace . . .").[46] Used more technically, it refers to the subject matter of a literal composition, as when Aurelius writes love laments: "Of swich matere made he manye layes, / Songes, compleintes, roundels, virelayes, / How that he dorste nat his sorwe telle" (V.947–49). In this compositional context, Chaucer sometimes uses it to signal the end of a narrative digression—"And turne I wol agayn to my matere" (II.322)—or to mark varying levels of discourse: "I wol nat han to do of swich mateere; / My tale is of a cok, as ye may heere" (VII.3251–52). Chaucer also uses the word "mateere" in the philosophical and rhetorical senses of a cause or argumentative reason for something else, as when the Parson calls "prosperitee" the "kyndely matere of joye" (X.491), or when Prudence advises

Melibee that a man should be temperate in self-defense so "that men have no cause ne matiere to repreven hym" (VII.1536). Finally, Chaucer employs the word suggestively to show the link between literal and allegorical "matters," in the sense of analogous tales. For example, the Prioress's story of the little clergeon calls to mind the legend of Saint Nicholas: "But ay whan I remembre on this mateere, / Seint Nicholas stant evere in my presence, / For he so yong to Crist dide reverence" (VII.513–15).

If we take these and other discussions of material causality seriously, then the invention of matter to which Geoffrey of Vinsauf refers at the beginning of the *Poetria Nova* is an enormously complicated process. It involved not only the selection of a literal subject matter with definite parts (beginning, middle, and end) that could be rearranged, but the selection of allegorical subject matters as well, which were also divisible into movable parts, and which could thus be coordinated with the literal subject, unit by unit, part by part, through the establishment of logical relationships between and among the various levels of meaning.

Once the narrative parts, literal and allegorical, were properly aligned in a horizontal and hierarchical fashion, they could also occasionally be exchanged for one another, to create disjunctures in the literal narrative. That is to say, a part of the allegorical narrative could be moved down, so to speak, to substitute for a part of the original literal narrative, which could in turn be displaced upward, to become a hidden, transplanted part of the original allegory. In Chaucer's "Nun's Priest's Tale," for instance, Chauntecleer alludes briefly and tellingly to the legend of Saint Kenelm, a veiled narrative that parallels the literal one and that mediates between the tale "of a cok" (VII.3252) and another veiled narrative, that of young King Richard II. From the end of the allegorical legend of Saint Kenelm, Chaucer takes the homely scene of the poor widow which literally begins the beast fable, displacing the opening in known analogues of the tale.

An exceptionally skilled allegorical poet could work with as many as five different narratives at once. As we shall see, the *Gawain*-poet, for instance, combines at different levels the narrative materials of the Arthurian legend, of events in the reign of Richard II, and of the lives of Saints Julian, Giles, and John the Baptist. As in Chaucer's "Nun's Priest's Tale," the hagiographic narratives serve to mediate between the literal tale and its political allegory, so that one thing is assimilated to another through a series of resemblances, until apparent opposites meet in a shock of discovery. Geoffrey of Vinsauf refers, I believe, to this multilayered process of invention and arrangement when he writes, "The next task is to decide by what balance to adjust the weights of the discourse, so that the sentence [*sententia*] will balance evenly."[47]

The Matter of Audience

The allegorist fails in his communicative purpose if his intended audience misses the message he has hidden. The inventive process, therefore, necessarily involved taking the audience into account as part of the *materia* of the poem. The very notion of polysemous composition implies, as medieval and modern-day scholars alike have noted, a complex definition of audience that includes multiple tiers of intended readers and listeners, who are capable of grasping the message of the work at various levels and whose responses have to be carefully anticipated and directed by the poet.[48] As Boccaccio puts it, "In a single discourse [*sermone*], by narrating [*narrando*], the poet discloses both the text and the mystery which underlies it. And thus at a single moment it tests out the wise at one level and reassures the ingenuous at the other."[49]

The audience was part of the *materia* that the poet invented, and he divided his implied audience(s) along lines roughly comparable to the levels of narrative with which he worked, anticipating their powers of recognition and recall, as well as their emotive responses and ethical judgments. Some *accessus* mention the intended audience explicitly as part of a work's material cause. In a discussion of Ovid's epistles from Pontus, for example, we read: "The author's friends, to whom he writes, are its subject matter— he sends each of them a different letter—or else the words he uses to plead with them."[50] Similarly, an *accessus* to Ovid's *Tristia* asserts: "His material is the description of the dangers [to which he is exposed], or the friends themselves to whom he sends letters, one by one."[51]

Sometimes, as we shall see, the distinction between "for whom" and "about whom" a poet writes is purposely blurred. This is certainly the case in the first recension of John Gower's *Confessio Amantis,* where King Richard II actually appears in the Prologue to the poem. The Prologue establishes the king as the *Confessio*'s primary historical auditor and commissioner, even as it fictionalizes him, making him literally a part of the poem. The outer audience must therefore imagine the king as constituting an inner audience, to whom the poem is directed and about whom it speaks, both directly and indirectly. As an auditor, Richard is certainly part of Gower's invented *materia*.

In his commentary on "The Monk's Tale," Chaucer's Harry Bailly calls his own capacity as an auditor for delight and instruction by the technical term "substance," a synonym for *materia*. There Bailly complains that the Monk's "talkyng" is so lacking in "game" that he has lost the attention of his audience and thus the power to instruct them. Bailly himself has almost fallen asleep listening to him: "Thanne hadde youre tale al be toold in veyn, / For certeinly, as that thise clerkes seyn, / Where as a man may have noon audience, / Noght helpeth it to tellen his sentence. / And wel I woot the *substance* is in me, / If any thyng shal wel reported be" (VII.2799–2804; emphasis added).

Every auditor possessed "substance" and thus was a material cause for the poet, but the allegorist also clearly recognized that his auditors varied in density. Although Harry Bailly finds the Monk's dreary recitation boring, the Knight listens to "The Monk's Tale" with passionate interest and discovers in its tragedies, particularly in its so-called "contemporary instances," a painful personal allegory. He interrupts the Monk and declares that he cannot bear to hear more stories of fallen nobles: "*I seye for me,* it is a greet disese, / Where as men han been in greet welthe and ese, / To heeren of hire sodeyn fal, allas" (VII.2771–73; emphasis added). As I will argue, this speech, which literally breaks off the Monk's narrative sequence, is but one indication among many that Chaucer composed "The Monk's Tale" as an intentional political allegory, directed at a particular audience, for which the Knight stands as a not-too-distant double.

Judson Allen writes, "For medieval theory the audience of poetry was in a sense absorbed into it by virtue of that constant reciprocity acting between ordinary ethical life and its reflection in words."[52] The audience, in turn, expected to see itself and its experience mirrored in the poem at some level. Such expectations, as Allen rightly insists, arise from the very circumstances of oral performance and are reinforced by the Horatian dictum that poetry both delights and teaches; by the related, regular classification of poetry under ethics in the *accessus ad auctores;* and, as I have argued in this chapter, by the polysemous understanding of the *materia* that the poet invents.

In Chaucer's *Canterbury Tales*—to cite a well-known example—we find ample evidence that the tale tellers consciously adapted their *materia* to fit their intended auditors, and that the auditors in turn expected the narratives to be in some sense about themselves and interpreted them as such. The Reeve immediately gets edgy when the Miller announces the topic of his tale: "For I wol telle a legende and a lyf / Bothe of a carpenter and of his wyf, / How that a clerk hath set the wrightes cappe" (I.3141–43). Later, when he is about to avenge himself by insulting the Miller in turn, he complains, "This dronke Millere hath ytoold us heer / How that bigyled was a carpenter—/ Peraventure in scorn, for I am oon" (I.3913–15). The Friar takes the Summoner's description of a friar in his tale as so literal a reference to himself that he interrupts him, exclaiming, "Nay, ther thou lixt, thou Somonour!" (III.1761). And Harry Bailly comically derives his own meaning from the tale of Melibee, wishing that his wife, Goodelief, had heard it, because "she nys nothyng of swich pacience / As was this Melibeus wyf Prudence" (VII.1895–96).

These fictional responses of the pilgrim auditors certainly serve directly and indirectly to guide the responses of Chaucer's own intended audience(s), but they are also mimetic of a culture in which the choice and oral performance of stories was understood to be a commentary on local events. Storytelling, whether on pilgrimage, in the local tavern, in the king's presence at court, or from the pulpit was an art with real-life references and applications. Chaucer's Pardoner, for instance, knows how to take revenge on an opponent by making occult and uncomplimentary references to him in the course of a sermon through the careful use of an exemplum: "For though I telle noght his propre name, / Men shal wel knowe that it is the same / By signes and by othere circumstances" (VI.417–19).

In a manuscript culture, poetry was intended to be read aloud, and we know that poems were often recited before audiences in public and private settings. The conditions of oral performance make it highly unlikely that poets failed to take their expected audiences into material account when they first conceived of their work. As Allen has observed, "That much poetry was performed . . . suggests that these readings were inevitably occasions, and must often have had, either in the language or the emphasis of performance, some topical significance." Indeed, "occasionality, whether in some general ethical sense or in the sense of some very particular and pointed observation about some human incident, story, or life, seems clearly one of the distinctives of medieval literature."[53]

If the invention of matter to which Geoffrey of Vinsauf refers in shorthand fashion in the *Poetria Nova* actually involves the discovery and selection of letter, allegory, and intended audience, then the poetic theory enunciated in the *artes poetriae* bears a much closer relationship to the practice of vernacular poets than many scholars have previously supposed. Allen rightly asserts, "The very stuff of which poetry is made—the stories and descriptions which are, literally, the words which poems are—cannot be taken . . . in isolation. . . . Considered as texts, poems are, as it were, locations in a tissue of assimilatio larger than themselves."[54]

In this volume I search into the large web of associations in which the writings of late medieval England participate as products of a given time and place. I take seriously the medieval notion that their subject matter, as invented and intended by their authors, is both literal and allegorical. It is my argument that major English writers—William Langland, John Gower, Geoffrey Chaucer, the *Gawain*-poet, and Thomas Malory—offered timely commentary on public events and political issues through their fictions. They did so, moreover, in artful ways that attest to a similar education, a shared theory of allegorical composition, and familiarity with a variety of current cultural codes. The allegorical *materia* of their writings is, to a large extent, still recoverable today through the same logical principles whereby it was originally concealed. The audiences for whom they originally wrote would, of course, have had easier access to this veiled matter than we do. The poets counted on their capacity to discover it and employed that very process rhetorically, as a strategy of instruction, delight, and persuasion.

The characteristic indirection we find in Chaucer's poetry and that of his contemporaries attests, according to Lynn Staley, to their "keen sense of political realities and consequently of the needs for compromise, for ambiguity, and for deflection. These may be strategies of self-protection, but they are also the tools of art."[55] Given the fate of John Ball, Staley is surely right to emphasize "self-protection" as a motive for political allegory. As I suggest in the following chapters, however, there are also other motives. The use of allegory can endow a poet with a prophetic ethos that enhances his or her moral and spiritual authority. It can win poets the admiration of their auditors, who see their artistry and are dazzled by it. It can serve to unite and empower the members of an inner audience, who gain their identity and sense of belonging, on the one hand, by being divided off from others and, on the other, by being mutually "in the know." Finally, it can effect moral change in an auditor through the self-awareness that comes when one suddenly discovers one's very self allegorically represented.

The chapters are arranged chronologically, according to the historical events to which the works under discussion refer. Chapter 2 centers our attention on the Peasants' Revolt of 1381 and the allegorical literature associated with it: John Ball's letters and the A and B texts of William Langland's *Piers Plowman*. Chapter 3 turns to John Gower's allegorical treatment of the Merciless Parliament of 1388 in his *Confessio Amantis*. In Chapter 4 I survey Geoffrey Chaucer's Ricardian allegories and trace his development as a political allegorist, a development that culminates in his brilliant handling of key events in the reign of Richard II in the conjoined tales of the Monk and the Nun's Priest. Chapter 5 systematically decodes *Sir Gawain and the Green Knight* as a political allegory and argues for a precise dating of the poem between the years 1397, when Richard of Arundel was beheaded, and 1399, when Richard II was deposed. In Chapter 6 I address Thomas Malory's *Morte Darthur* as a typological allegory answering in part to the uses of Jehannine prophecy in England's war with France.

Although the chapters deal with different works by different authors, they are united by a consideration of recognizable codes and procedures, the repetition of which builds a strong case for the artful and rhetorical character of late medieval allegory. The works under study here are shown to refer in remarkably similar ways to similar things—a feature that safeguards this approach against the (often justified) charge of wild arbitrariness that arises frequently in cases of allegorical criticism.

The allegorical preoccupation with similar issues signals what is most problematic, worrisome, and threatening in fourteenth-century England. Here the poets and the chroniclers are in agreement. In a very real sense, the allegorical arguments of the works before us address the pressing issues of the day: issues of royal succession, of social justice, of the balance of powers between king and parliament, of the definition of treason, of the justification for (and consequences of) taking revenge, of the definition of heresy and sanctity.

To the extent that the poets offer a solution through the imaginative creation of a possible world, they typically do so through the insertion of hagiography. They allude to the lives of saints whose historical choices in the face of similar challenges were often different from, and radically other than, our own. Their *legenda* function allegorically to mark personal and social alternatives. For a medieval Christian, after all, to claim a saint as a patron and model was to embrace a two-edged sword: a source of power, yes, but also a standard of judgment. Thus, even in fourteenth- and fifteenth-century England, the city of God remains (as it was for Augustine) distinct from the earthly city and a challenge to it. Albeit veiled within the *civitas terrena* and sharing in its temporal suffering, it functions as its political "other."

2

"Full of Enigmas":
John Ball's Letters and *Piers Plowman*

"Literature" and "politics" are recent categories, which can be applied
to medieval culture . . . only by a retrospective hypothesis.
Michel Foucault, The Archaeology of Knowledge

The letters of John Ball afford us with an obvious, albeit difficult, beginning point for our consideration of late medieval English political allegory. The *Anonimalle Chronicle* reports that at the outbreak of the
Peasants' Revolt in 1381, when "the commons of southern England suddenly arose in two groups, one in Essex and the other in Kent," the rebel
leaders in Essex "sent letters ('diverses lettres') to those in Kent, Suffolk, and
Norfolk, asking them to rise with them."[1] Presumably letters were sent in
reply. The cryptic messages that Thomas Walsingham and Henry Knighton
preserve for us, and that they attribute to a prominent peasant leader, John
Ball, may tentatively be identified with this correspondence.[2] Such an identification lends immediate force to the words "nowe is tyme," which are repeated four times in the extant letters.[3]

According to Walsingham's *Historia Anglicana,* John Ball, calling himself
"Johan Trewman" and "John Schep, som tyme Seynt Marie prest of ȝorke,
and now of Colchestre," sent a coded letter ("aenigmatibus plenam") to
the commons of Essex, urging them to finish the work they had begun.[4]
The letter was afterwards discovered in the pocket of a man about to be
hanged for his part in the uprising ("pro turbatione"). Ball later confessed
that he had written the letter in question, as well as many others like it
("pluria alia") and had sent them to the commons. For this and for other
treasonous acts, Ball was drawn, hanged, and beheaded in the presence of
King Richard II at St. Albans on July 15, 1381, and the four parts of his
body were sent, as his letters had been, to the four corners of the kingdom
("et cadaver ejus quadripartitum quatuor regni civitatibus").[5]

Knighton gives a slightly different account. His *Chronicon* preserves two
examples of John Ball's letters, following three short speeches, which were

supposedly addressed to the rebels at Smithfield by Jack Milner, Jack Carter, and Jack Trueman. Scholars have long suspected that Knighton's representation of the first three texts as speeches is erroneous. From a formal perspective, they display epistolary conventions and resemble letters patent. Ball's attested use of pseudonyms ("John Schep" and "Johan Trewman") and the obvious intertextual relationships among the letters and speeches, moreover, strongly support the view of R. B. Dobson, among others, that John Ball "wrote all six letters under various pseudonyms."[6]

As Steven Justice has forcefully argued, however, "the dialectal differences among the three John Ball letters put it beyond doubt that his letters were copied and recirculated by rebels other than himself."[7] They may well have been copied by priests, since many clerics are known to have taken part in the rising, but "even if priests did write the letters," they did so under the pen names of peasants, thus staking the "rhetorical claim . . . that lay rural workers had begun to write and were taking a part in the culture of literacy" from which they had formerly been excluded (p. 25). The letters' "signatures were personae that staged the rebellion" under the "ideologically informed image" of the literate and virtuous peasant whom William Langland had first named "Piers Plowman" (p. 126).

The survival of six of John Ball's letters in two chronicles, one of which (Knighton's) was composed fifteen years after the insurrection, suggests that the letters had been diffused widely; that they were plentiful, visible, and recoverable; and that some of them had been preserved in archives (pp. 27–28). Justice calls the letters "broadsides," maintaining that they had been publicly posted and that they were "what official documents elsewhere call *escrowez* or *schedulae*" (p. 29). As vernacular broadsides, they had the revolutionary potential to reach a large new audience of literate commoners.

If Justice is right, and I believe he is, how are we to reconcile the public nature of the letters as revolutionary broadsides with the chroniclers' characterization of them as coded communications? External evidence urges us to classify the letters as allegorical. We have the contemporary witness of Walsingham that Ball's letter to the commons at Essex was "full of enigmas" ("aenigmatibus plenam").[8] The dangerous occasion of the letters, the important role they seem to have played in the rebellion, and the harsh punishment meted out to Ball for having written and disseminated them all suggest that the letters cloak a seditious content. The precise meaning of the letters to their intended recipients, however, remains elusive to us, even as it apparently did to Walsingham and Knighton, who preserve the letters in the vernacular in the midst of their Latin chronicles, as if to call attention to their inability to translate them.

What is striking about the letters, given their supposedly treasonous tenor, is their conservative vehicle. As V. J. Scattergood remarks, "In the verses associated with the rising, . . . radicalism is notably absent."⁹ Ball's letters seem to consist of little more than a list of proverbial sayings and scraps of poetry, including a versified complaint about the prevalence of the seven deadly sins: "Now regneth pride in pris, / and covetys is hold[e] wys, / and leccherye withouten shame / and glotonye withouten blame. / Envye regniþ with tresone, / and slouthe is take in grete sesone."¹⁰ As Siegfried Wenzel has amply demonstrated, this stanza closely resembles complaint verses found in late medieval preaching handbooks, such as that of John Grimestone.¹¹ Following Wenzel's careful lead, Richard F. Green has concluded that the other expressions in Ball's letters similarly "reflect the world of the popular preacher, their proverbs and scraps of vernacular verse turning up in sermons, sermon notes, and preaching manuals throughout the fourteenth century."¹²

The conventional nature of Ball's letters *ad litteram* inevitably raises questions that are often asked about Middle English complaint poems: Do they (to echo Rossell Hope Robbins) "refer to an actual topical abuse or are they aphoristic and proverbial?"¹³ Or can they be at the same time proverbs *and* allegories? Are Ball's proverbial letters in fact allegorical, that is, intended to carry a specific timely message to the rebels? If so, how did they seek to communicate it? What would have enabled Ball's letters to convey something more, or something other, than their literal meaning? And what allegorical truth would the rebellious "true commons" have discovered beneath the veil of John Ball's writings?¹⁴

Some scholars have suggested that the actual sayings in the letters are of little or no significance. What is important about the letters, according to Susan Crane, is that they provided the peasantry "with documents of their own to pass from hand to hand" and thus served to unite a semiliterate underclass in relation to their better-educated oppressors: the lords, the clergy, and their lawyers. Crane casts doubt on the literacy of the letters' author(s) and readers alike, arguing that the allusions to Langland's *Piers Plowman* in the letters are references to a work that "they perhaps knew only slightly or imperfectly."¹⁵ Similarly, Scattergood has dismissed the idea that the letters are deliberate allegories, pointing to their proverbial simplicity as proof that the rebels were unskilled writers who "had no more appropriate way of speaking in verse."¹⁶

Like Crane, Justice emphasizes that the medium of the letters was the greater part of their message. "The motive for the writing and the copying of the rebel letters," he writes, "lay chiefly not in their contents, but in the activity of their production: they made their most important claim merely by *being* written documents that came (or claimed to come) from the hands of *rustici*" (p. 36). Unlike Crane and Scattergood, however, Justice insists on the rebels' "familiarity and competence with the forms of literate culture" (p. 41), as shown in their targeting of particular documents, but not others, for destruction. If the content of the letters remains veiled to us, "it is not because the rebels were operating in a medium that did not belong to them (as Crane suggests)" (p. 130). According to Justice, Crane's position, and that of many modern historians, reflects the same prejudice that led Knighton originally to mistake letters as speeches: "Knighton . . . knew that no layperson could write a letter" (p. 17).

Despite his own inclination to attribute a sophisticated literacy to the rebels, however, Justice stops short of viewing the letters themselves as coded, on the grounds that allegorical composition and decoding "would have been the merest didactic irrelevance to anyone wondering what archive to torch, which prelate to lynch" (p. 24). He prefers to call them "elliptical" in their mode of reference, observing that "the letters are elliptical because they did not need to be otherwise: they assume that their community of address, and its interests and purposes, sufficiently define the terms of that meaning and render them comprehensible to that community" (p. 130). What Walsingham (as an outsider) terms allegorical and enigmatic, the rebels (as insiders) would have readily understood.

The letters are surely elliptical, but their being so does not preclude their also being designedly full of riddles; rather, it defines the very nature of their allegory as a concealment to some and a communication to others. As Andrew Galloway has stressed, "Late medieval textual communities . . . defined themselves by riddling verses," using enigmas to provide "access to . . . the compiler's specific social and intellectual community" and to confirm or deny "the reader's participation in that specific interpretive group, however elusive the boundaries of such interpretive communities might ever be." Galloway sees this tendency manifested both in *Piers Plowman* and "on a fully political scale in the cryptic 'letters' circulating in the Rising of 1381."[17]

Indeed, the use of riddles, wordplay, and allegory in the writings of Langland and Ball suggest a generic basis for their complex intertextuality. As Maureen Quilligan, Mary Carruthers, Lavinia Griffiths, and others have emphasized, Langland's names for things are likely to be puns that simultaneously name something else and thus dictate the course of the narrative as a semantic unfolding.[18] Defining Langland's allegory in such a way that it sounds "like the definition of a pun," Quilligan finds the "literalness of allegorical action" in *Piers Plowman* to be so dominant that it militates against searching for hidden meanings, political and otherwise, in the poem.[19]

Quilligan's approach affords us with a novel tool for approaching the literal texture of Langland's text, but A. J. Colaianne rightly observes that it is also typical of recent criticism in the way it deemphasizes "the social satire for which *Piers* was once well known and with it the cultural situations that helped to shape the poem's original purpose."[20] Quilligan fails to consider the possible interrelationship between literal, paranomastic allegory, on the one hand, and topical political allegory, on the other, in *Piers Plowman*. The one does not necessarily preclude the other. I would argue, in fact, that the restless literal movement of Langland's poem—a movement reinforced by paranomasia, concordance, translation, commentary, quotation, and paraphrase—urges us to seek the poem's meaning outside itself and to see *Piers Plowman* instead in relational terms (to borrow a phrase from Morton Bloomfield) as "a commentary on an unknown text," a social text.[21] John Ball, for one, certainly interpreted the poem in this way in both his sermons and his letters.

Without wishing to deny the sign value of the letters themselves as vernacular documents,[22] I hope to show that the strong association of the letters with preaching argues for their allegorical status.[23] Knighton's distinction between the priest's "letters," on the one hand, and the peasants' "speeches," on the other, is surely mistaken, but his blurring of the generic categories of the address and the epistle is more right than wrong, for John Ball's sermons precede, penetrate, and contextualize his letters. Indeed, the proverbs and verses that constitute the letters are best understood as a kind of shorthand, meant to recall sermons that Ball had previously preached, during which he had used and interpreted those same texts in application to contemporary social and political conditions. The specific clerical model for such a practice was the tradition of pulpit commentary on Wisdom literature—in particular the explanation and hortatory application of biblical proverbs and prophetic dreams and their classical analogues. The letters themselves point to such an origin in their multiple allusions to the "Sayings of the Four Philosophers," their echoing of Sapiential texts, their use of code names and puns, and their sophisticated response to the A and B versions of *Piers Plowman* as an allegorical dream-vision.

John Ball's Allegorical Preaching

John Ball was a priest and, as Rodney Hilton has emphasized, behind Ball and the other "clerics named in the chronicles and the indictments, we have indications of a wider and anonymous grouping" of clergymen, especially in Kent.[24] The chroniclers point to a loose alliance between and among peasants, artisans, mendicant friars, and Lollards.[25] According to Hilton, the clergymen who were involved in the revolt were "well-to-do as well as poor," literate, "familiar with general concepts about the rights of men and the duties of government," and versed in the Bible and patristic texts. Their "religious radicalism" and social commentary were therefore all "the more explosive."[26] According to the *Fasiculi Zizaniorum,* Ball confessed himself to be a follower of John Wycliffe.[27] Knighton calls Ball a "precursor" to Wycliffe, and Walsingham similarly records that Ball taught "the perverse doctrines of the perfidious John Wycliffe."[28]

Ball was first censored for illicit preaching in the 1360s, at a time roughly coincident with the composition of the A text of *Piers Plowman.* According to Walsingham, "for twenty years and more" prior to his execution in 1381, "Balle had been preaching continually in different places such things as he knew were pleasing to the people, speaking ill of both ecclesiastics and secular lords." When he was "prohibited by the bishops from preaching in parishes and churches, he began to speak in streets and squares and in the open fields."[29] Finally excommunicated and imprisoned, Ball predicted his own release, which came about at the bloody beginning of the Peasants' Revolt. Delivered by his followers from prison, he preached an incendiary sermon at Blackheath on June 12, 1381, before a crowd of "two hundred thousand of the commons."[30]

That famous sermon—the only one of Ball's sermons that has come down to us, albeit in summary form and by a hostile reporter—tells us much about Ball's customary preaching style and about the veiled content of his letters. The "text" of his sermon was a rhymed proverb that was already then a commonplace among preachers: "Whan Adam dalf, and Eve span, / Wo was thanne a gentilman?" Ball began with this proverb and interpreted it for his auditors with specific reference to serfdom, urging them to overthrow the oppressive "yoke of long servitude" ("servitutis jugo diutinae") in accord with the will of God, who "had now appointed the time" ("iam tempus a Deo datum") for the restoration of Edenic liberty and equality.[31] Ball exhorted them, as a means to this end, "to be prudent, hastening to act after the manner of a good husbandman, tilling his field and uprooting the tares that are accustomed to destroy the grain."[32] Understood in accord with Ball's exegesis, this parable of the tares (cf. Matt. 13:24–30, 37–43) meant "killing the great lords of the realm, then slaying the lawyers, justices, and jurors, and finally rooting out everyone whom they knew to be harmful" to the egalitarian community envisaged for the future.[33]

There are obvious elements in common between this sermon, as reported by Walsingham, and the extant letters. Both include proverbial matter that stands in need of interpretation. Both refer to the time that is "now appointed" by God: "God do bote, for nowe is tyme."[34] In the sermon Ball urges the peasants to "be prudent," even as his letter charges them, "Be ware or ye be wo."[35] The sermon at Blackheath promises the peasants that they "would obtain peace and security, if, when the great ones had been

removed, they maintained among themselves equality of liberty and nobility, as well as of dignity and power."[36] Similarly, the "littera Johannis Balle"
exhorts the commons, "And seketh pees, and holde therynne."[37] The sermon counsels them "to act after the manner of a good husbandman, tilling
the field," whereas the letter "biddeth Peres Plouȝman go to his werke."[38]

However idiosyncratic may have been Ball's interpretation of *Piers Plowman*, of parables such as the parable of the wheat and the weeds, and of
proverbs such as "Whan Adam dalf, and Eve span," his basic method in employing them was certainly not unusual. As Wenzel has shown, fourteenth-
century English preachers regularly used verses in their sermons, not only
for decoration but also for a variety of other functions: as renditions of the
sermon theme, as expressions of the *divisio*, as proverbial proof texts giving "authoritative proof for a point made by the preacher," as message verses
within exempla, as prayers, and as "versifications of material the audience
was required to memorize," such as the Ten Commandments and the
Seven Deadly Sins.[39] Rather than merely summing up a preceding prose
passage as a mnemonic aid for their audience, English verses sometimes
determined the entire structure of a sermon. Thus, Wenzel relates, "the
work of preachers formed . . . a generative center for the production of
English verses."[40]

The so-called complaint verses also frequently originated among preachers and appear in sermon handbooks. These verses, like those found in
John Ball's letters and addresses, typically "talk about general aspects of
human behavior, including vices and virtues."[41] Although, as Thomas L.
Kinney observes, "the generalization of this verse hides the specific object
of complaint," its hidden reference can easily be supplied by the auditors
themselves, especially if the preacher guides their interpretation through
the use of contemporary examples.[42] In this fashion the timeless becomes
timely. Indeed, the traditional can become revolutionary, and the proverb
a watchword among rebels.

Kinney has called attention to the "ambiguous authority of the poet of
complaint," whose only "real power is in communion with his audience."[43]
Spoken by a preacher, the poetry of complaint assumes a prophetic qual-
ity, especially if he contextualizes those verses or sayings within an exemplum or dream-vision story related in the course of a sermon. In such a
case, the poet-preacher's use of a visionary dreamer as a persona serves to
enhance his authority by deriving it from a prophetic source other than,
and higher than, the established powers-that-be. At the same time, the
dreamer's voice—to the extent that it articulates sentiments commonly
held by his auditors—invests the audience itself with "popular authority"
by defining their view of contemporary conditions as truly visionary.[44]

As Anne Middleton has emphasized, the Ricardian poet's most charac-

teristic voice is "the common voice." Middleton is too quick to deny, however, that this "common voice" can be reconciled with divine authority: "It
is [the public poet's] task to find the common voice and to speak for all,
but to claim no privileged position, no special revelation from God or the
Muses, no transcendent status for the result."[45] Langland, for his part, uses
the voice of a visionary dreamer to impart to his audience messages from
Holy Church and from Truth, whereas Ball claims to speak and to act in
God's name and encourages his followers to do the same.

The ambiguous status of dreams answers to the poet's "ambiguous authority" in yet another way, however, because dreams can be false as well as
true. The use of an unreliable (because dreaming) narrator thus affords
the poet a rhetorical shield and protection from powerful enemies, even
as it signals to his friends that his complaint is *intended* allegorically. When
estates satire and complaint take place within a dream vision, that contex-
tualization can turn proverbial wisdom into something more. Indeed, it
can transform a seemingly timeless moral observation about human folly
and vice into a veiled reference to living persons and topical events.

Ball's Letters and the "Sayings of the Four Philosophers"

Notable among extant sermons that combine the use of verse with
specific historical references are those that feature the exemplum of the
Four Philosophers. Wenzel attests to its "great popularity with medieval
preachers" and points to its inclusion in "a collection of preaching materials in MS. Harley 7322 and in the *Speculum Christiani*" as well as the *Gesta
Romanorum*.[46] The Auchinleck MS, composed circa 1330–40, also includes
the exemplum as "vn sarmoun / Of iiij wise men þat þer were, / Whi En-
gelond is brouht adoun," setting it within a two-part poem, the first sixteen
lines of which deal with political events of 1311.[47] In 1381 John Ball, too,
apparently used the exemplum of the sages and their "Sayings" as a basis
for commentary on contemporary conditions. Green has pointed out that
the address Knighton attributes to "Iakke Mylner" and the first letter he ascribes to John Ball both rhyme "might" with "right"—a rhyme that is prominent in the "Sayings of the Four Philosophers."[48]

In order to understand the significance of the link between the "Sayings"
and the letters of John Ball as a clue to the allegorical status of the latter,
we need to recall the frame story within which the "Sayings" appear. MS
Harley 7322 gives the earliest extant version in Latin prose. It describes a
realm, which had formerly enjoyed peace and prosperity, that is suddenly
beset with misfortune: "bellum, fames, pestilencia, & huiusmodi."[49] Its

noble king seeks the counsel of four philosophers concerning the causes of the present distress. Each of them gives three cryptic answers in English verse:

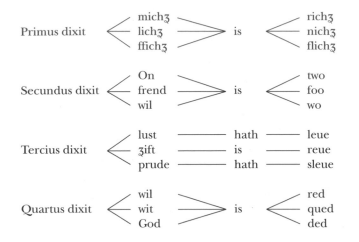

Primus dixit ← mich₃ / lich₃ / ffich₃ → is ← rich₃ / nich₃ / flich₃

Secundus dixit ← On / frend / wil → is ← two / foo / wo

Tercius dixit ← lust —— hath —— leue / ₃ift —— is —— reue / prude —— hath —— sleue

Quartus dixit ← wil / wit / God → is ← red / qued / ded

The king then asks them to explain: "Miscue sunt hec dicta que secundum vestrum intellectum exponatis." In the explanation that follows, Wenzel notes, "very often explicit references to England are made, and criticism is directed against such specific evils as oppression of the poor, pride of clothing, and the like."[50] The exposition includes illustrative exempla, such as the story of Jesus and his betrayer Judas (to explain the saying "God is ded") and that of the father who instructs his eight sons in the dangers of fraternal strife ("On is two") by breaking easily one stick, by breaking a larger bundle of four with difficulty, and by failing to break a bundle of eight.[51] It also incorporates English proverbs that correspond to the English "Sayings," using "wel fich₃t þat fleoþ," for example, to gloss "ffich₃ is flich₃."[52]

In the enormously popular *Speculum Christiani* (ca. 1400), an unnamed king similarly consults four philosophers about the cause of the "many myscheffys and myshapys" that have befallen his realm, asking in particular why they are more prevalent "in the peple in his tyme than in tymes of predescessours."[53] The sages reply in the same verse-answers found in MS Harley 7322. In the *Speculum*, however, the explanations of these verses typically take the form of compiled sentences from the Bible; from church fathers such as Ambrose, Augustine, Gregory, and Origen; from Seneca; and from theologians such as Saint Bernard and Robert Grosseteste. The author of the *Speculum* does nevertheless occasionally insert a personal explanation with a topical ring. For example, "*Frende is foo.* That may be vndyrstonde when grete worldly men, and namly myghty and ryche

men, strangle the true pees or rightwysnesse or holy chirche, in suche mys-
doers aȝen which ȝe aughten myghtily to stande and fighte for true pees
and right of al-holy chirche, principally for goddes cause."[54]

The insertion of this passage, with its direct address to its audience and
its call to them "myghtily to stande and fighte for true pees" against powerful lords, suggests the kind of commentary on the "Sayings" that John Ball
may have given. In one of his letters he urges his followers: "Knoweth ȝour
frende fro ȝoure foo" and "stondith togiddir in Goddis name."[55] Similarly,
Ball's "prima epistola" invokes the Blessed Trinity and bids them "stonde
manlyche togedyr in trewthe, and helpez trewthe, and trewthe schal helpe
ȝowe."[56]

In the English *Gesta Romanorum* the frame story that occasions the "Sayings of the Four Philosophers" specifies social conditions in Rome that are
strikingly parallel to those in fourteenth-century England: "This is redde in
the Cronycles of Rome, that in the tyme of Antynyane, the Emperour, in the
Citee of Rome befille a grete pestilence of men and bestes, and grete hun-
gre in all the Empire."[57] Like the "Cronycles of Rome," English chronicles
such as John Capgrave's depict plague, famine, and economic decline:

> 1349. In þe xxiii ȝere was þe grete pestilens of puple. First it began in þe
> north cuntré, þan in þe south, and so forth þorwoute þe reme. Aftir þis
> pestilens folowid a moreyn of bestis, whech had neuyr be seyn. For, as it
> was supposed, þere left not in Inglond þe ten part of the puple. Than cesed
> lordes rentis, prestis tithes; because þere were so fewe tylmen, þe erde lay
> vntilled. So mech misery was in þe lond þat þe prosperité whech was be-
> fore was neuyr recured.[58]

Assuming a tone of complaint, Capgrave looks back to a prosperous time
before the Black Death, even as the ruler in the story ponders the contrast
between his unfortunate realm and the peaceful, prosperous kingdom of
former kings.

In the exemplum in the *Gesta Romanorum*, plague and famine lead directly to revolt: "The comons risen agayn her lordes and agayn her Emperour."[59] The mention of the revolt of the commons against the lords
does not appear in either MS Harley 7322 or the *Speculum Christiani*, but
its appearance here indicates the adaptability of the frame story. Although
the Black Death of 1349 stands at best as a remote cause among a complex
of causes for the Revolt of 1381, the association of plague and revolt in
the *Gesta* would have provided a convenient means for a dissident
preacher such as Ball, in the course of a sermon on the "Sayings," to make
a comparative listing of causes for rebellion by the poor commons (*menues
communes*).

In the act of consulting the philosophers, the king in the *Gesta* seeks not only a diagnosis of the causes of misfortune but also a means of return and recovery through an active reversal of things: "The Emperour desired to wete the cause of the tribulacions and discases and disposed hym forto putte a remedie agayn the forsaid disease."[60] The exemplum of the Four Philosophers thus shares with John Ball's sermon at Blackheath—and indeed with the whole tradition of verse complaint—a "nostalgic evocation of the golden past" that is, as Kinney remarks, "darkly compared with present conditions."[61] Ball, however, looked farther back than most did—back to Eden itself—and that radicalism led him, as we shall see, to espouse his own version of the "Sayings of the Four Philosophers."

The popularity of the exemplum and its adaptability to various times and places encouraged preachers and poets to tell the story in different ways, and the extant versions hint at considerable fluidity within the tradition. As we have already seen, these versions specify slightly different misfortunes. Similarly, the king goes unnamed in the *Speculum Christiani* and in the Latin *Gesta Romanorum*, but he is variously identified elsewhere as Antoninus (in the English *Gesta*), as Varro (in MS Harley 7322), and as Hannibal (in MS Cotton Vespasian E.XII).[62]

The answers given by the philosophers and their explanations of them also vary. In the English *Gesta*, the four philosophers give verse answers, beginning with "Gifte is domesman," that differ from those in the *Speculum* and MS Harley 7322.[63] The Auchinleck MS preserves the "Might is right" version of the answers, adds a variant of the same, and inserts these triplets among stanzas rhyming *aabccb*, each of which gives an alternative version of the philosopher's reply. In this case, Wenzel remarks, we must "conclude that . . . the unknown poet has made a potpourri from three different though related things: his own verses and two forms of *Might is right*."[64]

In addition to variants with regard to the kingdom's misfortune, the king's name, the answers given by the philosophers, and the explanations of those answers, we need to note one other attested variation, in which the "sayings" appear as inscriptions. In MS Douce 95 there are four isolated lines of verse, two in Latin hexameters and two in English, that record what the "primus philosophus" wrote on the eastern gate of a city ("in porta orientali").[65] Similarly, in MS Cotton Vespasian E.XII, Virgil guides Hannibal to discover inscriptions carved in stone on the four gates of the city, each of which spells out three Carthaginian vices in answer to Hannibal's question about the underlying cause of his army's defeat by Rome.[66]

John Ball's letters give a fragmentary witness to his version of the "Sayings of the Four Philosophers." In the fourth letter in Knighton's *Chronicon* ("Exemplar epistolae Johannis Balle"), Ball urges his followers, "Nowe ryȝt and myȝt, wylle and skylle."[67] In the pseudonymous address of "Jakke

Mylner," the same four rhyme words appear in what is apparently an allegory of a mill.[68] Ball's choice of a mill is especially appropriate, as Justice notes, because "milling rights were a perpetual irritant between tenants and landlords" (p. 136). The four sails of the mill resemble the four gates of Hannibal's city, inscribed with cryptic answers, and they represent the qualities of Right, Might, Skill, and Will. The successful grinding of the mill of revolution depends on the turning of the sails in the proper order, an order that reverses the subordination of Right to Might and resists the identification of the two. Justice observes, "The letters' mill diagrams the moral basis of the rebels' claim in a schematically allegorical image" (p. 136). The "Might" of the wealthy can no longer be "Right," but neither can "Right" by itself be "Might." Rather, "Right," understood as social justice, must be furthered by "Might" in a show of armed resistance by the peasants:

> Iakke Mylner asketh help to turne hys mylne aright. . . . Loke thy mylne go ariȝt, with the foure sayles and the post stande in stedfastnesse. With riȝt and with myȝt, with skyl and with wylle, lat myȝt helpe ryȝt, and skyl go before wille and ryȝt before myȝt, than goth oure mylne aryght. And if myȝt go before ryght, and wylle before skylle, than is oure mylne mys adyȝt.[69]

Thus, not only does Ball offer a fourfold diagnosis of the causes of misfortune in England, but also he rearranges those same four terms to define its cure. In so doing he echoes the answer of the first philosopher, "Might is right," even as he transforms it.

The rhyme word "wyl" traditionally appears in the first answer of the fourth philosopher: "Wyl is rede." The word "skyl," with which Ball pairs it, does not appear, but it is related semantically to "rede" as an aspect of practical wisdom. The substitution of "skyl" for "rede" allows for the "skill"-"will" rhyme and enables Ball to follow his practice of converting a lamentatious listing of problems, such as we find in this couplet from *Speculum Christiani*, "To maynten syn som kan grete skylle, / And wronge prefe ryght for ȝiftes they wylle,"[70] into a battle cry for their solution: "with ryȝt and with myȝt, with skyl and with wylle."

In directing the tradition of the "Sayings" beyond the diagnosis of social ills to an activist prescription for their remedy, Ball follows an impulse that he shares with the author of MS Harley 7322. At the end of its explanations of the four philosophers' cryptic answers, the Harley author recalls another set of frequently allegorized words, the names of the four Daughters of God: Peace, Truth, Justice, and Mercy.[71] These he summarizes in "duo verba anglicana," *trouthe* and *reuthe*. The first, he says, includes the whole law and all of philosophy, whereas mercy (*reuthe*) is, as the Psalmist declares, above all of God's works.[72] Ball's Edenic vision is arguably no less apocalyptic in its revolutionary evocation of a striving for "pees" and "trewthe."

Other expressions in Ball's letters similarly reflect the tradition of the "Sayings." As I have suggested, his injunction "Knoweth ȝour frende fro ȝoure foo" transforms the second answer of the second philosopher, "Frende is foo."[73] Indeed, it translates that proverb into the watchword used by the rebels: "Wyth kynge Richarde and wyth the trewe communes."[74] Similarly, the exhortation "and loke schappe ȝou to on heued, and no mo" recalls the philosopher's saying "On es two."[75] It changes a commonplace complaint about societal divison into a call for united action by the peasants under the leadership of Wat Tyler. At the same time it comments on the crisis in leadership in England during Richard II's minority, thus giving a topical reference to the biblical sentence with which the *Speculum Christiani* glosses "On is two": "Euery kyngedome hauinge dyuision in hym-selfe schal be desolate and forsaken."[76]

Other intertextual relationships between the letters and the "Sayings" are more buried. Most obviously, perhaps, the aggressive action of the rebels against their oppressors literally reverses the philosopher's complaint that "fyght es flight." As the *Speculum Christiani* insists, it is "consent of erroure" and complicity with evil "to do wele, as so sey in thyn owne person, and not to forbede vnleful thynges in other."[77] In that spirit Ball urges the rebels to "do welle and bettre, and fleth synne" and to stand "togiddir in Goddis name" against injustice.[78]

The opposition of "trewþe" to "falsness and gyle" in the address of "Jak Trewman" and his references to bribery in the courts resemble a gloss on the answer of the first philosopher, "Gifte es domesman," or, in a different tradition, "Might is right." The *Speculum Christiani* effectively combines the two traditions by glossing "Might is right" with a sentence from the prophet Isaiah: "True dome es turned bakwarde. . . . Truth has fallen in the stretes, and equite myght not entre."[79] Similarly, "Trewman" complains, "Trewþe hat bene sette under a lokke, and falsnes regneth in everylk flokke. No man may come trewþe to, but he syng *si dedero*."[80]

The whole world of the medieval popular preacher stands, of course, as a background to John Ball's letters, even as it does to *Piers Plowman*,[81] and I do not mean to suggest that the "Sayings of the Four Philosophers" were Ball's only model. The exemplum would, however, have given Ball an important occasion for social commentary through exegesis in his sermons, as well as a means of allegorical communication with his auditors through letters composed of proverbial inscriptions resembling the words on the four gates of Carthage. The very intelligibility of the letters depends on their referring to something outside themselves, namely, to Ball's already familiar teaching in his sermons. The letters are indeed (to use Justice's word) "elliptical," but they are also (and for that very reason) "full of enigmas."

Ball's Allegorical Letters: Piers, Hobbe, and Jon

The letters, as we shall see, allude repeatedly to *Piers Plowman* in its A and/or B versions and provide us with the earliest surviving record of its reception. We cannot, in fact, understand what *Piers Plowman* meant to at least one of its contemporary audiences without paying close attention to John Ball's interpretation and appropriation of its words and images. As Anne Hudson remarks, judging by Ball's letters, "It seems impossible to avoid the conclusion that *Piers Plowman* had by 1381 gained sufficient fame amongst those likely to favour the Revolt to act as a rallying cry." The poem was plainly "perceived as an expression of sympathy with, if not of instigation to, action by such participants towards bettering their lot."[82]

Langland's Piers is named twice in the letters. In Knighton's *Chronicon* "Jack Carter" issues the following imperative: "Lat Peres the Plowman my brother duelle at home and dyʒt us corne, and I will go with ʒowe and helpe that I may to dyʒt ʒoure mete and ʒoure drynke, that ʒe non fayle."[83] Walsingham's *Historia* records a similar order from Ball, who "biddeth Peres Plouʒman go to his werke."[84] In the letters that work is associated literally with the fields, allegorically with the revolt itself, for the insurgent peasants and artisans are urged to "do welle and bettre" (in Walsingham) and to do "wele and ay bettur and bettur" (in Knighton). John Gower's *Vox Clamantis* offers some support (albeit ironic) for an association of Langland's Do-Wel, Do-Bet, and Do-Best with the actions of the rebels: "One man helped in what another man did, and another agreed that they would be bad, worse, and worst" (I.1121–22: "Iste iuuat quod et ille facit, consentit et alter, / Vt malus et peior pessimus inde forent").[85]

In addition to these obvious allusions, others have been proposed. Following Walter W. Skeat's suggestion, James M. Dean regards John Ball's pseudonym, "Johan Schep" as an allusion to the opening line of *Piers Plowman:* "In a somer seson, whan softe was the sonne, / I shoop me into a shroud as I a *sheep* weere."[86] Similarly, I would suggest, Ball puns on his own name in order to allude to Langland's Parliament of the Rats and their plan to bell the cat: "Jon Balle greteth ʒow wele alle and doth ʒowe to understande, he hath rungen ʒoure belle."[87]

Even more than the A text, the B text of *Piers Plowman* trains its auditors in allegorical interpretation and involves them in completing its meaning by supplying what is literally missing. In the B Prologue a "lunatik," an "Aungel of heuene," and a "Goliardeis" appear in rapid succession, each delivering in the king's presence a speech that is both proverbial and enigmatic (ll. 123, 128, 139). That scene in turn is interrupted as a swarming "route of Ratons" enters and assembles a "counseil for the commune profit" (ll. 146, 148). A "raton of renon" proposes to the assembled rats and mice that they, for the sake of "comune profit," buy "a belle of brasse or of briȝte sylver" to hang about the cat's neck (B Prologue, ll. 158, 168–69).[88]

At the Prologue's end, the narrator signals the allegorical nature of the whole dream sequence and involves his audience in its interpretation: "What þis metels bymeneþ, ye men þat ben murye, / Deuyne ye, for I ne dar, by deere god in heuene" (B Prologue, ll. 209–10; emphasis added). The rebel readers of this passage clearly took seriously this invitation to interpret. In *Piers Plowman,* Langland's rats and mice finally lack the courage to bell the cat, but in his letters Balle/Belle is ready to arouse the commons with a call to arms: "Nowe is tyme."

Ball's chief enemy corresponds to the "cat" in *Piers Plowman,* namely, John of Gaunt.[89] In the letters there are, in addition to Piers's name and Ball's pseudonymous names, two other proper names: "Hobbe the Robbere" and "Jon of Ba(n)thon." The references to the latter characters are negative, and I argue that they stand as code names for the two men whom Hilton has termed the "prime targets" of the rebels: Sir Robert Hales, the Treasurer, and John of Gaunt, duke of Lancaster.[90]

The first identification is not an original one. Others have suggested that "Hobbe"—an attested Middle English nickname for Roger or Robert—is a code name for the Treasurer, and that Ball's use of it with the epithet "Robbere" alludes to the "Robert þe robbere" in *Piers Plowman* (B V.469), who has stolen so much that he can never make the restitution (*reddite*) on which his forgiveness depends.[91] Langland describes the robber's weeping and his plea for mercy, but he leaves his fate unspecified: "What bifel of þis feloun I can nouȝte faire schewe" (B V.479). In a move that is characteristic of him, Ball fills the gap in Langland's text, finishing it with a vengeance. In Walsingham's *Historia,* Ball urges his followers to "chastise welle Hobbe the robber."[92] Knighton's "Jak Carter" also admonishes the rebels, "Lokke that Hobbe robbyoure be wele chastysed."[93]

On June 14, 1381, the mob seized the Tower of London and beheaded Sir Robert Hales, along with Archbishop Simon Sudbury and two others. On the previous afternoon they had set fire to the Temple Bar and to the Hospitallers' house in Clerkenwell, presumably because of Hales's position as High Prior of the Hospital of St. John of Jerusalem. Hilton observes that "the general attack on Hospitallers' property in London as well as in the country can be attributed to the Treasurer's unpopularity, for John of Gaunt was the only other leading personality whose property in London and elsewhere was systematically despoiled."[94] Indeed, the destructive route of the rebels in London links Hales with Gaunt. The *Anonimalle Chronicle* puts it succinctly: "On their way to the Savoy they destroyed all the houses which belonged to the Master of the Hospital of St. John."[95]

The behavior of the rebels during the attack on Gaunt's Savoy Palace has led some to view "Hobbe the Robbere" in Ball's letters as a reference not to Robert Hales, but rather to any thief among the peasants themselves whose greed would discredit their cause and result, in Ball's words, in the "lesyng of . . . grace" and of God's favor.[96] Walsingham reports, "In order that the whole community of the realm should know that they were not motivated by avarice, they made a proclamation that no one should retain for his own use any object found there [i.e., at the Savoy] under penalty of execution." Indeed, "if they discovered anyone guilty of theft, they would execute him, because they detested robbers."[97] According to Knighton's account, the rebels held to their word and tossed a looter into the fire at the Savoy, "saying that they were lovers of truth and justice, not robbers and thieves."[98]

One identification need not, however, exclude the other. The rebels are consistent in their punishment of robbers, noble and peasant alike. If they regarded Treasurer Robert Hales as an arch-robber and the virtual personification of thievery, what better way for them to signal the "otherness" of their opposition than through a double allegory? At one level, chastising "Hobbe" thus means taking vengeance on Hales. At another level, it uses his name as an allegory to signify what they were not and did not want to be, that is, a robber like him.

If "Hobbe the Robbere" does refer in a narrow and particular sense to Robert Hales, then the previously unidentified "Jon of Ba(n)thon" is almost certainly John of Gaunt.[99] The two men were the special objects of the rebels' hatred, and there are only two foes named in Ball's letters. The mysterious and potentially dangerous reference, moreover, appears in a context that strongly hints at allegory, at truth hidden under a veil: the letter of "Jak Trewman," who bewails the imprisonment of "trewþe . . . under a lokke."[100]

In this letter "Jon of Ba(n)thon" is a rich and bad counselor, whose sole advice is "Speke, spende, and spede." Justice terms this passage "the most explicitly topical reference in the rebel letters" (p. 133). Interpreted as a principle of policy, this threefold alliterating imperative links "Jon of Ba(n)thon" with the economic instability, monetary abuse, and rampant practices of bribery that *Piers Plowman* personifies in Lady Meed.[101] Meed, in turn, as scholars have long recognized, bears the features of Alice Perrers, the notorious mistress of Edward III, whose supporter John of Gaunt was held to be.[102] Gaunt, after all, had opposed the Good Parliament of 1376 and had effected the reversal of many of its decisions, including its dismissal of Perrers.[103]

More important, however, the letter of "Jak Trewman" blames the powerful influence of "Jon of Ba(n)thon" and the words he "quoth" for all the evils of the age: "*and therefore* synne fareth as wilde flode, trewe love is away, that was so gode, and clerkus for welthe worche hem wo."[104] Among Ball's contemporaries in 1381, only John of Gaunt could have been singled out by the rebels as the cause of England's ills, because of his enormous wealth, his role in foreign and domestic policy, and his privileged status as the young king's guardian. In 1381 Gaunt's power and influence overshadowed that of Richard, the boyking. Thus, as the *Anonimalle Chronicle* affirms, the rebels "directed their evil actions against the duke of Lancaster."[105] In Kent the rebels stopped pilgrims on their way to Canterbury and made them swear "that they would be faithful to King Richard and the commons and that they would accept no king who was called John."[106] Shortly thereafter, when Richard II declined to meet with the rebels assembled at Blackheath, "the commons of Kent sent him a petition asking him to grant them the heads of the duke of Lancaster and fifteen other lords."[107]

Supposing that "Jon of Ba(n)thon" represents John of Gaunt, how is the substitution of place names to be explained? What covert connection, if any, was there between Bath and Ghent? The answer to this question lies, I believe, in the idiom of the English wool workers and weavers who played a major part in the revolt. Although the precise relationship between the two cities in the everyday parlance of the weavers cannot easily be recovered, there are strong, albeit inconclusive, grounds for supposing that such an association existed and inspired Ball's code name for the duke.

One important indication of this comes from Geoffrey Chaucer, who was controller of the customs (that is, export tax) on wool, sheepskins, and leather and of the subsidy tax on these same items from 1374 to 1386, and who thus had close dealings with the organized weavers in London at the time of the revolt.[108] Wool was England's chief export, and the tax revenue from its trade paid the daily costs of government. Through his regular interaction with the collectors, Chaucer would have had access to the talk and the complaints of the wool workers.

In 1381 those complaints were numerous. According to T. H. Lloyd, "The fall in [English] exports which had begun in the 1360s continued unabated throughout the last quarter of the fourteenth century," partly a result of unwise policy concerning the staple, the taxation of exports, and monetary regulation, but also owing to the civil war which wracked Flanders from 1379 to 1385.[109] The weavers in Ghent arouse in revolt in September 1379, and "in the parliaments of January and November 1380 . . . the chancellor alleged that the revolt was discouraging the Flemings from buying wool and that in consequence the custom revenue was declining."[110] As the Flemish cloth industry moved from the towns to rural areas, the Flemish weavers used "cheaper native, Scots and Spanish wool at the expense of the English product," and the "same tendency is observable in Brabant."[111]

In England the discontent of the wool workers showed itself during the

Peasants' Revolt in a concerted attack on Flemish immigrants. As Hilton notes, the chronicles record "many attacks on the Flemish (among whom we should probably include Brabanters) who are assumed to have been weavers, rivals of the native craftsmen and organized separately from them."[112] The rebels included master weavers who were "jealous of the privileges the Flemings enjoyed," as well as "English journeymen employed by Flemish masters" whose "class antagonism" was "cloaked, consciously or unconsciously, by xenophobia."[113] Their violence was unrestrained. As the Monk of Westminster relates, the rebels "went on to the banks of the river Thames where the majority of the Flemings lived; and they beheaded all the Flemings they found without judgment and without cause. For you could see heaps of dead bodies lying in the squares and other places. And so they spent the day, thinking only of the massacre of Flemings."[114] The other chroniclers make similar reports, and Chaucer also alludes to the slaughter in "The Nun's Priest's Tale" (*Canterbury Tales* VII.4584–87). As Hilton observes, moreover, "the attack on the Flemings was not peculiar to London."[115]

The Flemish wool trade had its real and symbolic center in Ghent, where John of Gaunt was born in 1340.[116] There he was held at the baptismal font by Jacques van Artevelde, whom Anthony Goodman calls the "architect of the bourgeois alliance" with the English "woolmonger" king, Edward III.[117] His godfather was John, duke of Brabant. According to Goodman, throughout his life John of Gaunt cherished his ties "with the French-speaking princely families of the Low Countries and was always ready to acknowledge that he was of the comital family of Hainault."[118] Gaunt's very name, together with the fiscal and foreign policy he espoused, would have made him in the rebels' eyes a protector of the Flemish wool workers, whom they hated.

If the "Jon of Ba(n)thon" is John of Gaunt, and if Ball's letters were posted as broadsides in 1381, then that posting marks the second time that broadsides were used against the duke of Lancaster. As Justice notes, in 1377 "during the conflict between John of Gaunt and the city of London . . . broadsides in verse (*rhythmos*) appeared, claiming that Lancaster was actually son to a butcher of Ghent" (p. 29). According to the *Anonimalle Chronicle*, the story then circulated throughout England that a low-born Flemish infant ("fitz a une bowcher de Gaunt") had been substituted for Edward III's true son, who had been born deformed and killed at birth by his nurse. The broadsides that were posted throughout London protested that the supposed duke was Flemish rather than English, and therefore loved the Flemings twice as much ("amast plus les Flemynges qe les Engleis par cent double").[119]

In his poetry Chaucer uses the word "Gaunt" only in connection with Flemish cloth making. In Chaucer's English translation of Guillaume de

Lorris's *Roman de la Rose,* Ydelnesse wears a coat "of cloth of Gaunt."[120] More important for my analysis here, in *The Canterbury Tales* Chaucer figures the Wife of Bath as a weaver and through her associates the cities of Bath and Ghent ("Gaunt") as rivals in the wool trade: "A good Wif was ther of biside Bathe, / But she was somdel deef, and that was scathe. / Of clooth-makyng she hadde swich an haunt / She passed hem of Ypres and of Gaunt" (General Prologue, ll. 445–48).

Chaucer's association of the two cities in this passage has caught the notice of scholars, beginning with John Matthews Manly, who identified the Wife's residence "biside Bathe" with the parish of St. Michael's *juxta Bathon,* a parish largely devoted to weaving.[121] Historians affirm, moreover, that the city of Bath itself was heavily involved in the wool trade.[122] In Manly's view, Chaucer's comparison of Ghent with Bath represents some kind of local joke, because the "cloth of Ypres and Ghent and other cities of the Low Countries was for centuries held in the highest esteem," whereas the West Country weavers, including those of Bath in Somerset, enjoyed a poor reputation at home and abroad.[123] Manly cites the work of Henry Atton and Henry Hurst Holland, who point to a statute requiring that "West-Country cloth . . . be exposed for sale open, as merchants who had brought it by the bale and had taken it abroad had been in danger of their lives from the incensement of buyers who had found the bales deceptive."[124]

In his choice of "Jon of Ba(n)thon" as a code name for John of Gaunt, Ball was probably inspired by a current wool workers' joke similar to that which inspired Chaucer to make Alisoun of Bath a weaver whose cloth making surpassed that of weavers from Ghent. The joke, as the suspended "n" in Ba(n)thon suggests, may have originated in an incident of mislabeling or misreading, resulting from the orthographic resemblance of the capitals *B* and *G* and the suspension of *n* or *un*. Wool from "Ga(un)thon" could (momentarily at least) be mistaken for wool from "Bathon," and vice versa. The letter that veils Ball's allegory thus literally derives from cloth makers and wool dealers, even as Ball's pseudonym "Jon Schep" recalls both his priestly mission as a shepherd for his flock and his ties as a rebel leader to the organized weavers. This pattern of association, as I have already suggested, puts Ball's letters in dialogue with *Piers Plowman,* a political allegory that literally begins with the wanderer's body being garbed in wool: "I shoop me into a shroud as I a sheep weere" (B Prologue, l. 2).

John Ball's Allegorical Reading of William Langland

Langland's first-person narrator soon falls asleep, only to have a "merueillous sweuene," a dream-vision, in which he beholds a "fair feeld ful of folk" that is framed, on one side, by a tower raised on a hilltop; on the other, by a dungeon set in a "deep dale" (B Prologue, ll. 11, 13–17). Sheila Delany has noted that "this opening allegory . . . soon becomes indistinguishable from realistic satire."[125] The shifts throughout the poem "between various modes of representation," and especially the recurrent use of dreaming and waking as frames for Langland's social commentary, raise the question of the generic relationship between allegory, on the one hand, and complaint and satire, on the other. According to Delany, allegorical representation and analogical argument are "admirably suited to the needs of any ruling class which feels itself threatened by change; while those who desire change will tend to be wary of allegory."[126] Delany therefore regards the device of the dream and the use of personification as signs of Langland's conservative acceptance of hierarchical structures of governance; furthermore, she sees the mixture of these allegorical forms with realistic complaint as a sign of his "divided will" as a reformist.[127]

The pronounced use of allegory in Ball's letters and in certain Lollard texts, however, argues against Delany's too simple analysis of Langland's *Piers* and suggests that it was precisely Langland's overt use of allegorical forms that led rebel readers such as John Ball not only to interpret his complaints and satiric sketches as revolutionary, but also to appropriate his words as watchwords. English reformists in the late Middle Ages regularly interpreted in an allegorical sense what their opponents took literally, and vice versa. Allegory enabled them to agree superficially with their opponents, even when they actually disagreed; it afforded them, moreover, an effective means of covert communication, self-protection, and spiritual authority.

In the Lollard *Ploughman's Tale* (ca. 1396) we find, for example, an instance of personification allegory. There a Griffon (representing the papists) and the Pelican (representing Christ suffering in the persecuted Lollards) carry on an extended debate about the nature of the true church. The ploughman, who witnesses the fowls' debate and records their words, concludes with a declaration of his own innocence and a disavowal of the Pelican's angry complaints: "Witeth the Pellican and not me / For hereof I nill not auow."[128]

The 1407 inquiry of Sir William Thorpe before Thomas Arundel, archbishop of Canterbury, provides a more complex example of allegorical usage by a Lollard. Accused of preaching in Shrewsbury against the lawfulness of pilgrimage, Thorpe protests, "But, ser, I seide neuere þus, for I knowe þat þere is trewe pilgrimage and leeful and ful plesynge to God."[129] True pilgrimages, as he explains, involve taking one spiritual "stap" after another (not unlike Langland's *passus*) to God through prayers and good works, "steps" not taken by "þe moost parte of hem, boþe men and wymmen, þat gon now on pilgrimage."[130] Accused furthermore of denying the lawfulness of musical instruments such as organs in worship, Thorpe again responds by interpreting Scripture allegorically. Although David commends in the Psalms the use of "dyuersc instrumentis of musik for to presie wiþ God," Thorpe explains, "þese instrumentis wiþ her musyk owen to be interpretid goostly, for alle þei figuren hiȝe vertues and grete."[131]

A striking coincidence obtains, on the one hand, between Thorpe's objections to the practice of literal pilgrimage and Langland's repeated complaints against "Rome renneres" (B IV.128) and, on the other hand, between Thorpe's allegorization of pilgrimage and Langland's in Passus V-VI of the B text of *Piers Plowman:* "And ye þat seke Seynt Iames and Seyntes at Rome, / Sekeþ Seynt Truþe" (B V.56–57). There Piers substitutes for the well-traveled Palmer and guides the pilgrims seeking the Shrine of St. Truth not by literally journeying with them, but rather by allowing them to help him in his "at home" task of plowing, sowing, and harvesting. Such, at least, is the interpretation John Ball seems to have given Langland's poem, for, as Steven Justice notes, he affirms Piers's decision to work his half acre as an alternative to pilgrimage, telling him to "duelle at home."[132]

The Lollards, as is well known, objected to both the making of pilgrimages and the purchasing of pardons.[133] Langland's narrative argument notably links the two topics, for Piers's pilgrimage first turns into plowing, and then his plowing is rewarded by a pardon granted by Truth. John Burrow has brilliantly demonstrated how Langland uses a similar strategy of allegorization in his treatments of the pilgrimage and the pardon.[134] As we shall see, moreover, John Ball's allegorical reading of the latter scene parallels his interpretation of the former.

That Ball alludes to Langland's work is indisputable, but scholars disagree about how we are to characterize the relationship between Ball's letters and *Piers Plowman*. Walter W. Skeat long ago maintained that Ball had read *Piers* but had misinterpreted it, mistaking the passionate social satire of a conservative moralist for a political call to arms. According to Skeat, Langland "nowhere recommends or encourages revolutionary ideas, but the contrary, and he never could have intended his words to have roused the flames of rebellion. . . . His bold words were perverted into watchwords of insurgency."[135] That view is often repeated. Modifying Skeat's position somewhat, Rossell H. Robbins has argued that "fundamentally conservative" and "pro-Establishment" thinkers such as John Wycliffe and William Langland actually gave "the most dangerous and far-reaching manifestations of dissent" in their writings through the "*unconscious* formulations . . . of basically dissident positions" that later fueled the "open rebellion" of men such as Ball.[136]

More recently, David Aers has challenged Robbins's view that Langland was "unconscious" of his own dissidence, arguing instead that the insights of Langland's imagination ultimately led him, like the rebels, to reject a conservative ideology.[137] To this George Kane has replied that "the revolutionary implications" of Langland's poem and "of Ball's two 'letters' . . . have been exaggerated," and that "there is in fact no genuinely revolutionary writing in Middle English prose or verse, except that of Wyclif and the Lollards."[138] Kane's stance, in turn, has inspired opposite responses. Russell Peck, on the one hand, aligns both Langland and Ball as radical reformists with Wycliffe, while Richard F. Green, on the other hand, characterizes the leaders of the Peasants' Revolt as reactionaries far "to the right" on the political spectrum, and he associates them not with the Lollards but with the friars.[139]

A sophisticated recent analysis of Ball's reading of Langland is provided by Anne Middleton. Noting that "both reformers and orthodox men of affairs" discovered in *Piers Plowman* "a particularly powerful idiom for thought about the contemporary community," she insists that any partisan appropriation of the poem's meaning, including Ball's, results from mistaking "literary" for "rhetorically instrumental discourse."[140] Langland as author understood that his poem's "heteroclitic nature, its capacity to become a property of public discourse in several incommensurable ways at once, define[d] its social power and wholly *ad hoc* authority," and therefore he eschewed stability and closure, evading "the expectations and categories of his audience, in order to fulfill the needs of the literary public as he sees it" (p. 123). In short, Langland willfully (pun intended) allowed for and actually encouraged contradictory appropriations of his words by others through a wandering narrative, a multiplicity of guides, dreamlike disruptions, and "the absence of explicit initial declarations of intent and mode by the author in his own person" (p. 110). That absence required the audience to supply "an *ad hoc* classification of its own" (p. 110).

Impressive as Middleton's argument is, it depends on her own ad hoc classification of the poem's basic genre as a *chanson d'avanture*, a classification that allows her to identify Will as the poem's questing hero and to distinguish him from both Langland and Piers Plowman. As Middleton herself suggests, John Ball viewed the poem's basic genre to be not *chanson d'avanture*, but rather political allegory. Thus understood, the poem's silences, wandering, and dreaming are strategically self-protective; its riddles are rhetorical appeals to a particular well-known audience; its heroes (Will and Piers), author, and audience are virtually self-identical; and its impassioned complaints are calls to action. For Ball and the other rebel readers of the poem, *Piers Plowman* was not a *chanson d'avanture* but rather a compilation of allegorical forms—dream-vision, parable, personification, word-play, and coded messages—that gave rhetorical definition to their community and inspired their action.

Such an interpretation of *Piers* is especially sensitive to what Langland leaves conspicuously veiled and unsaid. As James Simpson has observed, "In the Prologue of *Piers Plowman* the narrator draws attention to his own voice often in order to say that he will *not* speak about various things." Given the existence of powerful restrictions "on the writing of satire and theological statement in the period 1378–1406, both from ecclesiastical and royal sources," there is good reason for us to "read the text as being informed by non-fictional constraints."[141] Ball certainly read the poem that way. He recognized that Langland was *not* saying something; he concluded that that something was politically dangerous and therefore deliberately left to be decoded and construed by others; he himself supplied what was missing in Langland's text.

If the rebels were, moreover, a coalition of dissidents and discontents, then the peculiar mixture of reformist and traditional appeals in Langland and Ball alike may have rhetorically engaged, rather than fictively evaded, the expectations of their audience. As recent investigations have concluded, those who participated in the Revolt of 1381 represented an ad hoc alliance of various subgroups, each with their own particular grievances and goals. In their quest for happier conditions, some looked backward, some forward, some simply "away." Thus in Ball, as in Langland, we find a call for both steadfast traditionalism and timely change, an amalgam mirrored in the sturdy post and revolving sails of Ball's allegorical windmill and in Langland's complex association of plowing with pilgrimage and quest.

Peck has called attention to a rhetoric common to Ball and Langland, both of whom make urgent appeals to a "spirit of Christian unity," to the service of "Truth," to "doing," and to "Conscience."[142] They object to the same societal ills and moral offenses. Dobson notes, too, that Langland's ideal of government by the king and the commons (as expressed in the B Prologue, l. 121) was "not too far removed from that of the rebels of 1381."[143] Kinney emphasizes that Langland, like Ball, voiced his complaints in the vernacular, and that his choice to "make Piers, a plowman, his spokesman" was "radical."[144]

Even more important, perhaps, Langland images a society that takes its directives not "from above"—that is, from the nobles represented in the person of the knight—but rather "from below," from a plowman who is acutely aware that the stability of a society depends in large part on its ability to clothe, feed, shelter, and protect the poor, to meet their material and spiritual needs, and to keep the able-bodied productively employed. Langland explicitly denies that the lives of Do-Wel, Do-Bet, and Do-Best correspond to class distinctions,[145] and he repeatedly affirms that the Gospel obligates the rich to dispossess themselves of their wealth, so that all persons receive their proper measure. Were Langland's dicta to be taken seriously, the end result might well be the same as the Eden that Ball sought to restore. As Anna P. Baldwin observes, "Even if the rebels were wrong to use Langland's hero as a type of chiliastic avenger (if this is what they were doing), they were right to believe him the champion of the poor."[116]

As many have noted, there is nothing in *Piers Plowman* to suggest that Langland would have approved the bloody vengefulness of the rebels' attack, and many of his revisions in the C text—most notably his deletion of the tearing of the pardon—work to distance him from their manifestos.[147] There remain, however, striking similarities between Langland's poem and Ball's letters which suggest that Ball and his followers did not simply misunderstand *Piers Plowman.* They may, in fact, have understood it very well. They certainly heard the poem speak their own language and express a kindred ideology, and they fashioned their own rhetoric out of Langland's. The rebel readers of *Piers Plowman* (to echo Justice) "derived authority" from Langland's poem, even as they "asserted authority over it, assimilating its language and imagery to a practical purpose already conceived and undertaken" (p. 118). Their literacy in reading the poem may have been variable and selective, but they read the poem with great attentiveness, filling in its gaps, and co-creating it in the process. As we shall see, key episodes in *Piers* confirmed their belief that laying claim to literacy necessarily meant asserting the right not just to read texts but also to interpret them.

Much careful work needs to be done before we can answer the question: What did *Piers Plowman* mean to John Ball and the rebel leaders? In order to begin to answer it, we must start with other, more precisely formulated questions: What basic genre and subgenres did they perceive in the work? How did they read and respond to particular passages in Langland's work? Leading the way in this direction, Justice has delineated in John Ball's reported sermon at Blackheath a commentary on, and response to, Wit's remarks about bastards in Passus 9.195–201 of the B text (pp. 102–10). In the final pages of this chapter, I concentrate on Ball's allusion to, and interpretation of, a notorious crux in Langland's poem: the pardon scene.

Langland's Messages and Ball's Letters

Langland's characteristic mingling of Latin and English plays upon the impossibility of translation without interpretation—so much so that many of the Latin expressions literally become allegories or message texts that overtly exclude one audience in order to draw in and thereby define another audience all the more effectively. Let me exemplify this practice by pointing to two such message verses that appear in both the A and the B versions of *Piers Plowman:* the macaronic pronouncement by Reason and the Latin pardon sent by Truth. As I hope to show, Langland establishes a firm parallel between them, sets them in dialogue, and purposely leaves their meaning open for interpretation. John Ball explains their veiled significance in a cryptic line in one of his letters, a line that glosses Langland's poem for his fellow rebels, even as it remains an allegory in its own right: "Johan the Muller hath ygrownde smal, smal, small; / The Kyngis sone of heuene shalle pay for alle."[148]

The first of the messages in question is spoken by Reason to the king: "For *Nullum malum* þe man mette wiþ *inpunitum* / And bad *Nullum bonum* be *irremuneratum*" (B IV.143–44). Although Reason has already paraphrased the saying in English (B IV.138–41), he renders it in Latin as an allegory, an oracle in need of correct interpretation: "Lat þi Confessour, sire kyng, construe it þee on englissh / And if þow werche it in werk I wedde myne eris / That lawe shal ben a laborer and lede afeld donge, / And loue shal lede þi lond as þe leef likeþ" (B IV.145–48). In response to Reason's request, the "Clerkes þat were Confessours coupled hem togideres / Al to construe þis clause" (B IV.149–50). Although, in the end, "Alle riȝtfulle recordede þat Reson truþe tolde," the motive for their decipherment of Reason's sentence is false, for the worldly clerics seek the king's (and their own) "profit," construing the clause "noȝt for confort of þe commune ne for þe kynges soule" (B IV.150–51). The clerics thus can translate Reason's macaronic message correctly into English according to its literal sense, but they cannot grasp its deeper meaning, nor can they convey it to the king, who remains dependent on Reason and Conscience and on the support of the commons.

The second message comes not from Reason speaking the truth, but from Truth itself in the form of the pardon sent to Piers. Like the first message, it comes in two lines of Latin that must be translated by a priest: "'Piers,' quod a preest þoo, 'þi pardon moste I rede, / For I shal construe ech clause and kenne it þee on englissh" (B VII.107–8). Even as Reason's message, taken from Pope Innocent II's *De contemptu mundi*, insists that no good act must go unrewarded and no evil deed unpunished, the translated pardon, which echoes the Athanasian Creed, renders the imperative "do wel and haue wel . . . / And do yuel and haue yuel" (B VII.116–17). The messages thus are similar in form and content and share an origin in Truth; they are both translated literally by a clergyman whose motivations prevent him from interpreting the message as Reason and Piers do, that is, as an allegory: "'Peter,' quod þe preest þoo, 'I kan no pardon fynde'" (B VII.115).

Piers has been content to receive the pardon as something literally veiled—because "unfolded" and unread (B VII.109)—and to substitute his own commentary or gloss for its literal meaning. When Piers lets the priest see the text, he himself beholds it apparently for the first time: "In two lynes it lay and noȝt a lettre moore" (B VII.111). At that moment Piers is forced to distinguish between his text and his commentary, partly because the priest's interpretation differs from his own. Piers has understood the message from Truth to be a pardon, whereas the priest does not. At the same time, as David Aers has emphasized, Piers realizes the discrepancy between his ninety-seven-line gloss and the actual two-line message.[149]

The scene that follows is a notorious crux. Critics generally agree that when "Piers for pure tene" tears the pardon "asonder," dividing its two lines in two, he is reacting in anger against the literal-minded priest, who despises Piers for his small knowledge of Latin, while he himself (as Piers objects) has only a superficial knowledge of the Bible.[150] It is also possible, however, that Piers's anger is at least partially directed against the "bulle" itself, for Piers tears it and substitutes for it another two lines in Latin from Psalm 23:4: "Si ambulauero in medio vmbre mortis / Non timebo mala quoniam tu mecum es" (B VII.110, 120–21).[151] Finally, Piers seems to be angry at himself, for he explicitly turns away from his former way of life at this point: "'I shal cessen of my sowyng,' quod Piers, '& swynke noȝt so hurde, / Ne aboute my bilyue so bisy be na moore; / Of preiers and of penaunce my plouȝ shal ben herafter, / And wepen whan I sholde werche þouȝ whete breed me faille'" (B VII.122–25).[152]

The meaning of Piers's violent action and of his abrupt turning away from a life that he had formerly believed to be virtuous is intended by Langland to be ambiguous and thus to require interpretation.[153] The narrator himself does not understand what the scene portends, and, having awakened from his dream, he muses upon it as he walks "metelees and moncilees" through the Malvern hills: "Many tyme þis metels haþ maked me to studie / Of þat I seiȝ slepynge, if it so be myȝte" (B VII.149–50). Although the narrator does not give a directly political interpretation of his dream, he suggests that such an interpretation is possible by comparing it, in curiously contemporary terms, to the biblical dream of Nebuchadnezzar, which the prophet Daniel interpreted to mean "That vnkouþe knyȝtes shul come þi kyngdom to cleyme; / Amonges lower lordes þi lond shal be departed" (B VII.161–62).

The narrator's observation that "þe preest preued no pardon to dowel" (B VII.174), coupled with Piers's own apparent rejection in the *visio* of his former life as a feudal plowman, raises the twofold question whether Piers has in fact been doing well in patiently plowing his halfacre and whether such a conservative stance can merit "pardoun *a pena & a culpa*" (B VII.3) for Piers and his co-workers. The readiness of Piers to walk in the dark valley like the Psalmist, but also like a day laborer, trusting in Providence, foreshadows the quest of the dream-troubled narrator, now suspiciously "yrobed in russet," who roams about "for to seke dowel" (VIII.1–2).

As David Aers has argued, both Piers at the end of the *visio* and the narrator at the beginning of the *vita* resemble the footloose "wasters" against whom the Statute of Laborers had first been enacted in 1351.[154] Piers receives the "pardoun" (which is and is not an indulgence), after all, as an apparent answer to his predicament at the end of Passus VI, when Hunger and famine have proven to be the only effective means for protection against wasters and, more generally, for the enforcement of the statute: "Ac whiles hunger was hir maister þer wolde noon chide / *Ne stryuen ayeins þe statut,* so sterneliche he loked" (B VI.319–20; emphasis added). Such a solution, as Piers himself realizes, is horrific, and the passus ends with a Saturnine oracle of impending disaster: "And so seiþ Saturne and sente yow to warne. / Whan ye se þe mone amys and two monkes heddes, / And a mayde haue þe maisterie, and multiplie by eiȝte, / Thanne shal deeþ wiþedrawe and derþe be Iustice, / And Dawe þe dykere deye for hunger / But if god of his goodnesse graunte vs a trewe" (B VI.326–31).

The pardon *a culpa & a pena* that is sent by Truth seems to be the "trewe" granted by God's goodness, but both Piers and the priest misunderstand it.[155] Piers, on the one hand, is too quick to interpret the well-doing that merits an indulgence (in this world and the next) as a feudal continuance in strict keeping with the Statute of Laborers (although, as Anna Baldwin notes, Piers tends to be more merciful to wasters than the statute warrants).[156] The literal-minded priest, on the other hand, does not understand in what sense the striving to do well can entail a pardon at all. Thus they both remain in the Saturnine valley, which is overshadowed by death (*umbra mortis*). When Piers tears the "bulle" and turns away from his former understanding of doing well, his action implies his own protest against the Statute of Laborers, a "statut" that he had previously upheld and defended; it does so, moreover, in an uncanny foreshadowing of the rebels' angry wholesale destruction of legal documents in 1381.[157]

The impassioned resolution of Piers to behave differently in the future and the narrator's subsequent waking and dreaming quest for Do-Wel mirror the process the poem evoked in its fourteenth-century readers as they interpreted the *visio*. Many of them viewed it as an intentional political allegory veiling a call to action. As the letters of John Ball indicate, some of Langland's contemporaries found their own definition of well-doing in open and violent revolt, acting "as god biddeþ" to restore an Edenic order. In their view, sometimes ("tyme is nou") one does well to rebel. Indeed, as Justice reminds us, the rebels who beheaded Archbishop Simon Sudbury declared even as they did so that it was "the hand of the Lord" that was executing him, an "astonishing assertion [that] can only mean that the rebels understood their collective action as the instrumental expression of God's imperative of reform" (p. 97).

What, then, did Ball understand by the enigmatic pardon scene? Ball's

letters suggest an answer to that question in the form of a previously unnoticed gloss on Langland's poem. Just as Langland links the threat of
famine with Truth's sending of the pardon, Ball writes the chilling couplet:
"Johan the Muller hath ygrownde smal, smal, small; / The Kyngis sone of
heuene shalle pay for alle."[158] Likening the rebels' causes of bitter discontent to a famine as experienced by rural peasants, Ball urges the rebels
to act like millers, grinding their oppressors instead of grain. Having insisted in his sermons that their revolt was God-willed, Ball looks to Christ
for an indulgence that will "pay" for the material goods they need, as well
as cover the spiritual and material cost of their violent actions to secure justice. What the rebels were seeking, after all, was both a this-worldly and an
otherworldly "pardoun *a culpa & a pena.*" The bloody payment of Christ
on the cross, which won the pardon for sinners from which every indulgence derives, is here invoked in Ball's letter as a pledge for better times
and as a guarantee of redemption for the rebels who do their "work" well,
including the divinely commissioned work of beheading their enemies.[159]

Certainly not all of Langland's contemporaries interpreted *Piers Plowman* as John Ball did. As Ball correctly recognized, however, Langland had
written an allegory, the significance of which could be known only (as Judson Allen has astutely observed) if it were *already* known.[160] Ball had his
"trewþe," and he could readily discover it in Langland's words and images.
For him, therefore, the poem's allegory was revelatory. Langland himself,
moreover, explicitly encouraged Ball and his other readers to find in his
poem a meaning that he dares not say (cf. B Prologue, ll. 209–10), a potentially dangerous meaning. In many ways *Piers Plowman* is as proverbial
and as enigmatic a text as John Ball's letters are, and it may be so for the
same life-threatening reason.

The use of Langland's Do-Wel, Do-Bet, and Do-Best by Ball and his followers as a code for revolutionary action has long been recognized. Their
use of Piers as a figure for themselves is also unquestionable.[161] The interpretive process by which they derived these watchwords from Langland's
poem has, however, received virtually no attention, on the scholarly assumption that they simply misinterpreted *Piers Plowman.* Justice has insisted,
however, that we cannot "gauge the sense the rebels made of Langland"
unless we also "reconstruct the *kind* of sense they looked for" (p. 120). The
preceding discussion has, I hope, shown that Ball read Langland's poem
as a political allegory, that he did so with considerable sophistication, and
that Langland himself provided Ball with cues to encourage such an interpretation.

As we have seen, allegorical texts are often regarded as "nonrhetorical," or
even "antirhetorical," because their meaning by definition is veiled and
cannot be declared openly in the marketplace, in the public arena (*agora*).

Partly for that reason, perhaps, *Piers Plowman* has been the subject of little rhetorical criticism, apart from an occasional study of Langland's wordplay and general style.[162] The letters of John Ball, however, give us an extraordinary opportunity to recover one of Langland's contemporary audiences, even as they afford us a measure for the success of his poem's rhetorical appeals. Written in plain style, deceptively abecedarian in their estates satire and social complaint, and profoundly allegorical in their topical application, *Piers Plowman* and the letters of Ball have the warrant of history for the moving power and the public impact of political allegory in the form of poetry. At once the least rhetorical and the most rhetorical of medieval allegories, they found and formed an audience and inspired an action: the uprising of 1381. Few public speeches have proven as powerful.

3

Gower's Arion and "Cithero"

The allegory does not simply disguise an historical reference: it analyzes
it and . . . gives it meaning.
                William Oram, "Elizabethan Fact and Spenserian Fiction"

Whereas the A and B texts of *Piers Plowman* antedate the Peasants' Revolt of 1381 and helped to inspire it by articulating the causes of
discontent, John Gower's *Vox Clamantis* describes the revolt in retrospect
and urges the social reforms necessary to prevent its recurrence. Gower
himself decodes his allegory for his readers. In the Prologue to Book I of
Vox Clamantis, he announces his intent "to describe how the lowly peasants
violently revolted against the freemen and nobles of the realm" and to do
so by reporting the "true dream" he had, in which he "saw different throngs
of the rabble transformed into different kinds of domestic animals," all of
which then assumed the ferocity of wild beasts.[1] As Steven Justice and others have argued, Gower's plan thus anticipates Chaucer's use in "The Nun's
Priest's Tale" of a barnyard beast fable, which includes a true dream of a
predator, to refer explicitly to the murderous uprising in London led by
"Jakke Straw and his meynee" (*Canterbury Tales* VII.3394).[2]

At first sight, the differences between Gower's nightmarish allegory and
Chaucer's merry fable are so great that any comparison of the two seems,
in John Fisher's words, "downright wrongheaded."[3] Similarly, critics have
been loath to liken Gower's overtly political writings to his *Confessio Amantis.* Written in Latin and addressed to a clerical audience, Gower's *Vox Clamantis* and his *Cronica Tripertita* are generally regarded as political writings
of little literary value, fashionably allegorical in style. Gower's Middle English *Confessio* has often been viewed as something quite different: exemplary rather than allegorical; amatory rather than political; poetic and entertaining rather than rhetorical. As Fisher observes, "The *Confessio Amantis*
has been traditionally regarded as a poem whose chief subject is courtly
love."[4] Even those critics who stress the importance of the estates satire in
the Prologue, who see the Aristotelian lore in Book VII as central to the

Confessio, who treat the question of the poem's various dedications, and who view the work as a whole as offering generic instruction to the king generally fail to address the specific, related questions of audience, political allegory, and rhetorical appeal in the work.

Evidence both external and internal suggests that the *Confessio* was not simply dedicated to King Richard in 1390 and then rededicated to Henry of Lancaster, the future King Henry IV, in 1392–93; rather, the poem was directed from the start toward a complex, heterogeneous audience with multiple circles inclusive of Henry and others, at the center of which Richard is imagined as the primary addressee. An identifiable topical reference, hitherto unnoticed, allows us to date the first recension not to 1390 but rather to the same date attributed to the third—that is, 1392–93—and thus to account for the differences between them in rhetorical terms, with a view to their intended audiences. As we shall see, such a definition of Gower's audience establishes a much closer link between the *Confessio* and the *Cronica Tripertita* than has previously been recognized, a link that affects interpretation not only of the Ciceronian exemplum of the Roman parliament in Book VII of the *Confessio,* but also of many other exempla. Indeed, the parallels between Gower and "Cithero," on the one hand, and between Gower and Arion, on the other, encourage us to reconsider the relationship between rhetoric and poetics in the *Confessio* as a whole.

The Questions of Audience

Recognizing the political significance of Gower's *Confessio* depends on our taking seriously the rhetorical *circumstantiae* that Gower himself supplies in the first recension. In the Prologue he specifies for whom the poem was written and why. It is, he declares, a "bok for king Richardes sake, / To whom belongeth my ligeance, / With al myn hertes obeissance" (ll. 9–11*).[5] Gower goes on to tell how the king met him by chance one day as he was taking a boat ride on the Thames, invited him aboard the royal barge, and commanded him to write "som newe thing . . . / That he himself it mihte loke" (ll. 51–53*). In the Prologue and at the end of Book VIII, Gower prays for King Richard. The so-called epilogue commends Richard's virtues and humbly presents to his "hihe worthinesse" Gower's "povere bok" (VIII.2988–3035*, 3050–51*).

Richard, then, occupies the first seat in Gower's audience. Even in the first recension of the *Confessio,* however, Gower imagines additional circles of auditors who observe his interaction with the king, who overhear his instruction of the young monarch, and who may learn more readily than Richard the lessons which the poet imparts. Indeed, Gower recites the story of the work's commission by Richard for the benefit of these implied, and largely unnamed, auditors—his potential detractors (Prologue, ll. 57–75*) and his friends (such as Chaucer, whom Venus names in VIII.2941–57*), both the "wise," for whom the book "may be wisdom," and the foolish "that lust to pleye," for whom the book will be only entertaining "pley" (Prologue, ll. 82–84*). Among his intended auditors Gower explicitly names the earl of Derby. G. C. Macaulay notes, "Even the first issue of the *Confessio Amantis* had a kind of dedication to Henry of Lancaster in the Latin lines with which it concluded, 'Derbeie comiti, recolunt quem laude periti, / Vade liber purus sub eo requiesce futurus.'"[6]

These Latin lines, which send Gower's book on its way to the earl of Derby, appear, Peter Nicholson emphasizes, in "at least eight of the surviving manuscripts" of the first recension.[7] Although (by Fisher's count) thirteen late manuscripts based on the Fairfax MS indicate that "Henry of Lancaster" replaced Richard II as the primary dedicatee of the *Confessio* as early as 1392–93, the "yer sextenthe of Kyng Richard" (Prologue, l. 25), thirty-one manuscripts preserve the original dedication to Richard—evidence which suggests, Fisher and others have argued, that the first recension of the *Confessio* "continued to be the official version" of Gower's work until after Richard's deposition in 1399.[8] "It may well be, as Macaulay proposed (II, clviii)," and as Nicholson explains, "that only after Henry's accession were the revised prologue and epilogue, originally written only for private presentation, first released for general circulation with the rubrics and colophon explaining how they came to be composed."[9]

The evidence provided by the manuscripts is complicated, and the very idea of three distinct recensions is challenged by their composite nature.[10] What is certain is that the *Confessio* existed in various versions, addressed to different audiences. In its first recension, the poem marks itself in the Prologue as commissioned by Richard and in the conclusion as presented either to him alone or (via the Latin *explicit*) to both Richard and Henry of Derby. Macaulay notes that the second recension is distinguished by "additional passages of the fifth and seventh books, with a rearrangement of the sixth book . . . , while the conclusion has been rewritten so as to exclude the praises of the king, and in some copies there is also a new preface with dedication to Henry of Lancaster."[11] In the third recension the poem is dedicated to Henry in the Prologue, the conclusion has been revised, and the additional passages found in the second recension are absent.

Despite the various dedications, the complex rhetoric entailed in the definition of different audiences for the poem has gained little critical attention. Most scholars have discussed instead the "alternative dedications" that distinguish the first and third recensions, doing so from the biographical perspective of Gower's apparently shifting political allegiance. Observing that the actual text of the *Confessio* remained virtually unchanged despite the dedicatory changes in the Prologue and at the poem's conclusion, other scholars, more interested in questions of audience and rhetorical strategy than in biographical issues, have concluded that Gower actually addressed his poem neither to Richard nor to Henry but rather (in Anne Middleton's words) "to the entire community—as a whole and all at once, rather than severally."[12]

"The King," Middleton asserts, "is not the main imagined audience, but an occasion for gathering and formulating what is on the common mind."[13] Similarly, Paul Strohm points to the altered dedication as evidence of Gower's "independence of any particular faction" and sees in his poetry "an attempt to forge a perspective which moves beyond faction."[14] Nicholson, for his part, sees the dual dedication as purely a matter of literary patronage and urges us "to disassociate the original composition of the poem from the [specific] political controversies of the period."[15] Larry Scanlon reaches a similar conclusion, insisting that "if it were possible to retain essentially the same poem, while changing the dedicatee, then it must be the case that Gower was more concerned with the general, public, and institutional aspect of kingship, and less interested . . . [in] any particular king."[16]

Scanlon's "if" clause is, however, precisely what is at issue. Was it possible for Gower to change the real or imagined audience of the *Confessio* and yet "retain essentially the same poem"? I would reply no. Even if the literal text of the poem remained stable for the most part after Richard's deposition (as it admittedly did), its political allegory—that is, the contemporary associations a person would have been likely to make as he listened to, or read, Gower's book in Richard's physical presence (whether in reality or in the auditor's imagination)—certainly changed. With the loss of Richard as an auditor whose presence informed the response of other auditors, the actual "matter" of the *Confessio* was profoundly affected. As we have seen, medieval literary theorists recognized the "matter" of any work to be both literal and allegorical. Thus, to change a poem's audience was to alter its very meaning from the viewpoint of both authorial intention and the poem's actual effect (*causa finalis*).[17] In the present instance, the "revision of only 69 lines," which distinguishes the third recension from the second, has (in the words of Hans-Jürgen Diller) "brought about an astonishing change in the explicit function of *Confessio Amantis*."[18]

The political interpretations I advance in this chapter support R. F. Yeager's claim that the "early connection [of the *Confessio* to Richard] adds resonance and specificity to subsequent discussions of proper kingship which appear throughout the *Confessio*. Many statements, if we imagine for them a royal audience, acquire a special point."[19] Indeed, "we must look carefully at the role played by . . . King Richard in shaping the *Confessio* in order to understand Gower's poetic generally, his marital metaphors, and the Arion figure in specific."[20]

The Politics of Arion

The first recension links the figures of Gower and Richard II in the opening lines of the Prologue, making the king, as Gower's imagined patron and auditor, literally a part of the poem's narrative *materia*. The Prologue's closing lines carry the argument one step further, identifying Gower with the legendary poet Arion. The Prologue's ending circles back to its beginning, enabling Arion, as it were, to take Gower's place on Richard's barge. The transposition is a crucial one that gives us a more precise insight into Gower's rhetoric and poetic than we have hitherto attained.

Yeager has shown that Gower's use of Arion, rather than "better known musician/poet figures such as Amphion, David, and Orpheus," is very unusual in Middle English literature. Indeed, considering the rarity of the Arion figure, Yeager has concluded that the recondite "Arion offered in effect a clean slate" to the poet and an original self-representation as he endeavored to write his vernacular love song.[21]

Yeager's question "Why did Gower choose Arion?" has, however, a more prosaic and topical answer, an answer with enormous implications for our consideration of the various recensions of the *Confessio*, all of which employ Arion as a poetic figure. The only date that one can attach with certainty to the composition of the *Confessio* is 1392–93, "the yer sextenthe of kyng Richard" (Prologue, l. 25), to which Gower refers within the poem itself in the text of the third recension. That date closely correlates with an unusual event in London that surely inspired Gower, as well as the general populace, to think of dolphins and to recall the legends attached to them, including that of Arion.

With dramatic gusto, Thomas Walsingham records the historical appearance of a real dolphin in London during Yuletide 1391–92. During the holiday season in the fifteenth year of Richard's reign ("anno gratiae millesimo trecentesimo nonagesimo secundo, qui est annus regni Regis Ricardi, a Conquaestu Secundi, quintus-decimus"), when King Richard and Queen Anne were celebrating the birth of Christ with a magnificent feast ("tenuit Rex Natale magnificum, cum Anna Regina"), a ten-foot-long dolphin created a stir by swimming down the Thames River all the way to London Bridge ("Ipso die Natalis, delphinus, de mari veniens, lusit Londoniis in Tamisia, perveniens usque ad Pontem").[22]

Walsingham elaborates on this remarkable and unusual occurrence, inserting into his chronicle a long commentary on the nature of the dolphin, taken from Pliny's *Historia Naturalis*. Following Pliny, the chronicler emphasizes the dolphin's attraction to the sound of musical instruments, its tendency to follow human voices, and the characteristic gathering of dolphins at the hearing of a symphony ("Sunt autem delphines marinae belluae, quae voces hominum sequuntur, et gaudent cantibus tibiarum, et ad symphoniam solent gregatim advenire"). Walsingham goes on to include, among other legendary accounts, the story of a boy "sub Augusto Caesare" who fed a dolphin and dared to mount its back. The dolphin carried him safely for a great distance through the water ("per aquarum magna spatia").[23]

Walsingham does not mention Arion directly, but his source does. Pliny concludes, after a long list of historical accounts about the friendly interaction of humans and dolphins, that such reports "make it credible that also the skilled harper Arion, when at sea the sailors were getting ready to kill him with the intention of stealing the money he had made, succeeded in coaxing them to let him first play a tune on his harp, and the music attracted a school of dolphins, whereupon he dived into the sea and was taken up by one of them and carried ashore."[24]

If the exotic appearance of a dolphin in London at Yuletide led Walsingham to mention the event in his chronicle and to quote Pliny at length, we may well imagine that it was the talk of the town. Grammar school teachers throughout the city probably seized the opportunity to expound on the subject of dolphins to interested students, while lay clerks like Gower recalled and discussed pertinent passages not only in Pliny's *Historia* but also in Ovid's *Fasti*. Because of the dolphin episode in London in late December 1391 or early January 1392, Gower could, in short, count on his audience's immediate familiarity with the previously less well known story of Arion and depend on them to notice his allegorical transformation of that tale.

Since the three recensions of the *Confessio* all employ the figure of Arion in the Prologue, albeit in different ways, it is almost certain that all three of them were composed after Yuletide 1391–92. The third recension is explicitly dated 1392–93 (for complicated reasons to which I will return), and there is no strong basis for dating the first recension to 1390, despite the scholarly habit of doing so. The only evidence, in fact, in support of a 1390 date are two marginal notes found in fifteenth-century manuscripts. The first of these marginal notes, "Anno domini Millesimo CCC⁰ Nonagesimo," which appears in the Prologue at the side of line 331 in manuscripts of the first and second recensions, simply provides a date for the schismatic papacy at Avignon, not for the composition of the poem. The second marginal note, which appears in some second- and third-recension manuscripts at the side of lines 2973–77 in Book VIII, dates not the *Con-*

fessio but rather an appended prayer that Gower as author offers for the unity of the realm: "Hic in anno quarto-decimo Regis Ricardi orat pro statu regni."

The putative 1390 dating of the first recension of the *Confessio,* which rests on the meager evidence of these two marginal notes, belongs, of course, to a larger interpretive scheme. Regarding the first recension as commissioned by Richard II and as complimentary to him, scholars have been inclined to assign it a relatively early date, during a relatively untroubled and hopeful time in his reign. Since the third recension is explicitly dated 1392–93 and dedicated not to Richard but to Gower's "oghne lord, / Which of Lancastre is Henri named" (Prologue, ll. 886–87), it has been viewed not only as later than the first but also as possibly signalling a shift in Gower's political allegiance from King Richard to Richard's cousin, the man who would later usurp him.

The dolphin episode in London, however, urges a very different dating and interpretation. If all three recensions date from sometime after Christmastime 1391–92, as the references to Arion suggest, then their variety most probably marks not a dramatic shift in Gower's personal and political attachments, but rather a shift on his part from one intended audience (or set of audiences) to another. The audience in each case constitutes part of the *materia* with which Gower is working.

The idea of directing his work in different versions toward several different principal auditors—Richard, Henry, or both Richard and Henry—may have been suggested to Gower by his Ovidian source for the tale of Arion.[25] The *Fasti,* written by Ovid during his exile, is one of the better-known examples among classical texts of dual (or alternative) dedication. According to his own account in the *Tristia* II.549–52, Ovid wrote and dedicated the *Fasti* to the Emperor Caesar Augustus.[26] The extant manuscripts of the *Fasti,* however, all dedicate the work not to Augustus but rather to the emperor's younger cousin Germanicus: "Excipe pacato, Caesar Germanice, voltu / hoc opus et timidae dirige navis iter" (1.3–4: "Caesar Germanicus, accept with brow serene this work and steer the passage of my timid bark"). Medieval commentaries on the *Fasti* indicate awareness that Ovid had more than one audience in mind, and that he hoped to placate the emperor and those readers who had been offended by his erotic compositions not only through the writing of an edifying work but also through the personal mediation of Germanicus.[27]

The example of the *Fasti* helps, albeit in a limited fashion, to explain the rhetoric not only of Gower's separate dedications of the *Confessio* to Richard II and to Richard's cousin, Henry of Derby, respectively, but also of his apparent double dedication to them both. As Macaulay, Fisher, and Nicholson have emphasized, the *explicit* found in eight manuscripts of the first recension sends the *Confessio,* which has been dedicated to the king, to Henry: "Go, dear book, to the Count of Derby, well considered by those versed in praise; upon him rest your future" ("Derbeie Comiti, recolunt quem laude periti, / Vade liber purus, sub eo requiesce futurus").[28] We know, moreover, that Gower actually gave a copy of *Confessio Amantis* to Henry upon his triumphant return to London in 1393, because household records of the Duchy of Lancaster indicate that Henry rewarded Gower with the gift of a collar.[29]

Whereas Ovid desired Augustus (or Tiberius) to overhear him as he praised Caesar's altars and instructed Germanicus in the origin and observance of religious festivals,[30] Gower wished the young and ambitious earl to observe and overhear his instruction of King Richard through the fictive mediation of other instructors: Genius guiding Amans and, at a further remove, Aristotle instructing Alexander. Ovid's purpose, to be sure, differed greatly from Gower's, but Gower arguably imitated both the *Fasti* (as a corrective to the *Amores*) and the *Metamorphoses* in the *Confessio* by combining a religious genre (the penitential treatise) with a series of illustrative amorous tales.

Within this large intertextual context, we need to look more closely at the figure of Arion. The exiled Ovid's nautical reference in the dedication of the *Fasti,* when he invites Germanicus to "steer the passage of [his] timid bark," anticipates the homeward voyage from Sicily of the lyre's master, Arion: "inde domum repetens puppem conscendit Arion" (*Fasti* II.95). Ovid thus forges an identification between himself, as a poet in exile, and Arion. Similarly, the nautical imagery of the opening scene in the *Confessio's* Prologue anticipates the prophecy of "an other such as Arion" (Prologue, l. 1054).

Gower's charming account depicts the poet rowing a boat in the Thames River when King Richard beckons to him: "And so befel, as I cam nyh, / Out of my bot, whan he me syh, / He bad me come in to his barge" (Prologue, ll. 43–45*). As many have noted, the scene bears an integral relation to the Arion passage; foreshadows the moving account of Thais, singing and playing her harp in the dark hold of Apollonius' ship in order to console the grieving king (VIII.1659–89); and guides a philosophical readership to see Gower himself as a latter-day Arion: "Quam cinxere freta, Gower, tua carmina leta / Per loca discreta canit Anglia laude repleta."[31]

When Arion actually appears in the *Confessio* (Prologue, ll. 1053–77), however, Gower makes no mention of boats, ships, and seafaring. He follows Ovid in praising the singer's power to soothe "bestes wilde" and expands on Arion's ability to reconcile "the comun with the lord, / And the lord with the comun also" (Prologue, ll. 1057, 1066–67), thereby making him a rhetor as well as a poet,[32] but he omits the Ovidian narrative that parallels the Ricardian barge episode. That blatant omission serves to link the two passages, calls attention to Gower's use of artificial order in retelling Ovid's story, and invites a reinterpretation of the opening scene on the Thames, which is now observed to complete, in a literally preposterous way, the unfinished tale of Arion.

In Ovid's *Fasti* the ship that Arion unwittingly boards, and upon whose deck he sings and plays in a calculated attempt to save his own life, is a pirate's vessel, whose helmsman and crew threaten the singer with drawn swords. Arion sings before the pirates, who form his primary audience, but his swan song (for it is apparently his last) is miraculously overheard by a dolphin, who bears him safely across the waves when he leaps from the deck.

Gower leaves out the story of Arion's rescue by a dolphin from the pirate captain and his crew. In omitting this part of the Arion legend, even as he includes the story of his interview on King Richard's barge, Gower raises the question whether the king to whom and for whom he sings is a trustworthy helmsman, wise in statecraft, or a pirate commanding a dangerous crew and about to steal the poet's life and goods. Interpreted allegorically and intertextually, the Prologue to the so-called first recension of the *Confessio* is much less complimentary to the king than it seems at first sight. Indeed, as Fisher has forcefully argued, Londoners in 1392–93 were likely to have seen the king precisely in piratical terms: "On June 25, 1392, at the beginning of 'the yer sextenthe of kyng Richard' . . . , the mayor of London, the sheriffs, and aldermen were arrested and fined 3000£, and the liberties of the city were suspended until it should pay the enormous fine of 100,000£."[33]

It is no accident that the first recension of the *Confessio,* the version of the poem that handles its Arionic materials most artfully, that is addressed overtly to Richard, and that requires an allegorical interpretation, also includes Geoffrey Chaucer explicitly among its intended auditors. Like the supposed shift of dedication from Richard to Henry, the omission in the third recension of the lines in the first (VIII.2941–57*) that name and praise Chaucer has been taken as a sign of a quarrel between the poets.[34] I would argue instead that Gower's allegorical play and veiled political meaning in the first recension is such that it implies and invites a sophisticated auditor such as Chaucer, who would be certain to notice and appreciate Gower's art of reordering, implied analogy, and omission. The third recension, which relies more on exemplarity and less on allegory for its rhetorical effect, is directed toward a less sophisticated and topically informed audience, which does not, by definition, include Chaucer. Indeed, despite the dating in the revised Prologue, the third recension may very well have been written after Chaucer's death in 1400, in which case a personal compliment to him of the sort included in the first recension would have been pointless.

We do not know what version of the *Confessio* Gower presented to Henry in 1393. His presentation copy of the poem may have been (as most scholars have supposed) a copy of the third recension *Confessio*, which names him in the Prologue. There are very good reasons, however, to believe that Gower composed the third recension only after Henry's ascension to the throne in 1400, and that he predated that later version in the "sextenthe yer of kyng Richard" (Prologue, l. 25) to make it match the date of his actual completion of the *Confessio* and of his earlier presentation of it to Henry. A marginal note at line 22 of the revised Prologue observes:

> Hic in principio declarat qualiter in anno Regis Ricardi secundi sexto decimo Iohannes Gower presentem libellum composuit et finaliter compleuit, quem strenuissimo domino suo domino *Henrico de Lancastria tunc Derbeie Comiti* cum omni reuerencia specialiter destinauit. (emphasis added).

> [Here at the beginning it states how in the sixteenth year of King Richard II John Gower composed and completed the present book, which he intended especially for his most vigorous lord the lord Henry of Lancaster, then earl of Derby, with all reverence.]

This note emphasizes that Henry is now "Henry of Lancaster," but that he was "then"—that is, in 1393, when the *Confessio* was completed—"earl of Derby." Similarly, Gower's revised colophon, which reviews his literary oeuvre, indicates that the *Confessio,* his third major work, was composed in English "out of reverence for his most vigorous lord the lord Henry of Lancaster, then earl of Derby" ("ob reuerenciam strenuissimi domini sui domini Henrici de Lancastria, *tunc Derbeie Comitis*"; emphasis added). As Nicholson rightly observes, "The very form of Henry's name . . . is enough to indicate that both colophon and rubric were written much later than the original presentation to Henry."[35] What Nicholson stops short of observing and arguing is that "the very form of Henry's name" in the third recension Prologue, where Gower sends his "amended" book to his "oghne lord, / Which of Lancastre is Henri named" (ll. 86–87), also dates the revised Prologue much later than 1393, when the original version was completed. If we can judge by the evidence of the colophon and the marginal note, Gower was careful to call Henry "Henry of Lancaster" only after the death of John of Gaunt, which occurred shortly before Henry's usurpation of Richard's throne.

The presentation copy that Gower gave to Henry in 1393, then, was almost certainly a manuscript of the first recension text, perhaps concluding with the two-line Latin *explicit* that names and compliments him: "*Derbeie Comiti* . . . / Vade liber purus" (emphasis added). If this was in fact the case, then Gower attributed not only to Chaucer but also to Henry the ability to decipher his Ricardian allegory of Arion.

A double dedication, after all, implies at least a two-tiered audience, such as Arion enjoyed when he sang both for the pirates at hand and for the more distant dolphins whom he summoned by his singing. In 1392–93 Henry of Derby stands, dolphin-like, in the second tier of Gower's original intended audience. From him the poet seeks rescue for himself and the realm, should Richard prove to be a pirate after all and inattentive to the song of "an other such as Arion" (Prologue, l. 1054).

When Henry replaces Richard as the primary addressee in the third recension of the *Confessio,* he does not and cannot substitute for Richard as the poem's commissioner on the barge in the Thames. This does not necessarily argue, as Yeager suggests, that "the tête-à-tête on the Thames was real and well enough known to prevent transference."[36] Rather, what makes a simple substitution impossible is the political allegory that casts Richard in the role of the Ovidian pirate captain, a role unsuited for Gower's hero, Henry.

During Richard's quarrel with the city of London, Gower must have doubted whether the reformation of the king, initiated by the Merciless Parliament, would be lasting in its effect. Although he could not have foreseen Richard's bloody 1397 reprisals against the Appellants, he was certainly able to witness in 1392 the king's wrath against, and heavy-handed treatment of, his opponents. If the first recension dates, as the third recension specifies, from 1392–93, then Gower's Arionic allegory of Richard is ironic in its praise of the king for his recent practice of justice, largesse, and pity, and for his restraint in dealing with Derby and the other Lords Appellant: "For he *yit nevere* unpitously / Aycin the liges of his lond, / For no defaute which he fond, / Thurgh cruelte vengaunce soghte" (VIII.2994–97; emphasis added).

The Rhetoric of the Two Parliaments

My approach to the rhetoric of the *Confessio* insists on the interrelatedness of audience and allegory. Gower himself invites such a rhetorical interpretation of the *Confessio* through an unusual discussion in Book VII of "rethorique" as an art and science. It is, James Murphy has noted, the "first known treatment of the subject in the English language," but it differs significantly from the introductions of rhetoric found in earlier encyclopedic and didascalic works. Indeed, Murphy has argued that "the manner in which it is derived from [its source] Brunetto Latini's *Tresor* would seem to indicate ignorance of the subject rather than knowledge."[37] In Murphy's view, Gower must have known very little about rhetoric because, apart from confused references to Marcus Tullius Cicero as two persons—"Tullius" and "Cithero" (in Books IV.2647–51 and VII.1588–1614)—and a non-technical use of the word "colour" to mean "semblance or outward appearance" (VII.1625), he "does not name any other terms of rhetoric, any other rhetoricians, or in any other way display a knowledge of rhetoric in its derivative forms."[38]

Murphy's conclusions have been challenged by others, notably the German scholar Götz Schmitz, on the double ground of Gower's own rhetorical achievement as a poet and our knowledge of his sources.[39] If, as Murphy acknowledges, Gower knew and understood the *Tresor* well enough to follow it closely in lines 1588–1640, where he gives the example of the opposed speeches "of Julius and Cithero" (VII.1597) in the context of the Catilinian debate,[40] then he could easily have derived from Brunetto a treasure trove of other rhetorical lore—for example, the definitions of rhetoric given by Plato, Aristotle, Gorgias, Hermagoras, and Cicero; the five parts of rhetoric (invention, arrangement, style, memory, and delivery); the four kinds of issues giving rise to controversy; the distinction between natural and artificial order; strategies for amplification and abridgment; the six parts of a speech and the five parts of a letter; the variety of appeals appropriate for use in a prologue; and so on. The absence of this material in Genius' Book VII summary of Aristotle's instruction of Alexander points not to Gower's ignorance of what belongs to a proper rhetorical curriculum, but rather to his conscious choice to abridge his French source and to use it selectively for his own poetic and rhetorical ends.

Gower's careful abridgment of his source material serves to bring to the fore negative and positive exempla of rhetoricians in support not only of his own plain style but also of his commitment to the "deth" of traitors, whether noble or peasant.[41] Not unlike the freedom-loving Dante of the *Convivio*, who saw Cicero, "a new citizen of lowly condition," as a divinely appointed hero who dared to defend "Rome's freedom against Catiline, a citizen of the highest rank,"[42] Gower implicitly likens himself to "Cithero" in his plainspoken opposition to the abuses of licentious nobles and riotous peasants. Indeed, Gower's depiction of the Roman parliament in the *Confessio* anticipates his approving account of the Merciless Parliament of 1388 in the *Cronica Tripertita* (1400). Viewed against this allusive background, the treatment of "rethorique" in Book VII actually introduces the lengthy exposition of the five points of policy, the exempla of which offer a comprehensive mirror to Richard II, the young king whom the Merciless Parliament aimed to reform through the execution or exile of his favorites.

Gower's relatively brief treatment of rhetoric as one of the three principal divisions of philosophy bridges his extensive surveys of "theorique," on the one hand, and of "practique," on the other. More powerful than plants and stones, whose virtues fall under the purview of physics as a theoretical science, words define the subject matter of rhetoric, the verbal art that Gower puts at the head of the trivium.[43] Genius begins with an account of the power of "wordes" either for good or for evil (using Ulysses' seduction of the Trojan traitor Antenor as an example of the latter),[44] and then proceeds to illustrate Ciceronian rhetoric as a whole with a second example: the case of the Catiline conspiracy (65–62 B.C.) and the debate it inspired.[45] Unlike his source, Brunetto Latini's *Tresor,* which praises Julius Caesar's skillful rhetoric in urging leniency for the conspirators, Gower's treatment approves instead the unadorned speech of "Cillenus" and the unequivocal condemnation of Catiline and his followers by Silanus, "Cithero," and Cato.

Given Gower's political leanings, he would have perceived multiple similarities between the Catiline conspiracy of classical Rome and the Ricardian conspiracy that supposedly occasioned the Merciless Parliament. In the *Cronica Tripertita* he condemns the youthful Richard as a tyrant and attributes to him and his associates crimes similar to those of which the patrician profligate Catiline stood accused. Catiline and his adherents had allegedly contrived to murder Cicero, the Roman consul. Richard similarly stood under suspicion of having plotted the deaths of his chief opponents—Thomas of Woodstock, duke of Gloucester; Richard, earl of Arundel; and Thomas Beauchamp, earl of Warwick.[46] As Gower relates, "There were three venerable nobles whom the wrath of the king took special note of, and he vowed to kill them."[47] Catiline had also planned a treasonous attack on Rome itself, and he eventually led an army against the city. Richard, a latter-day Catiline, authorized Robert de Vere, earl of Oxford and duke of Ireland, to gather an army in Cheshire and to march on London.[48]

Other chroniclers indicate that the Lords Appellant had previously threatened Richard with deposition and assembled their own forces to march on London, and that de Vere's desperate move, which ended in his defeat by the Appellants at Radcot Bridge on December 20, 1387, was a defensive action taken in response to theirs.[49] John Capgrave, for instance, records that Gloucester's forces first gathered outside London in Hakeney woods: "Whan þe kyng wyst þat þei were þere he dred mech þat gaderyng, and with his councel took avisament what myte best he do in þis mater. Than sent he þe duke of Erlond into Lancastirschere and Chestirschere to gadir him puple, with whech puple he myte make resistens ageyn þese lordes."[50] Gower, for his part, emphasizes de Vere's wicked initiative. An "insidious plotter" against loyal and good Englishmen, de Vere is said to have "sought for ruses, tricks, and deadly lurking places, in order that the realm might perish" under the king's "arrogance."[51] Gower charges de Vere, in particular, with having incited "the people" under the king's banner "to carrying arms, in order that by means of them he might freely pursue the nobles and utterly scatter them" (*Chronicle*, p. 292).[52]

Inspired by the implicit historical parallels between the Catilinian and Ricardian conspiracies, Gower uses the Roman parliament in the *Confessio* not only as an exemplification of Ciceronian rhetoric but also as an analogue for the Merciless Parliament. Doing so, however, requires him to depart in conspicuous ways from the account given in the *Tresor*. Following Sallust, Brunetto focuses on the remarkable rhetorical achievement of Julius Caesar, who scored his triumph over Cicero, the rhetorician par excellence, by speaking "masterfully in a concealed way" ("*par* coverture maistrielement") in defense of the conspirators whom Cicero had accused and prosecuted and for whom Decimus Silanus had urged the death penalty.[53] Brunetto first gives the full text of Caesar's speech and then analyzes it rhetorically. Gower, by contrast, gives short shrift to Caesar's speech, treats the opposition between Julius and Cicero and company as a fairly even contest—"Nou tolden thei, nou tolde he" (VII.1622)—and praises not the "wordes wise" (VII.1615) and cunning indirection of Julius, but rather the "tale" of Silanus, Cicero, and Cato, who held themselves accountable "to trouthe," upheld the "comun profit" (VII.1608–9), and spoke "plein after the lawe" (VII.1623) in calling for a "cruel deth" for those guilty of "tresoun" (VII.1610–11).

Gower's strategy here in Book VII of the *Confessio* is not unlike the one he employs in Part 1 of the *Cronica Tripertita*, where he represents the guilt of the Ricardian conspirators as self-evident under the law and clearly deserving of death, denounces those who called for leniency in their punishment, and either fails to mention, or represents disapprovingly, the speeches made in defense of the accused. Gower notes that Michael de la Pole, earl of Suffolk and Chancellor of England until the so-called Wonderful Parliament of 1386 dismissed him, fled the country before the Merciless Parliament was convened on February 3, 1388, because "he sensed that he was guilty" of the treason of which he stood accused by the Lords Appellant (*Chronicle*, p. 294). Similarly, Gower records that the king's confessor, Thomas Rushook, bishop of Chichester, "left his own region in flight and sought out foreign parts, conscious of his own guilt" (*Chronicle*, p. 294).[54]

These men—along with Robert de Vere and Alexander Neville, archbishop of York, who had also fled the country—were condemned as traitors in absentia and without trial by the extraordinary action of Parliament.[55]

Others of the accused were arrested, adjudged guilty, and punished. As Gower puts it, "Parliament proceeded step by step with particulars against those who had been the infamous favorites of the infamous King" (*Chronicle*, p. 295).[56]

Gower pays special attention to the fate of the justices who, in response to the questions posed to them by Richard at Nottingham on August 25, 1387, had rendered the formal opinion that the dismissal of de la Pole and the establishment of the Commission of Governance, which had been effected by the Parliament of 1386 at the urging of Gloucester, Warwick, and Arundel, were actions unlawful in their infringement on royal prerogative; and that those responsible for such actions were liable for treason.[57] Among the justices who affixed their seals to this opinion, Sir Robert Tresilian, Chief Justice of the King's Bench, was singled out, as a wicked "scoundrel" and a criminal, to pay the harshest penalty: "Because of a crime outstripping what he had committed before, he was stretched on a gallows and overcome by hanging there" (*Chronicle*, p. 296).[58] Gower clearly wishes that a similar fate had been accorded to Tresilian's fellow justices, who were condemned not to death but to exile in Ireland: "There was no punishment which would have been sufficient for these wrongdoers, and the voice of the people said this openly and firmly. But out of feigned piety the King's priests quite presumptuously mitigated the punishment from due course of law" (*Chronicle*, p. 296).[59]

Gower's condemnation of the justices in the *Cronica* echoes the words that Genius attributes to Silanus, Cicero, and Cato in the Roman "parlement": they "seiden that for such a wrong / Ther mai no peine be to strong" (VII.1604, 1613–14). Similarly, the "feigned piety" of the king's priests in their plea for leniency recalls the deceiving "colours" (VII.1625) of Julius Caesar in the *Confessio*, when he "with wordes wise / His tale tolde al otherwise, / As he which wolde her deth respite / And fondeth hou he mihte excite / The jugges thurgh his eloquence / Fro deth to torne the sentence / And sette here hertes to pite" (VII.1615–21).

Gower draws selectively from his source, reporting how the crafty Julius spoke and with what intent, but omitting what he actually said. To report the speech verbatim would, after all, involve the rhetorical risk of evoking the very "piety" and "pite" that he wishes to suppress and undermining the strict, merciless justice he approves. Brunetto's *Tresor*, by way of contrast, quotes both Catiline's words, spoken in self-defense, and Caesar's speech in its entirety, and comments on their effective use of ethical appeals.

According to Brunetto, Catiline "named his ancestors and their good deeds before the senate when he wanted to conceal the conspiracy in Rome, and when he told them that it was not for evil, but rather to help the feeble and powerless, as had always been his custom."[60] Caesar, for his part, acknowledged Catiline's guilt, but pleaded for leniency in punishment. In his speech, Caesar cites the good examples set by "wise men of old" in Rome ("li sage home de ceste cité"), when they spared the city of Rhodes and showed mercy to the Carthaginians, and he uses these exempla to convince his fellow senators that "the perfidy and the crime of those who have been arrested should not surpass our dignity and our kindness; we must have a higher regard for our good reputation than our anger."[61] Caesar goes on, moreover, to warn the Senate against taking rash action, giving two examples of cases in which strict justice was exacted, with the regrettable result that greater evils ensued:

> When the Lacedaemonians had taken Athens, they placed in office thirty men who were masters of the community; these men executed in the beginning the worst disloyal men without giving them a trial: the people were pleased and said that this action was good. After this, they gradually acquired the custom and the license to execute the good and the bad as they saw fit, to such an extent that . . . the city fell into . . . servitude. . . . Lucius Silla was greatly praised for his condemnation and execution of Damassipus and others who had been against the commune of Rome; but this action was the beginning of great evil.[62]

Not by accident does Gower omit these admonitory examples from Caesar's speech—exempla that would clearly have impugned the ruthless action of the Parliament of 1388, which, as Louisa D. Duls reminds us, pronounced "sentence of death . . . upon at least seventeen persons"[63] and thus prepared the way for "great evil": the retaliation taken by Richard in 1397, civil war, usurpation, and regicide.

A similar pattern of omission is evident in the *Cronica Tripertita,* where Gower makes no mention of the protracted efforts by Richard and others to maintain the innocence of Nicholas Brembre, the former mayor of London, and of Sir Simon Burley, the king's chamberlain and former tutor, both of whom were condemned to death as traitors, but only on dubious legal grounds, after extended debate, and through the evident coercion of the three senior Appellants.[64] According to the misleading account in the *Cronica,* the guilt of the two was self-evident, and Queen Anne pleaded on her knees in vain for Burley's life, not because she upheld his innocence, but solely out of compassion for his old age and ill health.[65] Gower's own judgment unambiguously approves the hanging of Brembre (the "Bramble") and the beheading of Burley: "When it is not virtuous, old age is the more to be blamed" (*Chronicle,* p. 295).[66]

According to the *Cronica,* the Merciless Parliament succeeded in a thorough cleansing of the royal establishment: "Gone was the flatterer, the villain, the plotter, the false counselor, the schemer, the envious promoter" (*Chronicle*, p. 297).[67] The parliament in effect accomplished what Richard's father confessors had failed to do when they, remiss in their priestly duties, had let the king's faults go "unchecked," without imposing a proper penance for his "guilt" or requiring him to make amends (*Chronicle*, p. 297). Supplying the virtue these "ungodly friars" lacked, the undivided secular trinity of Gloucester, Arundel, and Warwick "stood firm, consolidated the realm, strengthened the law, and routed corrupt practices," and thus "molded a reformed, reinvigorated king" (*Chronicle*, p. 297).[68]

When Gower penned his *Confessio Amantis* in the early 1390s, using the figure of Genius as a confessor and the outline of a penitential manual to fulfill what George Coffman has called his "most significant role"—namely, to be a "mentor for royalty"—he aligned his poetic and rhetorical project with the reformist program of the Lords Appellant.[69] Through the mouth of Genius, Gower sought to play the part of an Aristotle for Richard, England's young Alexander. The unforgettable and ever-threatening lesson he offered to Richard was that of the Merciless Parliament, thinly veiled under the exemplum of the parliament in Rome.

The rhetoric he tried to impress on the king was not the "soubtil cautele" and sophistry of a Julius Caesar pleading for leniency but rather the speech of a "trewman" (VII.1639–40), such as Decimus Silanus, who, according to Brunetto, "proceeded quickly with few words and without a prologue and without any concealment whatever, because his subject matter dealt with an honest thing, that is, condemning to death traitors against the republic of Rome."[70] Gower points approvingly to "Cithero" and his party, who "spieken plein after the lawe" (VII.1623), who form their "Argument" in such a way that "may the pleine trouthe enforme" (VII.1638), and who teach their student "in what wise he schal pronounce / His tale plein withoute frounce" (VII.1593–94).[71]

The treatment of rhetoric thus directly prepares for, and actually leads into, the extended discussion of practical philosophy which concludes Book VII: "Practique stant upon thre thinges / Toward the governance of kinges" (VII.1650–51). As a mirror for princes within the larger mirror of the *Confessio* as a whole, the concluding section of Book VII deals briefly with ethics (self-rule) and economy (household rule) before dwelling at length on policy or statecraft. Genius elaborates the five points of policy, using multiple exempla to illustrate each one. Not surprisingly, he begins with truth, the first point and the greatest of kingly virtues, followed by liberality, justice, mercy, and chastity. The good king is, above all, true to his word, guided by good counsel, and honest in his dealings with others—"regis ab ore boni fabula nulla sonat"—and thus a "trewman" like the rhetor Cicero and Gower, the plainspoken poet of the *Confessio*.[72]

The Rhetoric of "Trouthe"

But what does it mean for a king to be "trewe" in his speech? The exemplum which Genius uses to illustrate the meaning of truth records a debate in the Persian court of King Darius concerning what is strongest: "the wyn, the womman, or the king" (VII.1813). In the end, truth proves to be the strongest ("veritas super omnia vincit"), for, as Zorobabel argues, "trouthe" alone is "schameles" and empowering: "ther is no myht / Withoute trouthe in no degre" (VII.1966, 1968–69).

Gower relates the very same exemplum in his Anglo-Norman *Mirour de l'Omme* (1376–79). There, in the context of a general examination of the estates, Gower devotes a chapter to the state of the kings ("l'estat des Roys").[73] Addressing an imagined but nameless king directly ("O Rois"), Gower exhorts him to fulfill his threefold duty: "first, to love and serve God, and to uphold Holy Church, and to safeguard the laws."[74] If the king remains true to his coronation oath, Gower affirms, he will avoid the fate of King Nebuchadnezzar's son, King Belshazzar (Daniel 5), who lost God's favor and his kingdom. Gower explicitly uses the king's crown as the outward sign of his oath: "Do that which pertains to your crown" (*Mirror*, p. 297).[75] The king who is "false" to the oath he "made to God and Holy Church on the day of [his] coronation . . . is unworthy to hold his office" (*Mirror*, p. 296) and thus, Gower implies, subject to deposition.[76]

In Book VII of the *Confessio*, Gower is less direct. There Genius relates how Aristotle taught Alexander to "kepe his tunge and to be trewe" (VII.1739), without referring specifically to the coronation oath. The veiled connection between the king's "word . . . trewe and plein" (VII.1731) and the king's oath of office is nonetheless strongly suggested by Genius' extended interpretation (VII.1751–73) of the "corone" as a token of kingly virtue and responsibility, a "figure," and a "verrai Signe" that a king should "holde trewly his beheste / Of thing which longeth to kinghede" (VII.1762, 1764–65) if—the "if" is implied—he wishes to "kepe and guye" the land that stands "under his Gerarchie" (VII.1773).

Truth to his coronation oath is thus the first point of policy because it literally determines the king's right to rule. The king receives the crown, as well as other regalia, as the outward sacramental sign of the binding power of the word he has spoken. While such considerations have a general validity, Gower's pointing to "trouthe" and to the crown has a particular significance if we follow his poetic directives and imagine King Richard in 1392–93 as the primary auditor of the *Confessio*.

Already in 1386 Richard II had been threatened with deposition.[77] Although the historical evidence is inconclusive, there are strong grounds for believing that he was actually deposed by the Gloucester party for three days at the end of December 1387.[78] The Merciless Parliament of 1388 required him at its conclusion to take his coronation oath for a second time. John Capgrave relates: "In þis parlement þe lordes desired of þe kyng to make his sacramental oth byfore þe puple, because þe oth whech he had mad before was in his childhod. And so dcd þc kyng, and all þc lordis and states of þe parlement mad her new othis to be trewe ligemen to her kyng."[79]

Richard took this second oath while still in his minority. Approximately a year later, on May 3, 1389, he declared himself of age. Shortly thereafter he dismissed the duke of Gloucester and the earl of Warwick from his council. In the early 1390s, therefore, Gower's admonition of the king to preserve "trouthe" and his allegorical interpretation of what the crown "betokneth" (VII.1751) would have served to recall forcibly the object lesson the Appellants had only recently given the young king.

"Cithero" and "Tullius": Gower's Rhetoric and Poetics

Gower's rhetoric in the *Confessio* is the rhetoric of a poet rather than an orator. Splitting the "Marcus Tullius Scithero" (*Canterbury Tales,* V.722) of Chaucer's Franklin into two persons, Gower embraces the political stance of "Cithero," while rejecting the ornate doctrine of "Tullius," who knows "wordis forto peinte and pike" (VIII.3118). Opting to speak in a low style, using "rude wordes and . . . pleyne" (VIII.3067*), he rejects "the forme of rethoriqe" and "the forme of eloquence" (VIII.3117, VIII.3065*), while at the same time retaining its substance, its truth. This truth is "wisdom to the wise" (VIII.3059*) for those who know how to interpret the tales of the *Confessio* as allegories and exempla. For others, however, the poem's only value will be its entertainment, "as for to lawhe and forto pleye" (VIII.3057*). Thus thc pocm itsclf litcrally "stant *betwene* ernest and game" (VIII.3109; emphasis added) as a vehicle that mediates various meanings to different audiences.

Gowcr clcarly hopcs that thc rcadcrs of his poem will be delighted *and* instructed by it. Indeed, Gower indicates that King Richard's failure to interpret the *Confessio* properly—that is, allegorically—will incur for him a heavy penalty. Gower sounds this warning in the first exemplum that Genius relates in Book I, namely, that of Diana and Acteon. Whereas Ovid famously applied the tale to himself in *Tristia* II.103–6, with reference to the crime that offended Caesar and led to his exile, Gower invites his royal auditor, in the person of Amans, to identify with Acteon.

The tale appears in the context of an examination of Amans' "wittes fyve"

(I.296), which, taken as a whole, serves as a prelude to Genius' discourse on the first of the seven capital sins, pride. Genius tells only stories about seeing and hearing, however, omitting the other three senses, including touch (a sense that is of obvious importance to a lover's shrift). As the late Jerome Taylor once suggested to me, the exclusive focus on sight and audition indicates that these introductory tales do not primarily concern themselves with the psychology of love, nor do they simply anticipate the illustration of pride. Rather, their main purpose is to teach the reader and/or auditor how to take into one's heart and mind, through "the gates" of eye and ear (I.299), the exempla that follow. Gower, in short, offers his primary pupil, King Richard, and all of us through him, introductory lessons in how to understand the *Confessio.*

The first four exempla all warn against a merely literal, superficial interpretation of the tales. Acteon sees Diana naked, and "his yhe awey ne swerveth / Fro hire" (I.366–67). He fails to see her and her nymphs "veiled," and thus he makes the typical mistake of the carnal reader of an allegorical text. By way of contrast, Perseus refuses to look directly on Medusa, and, covering his face with the "Schield of Pallas" (I.431), goddess of wisdom, he succeeds in slaying the Gorgons, the direct sight of whom has petrified many others.[80] Finally, the tales of the prudent serpent and of Ulysses and the Sirens warn a person to close one's ears, lest one succumb to the dangerous attractions of verbal "enchantement" and beautiful "melodie" (I.477, 494).[81]

If we imagine Richard II and Henry of Derby as particular members of Gower's audience, the first of these tales teaches them a pointed lesson about the importance of reading allegorically and of finding a message veiled behind the obvious one. A proud Acteon, hunting in the woods, seeks "to finde gamen in his weie" (I.347) and looks steadfastly upon a naked Diana. In these actions, Gower's Acteon differs from Ovid's in *Metamorphoses* III.138–252.[82] He resembles instead those who discover only "game" in Gower's poem because they read it superficially, without making the proper personal applications. As a consequence of his transgression, Acteon is turned by the angry goddess into "the liknesse . . . of an Hert" (I.371), upon which he is put to the chase and cruelly torn apart by "his oghne houndes" (I.377).

This traditional Ovidian tale assumes an ominous, threatening tone when one recalls that, already by 1390, King "Richart" was using the hart as his personal device and dressing the members of his extended household in his livery.[83] And perhaps by 1393, but certainly by 1400, political poets and chroniclers were referring to Henry Bolingbroke as the Hound.[84] Should Richard fail to grasp the deeper import of Gower's imaginative Aristotelian lessons in ethics, economy, and statecraft, and should he fail to put them into practice, he can expect to share Acteon's terrible fate. Unlike Ovid, who raises questions in the *Metamorphoses* about the harshness of Diana's punishment, Gower quietly insists on its justice.[85]

The dark, allegorical undertow of the exempla we have surveyed—those of Arion, of the Roman parliament, of truth, and of Acteon—suggests that Gower's outspoken Lancastrian stance in the *Cronica Tripertita* does not reflect a sudden shift of allegiance. Rather, whatever hopes Gower may have entertained in 1392–93 about the king's ability to take instruction, the *Confessio* clearly continues and supports the program of Ricardian reform initiated by the Lords Appellant during the Merciless Parliament. Gower's dual dedication to Richard and Henry finds its meaning in that rhetorical context. When Henry of Derby became King Henry IV, the *Confessio* remained a mirror for princes and a "bok for Engelondes sake" (Prologue, l. 24), but it was no longer a "bok for King Richardes sake" (Prologue, l. 24*). It retained its general audience and its commonplace, exemplary meaning, but the loss of its particular addressee in the person of Richard and the related change from a "dual" to an "alternative" dedication meant nothing less than the loss of its timely allegory. With that loss, the poem certainly ceased to be the same.

4

Chaucer's Ricardian Allegories

> A rhetorical reading of Chaucer does not dismiss life and feeling but
> rather redirects emphasis from the verisimilitude of realistic content
> and dramatized characters to the labor itself of writing and composing
> poetic narratives.
>
> Robert M. Jordan, *Chaucer's Poetics and the Modern Reader*

In this study of late medieval political allegory, John Gower himself leads us to Geoffrey Chaucer. The first recension of Gower's *Confessio
Amantis* (which, I have argued, must be dated 1392–93, not 1390) includes
a farewell speech by Venus in which the goddess of love sends a grateful
personal greeting to Chaucer, her "disciple" and "poete," and a message
that he, "upon his latere age," should "sette an ende of alle his werk" and
complete his "testament of love" (VIII.2941–55*).[1]

The procession of famous lovers, including Alceste and Admetus (VIII.
2640–47), which shortly precedes Venus' speech, not only offers a review
of Gower's poem as a whole, but also invites a comparison between it and
Chaucer's unfinished *Legend of Good Women,* the "testament of love," which
is still to be recorded in Venus's "court" (VIII.2955–57*). Both works are
collections of amatory stories, heavily marked by Ovidian influence. Both
represent the poet as a lover on trial in a court of love. Both works, moreover, combine an erotic theme with topical allegory and explicit advice to
King Richard. In each case the king is a material cause for the poet, both
as part of his historical audience and as his literal and allegorical subject
matter.

Chaucer portrays Richard II allegorically at least thrice: as one of the
three royal tercel eagles who contend for the hand of a beautiful formel in
the *Parliament of Fowls;* as the god of Love in the Prologue to the *Legend of
Good Women;* and, as I hope to show, in various guises in the linked tales of
Chaucer the Pilgrim, the Monk, and the Nun's Priest in the *Canterbury
Tales.* The first two allegories have received considerable scholarly atten-
tion; the third, an allegory in three parts, has gone relatively unnoticed.
The discussion in this chapter offers a comparative survey of these three

Ricardian allegories from the viewpoint of Chaucer's developing, and increasingly sophisticated, allegorical technique.

Allegories of Similarity and Difference: the *Parliament of Fowls* and the *Legend of Good Women*

In the *Parliament of Fowls* (ca. 1380), Chaucer employs an allegory of resemblance to support a basic narrative argument from similarities. Richard II, like the eagle, was a royal suitor. As Larry D. Benson and others have observed, the young king's betrothal to Anne of Bohemia was settled only after protracted negotiations (1377–81), during which Richard, again like the eagle, had to contend with the rival suits of two others, Friedrich of Meissen and the Dauphin.[2] Through the comic impatience of the other birds, assembled for mating on St. Valentine's Day, Chaucer expresses a veiled wish for the prompt settlement of the affair, for the sake of "commune profyt" and "comune spede" (ll. 47, 75, 507) in a world where a king's marriage, love life, and ability to produce an heir profoundly affected the stability of the country as a whole.[3]

Approximately a decade later, in the F Prologue to the *Legend of Good Women*, Chaucer constructs a more detailed and personal allegory of Ricardian resemblance. He then goes even further, superimposing on that basic allegory of similarity, which likens Cupid to Richard II, an allegory of difference, according to which Cupid also stands for Richard's enemy, Richard of Arundel. The intertextual gap that results from the combination of oppositional allegories requires the reader to fill in, and thus discover, the "sentence" that is missing. Moreover, whereas the *Parliament of Fowls* merely depicts Richard in a veiled way, the *Legend* actually addresses him, albeit indirectly, in order to offer political counsel.

When Chaucer literally substitutes the god of Love for Admetus, the legendary husband of Alceste, he sets in motion a series of allegorical substitutions. Whereas the resemblance between Richard and the tercel in the *Parliament* is general, based on his status as a king and his action as a suitor, the likeness between Richard and the god of Love in the *Legend* is very particular. As many have noticed, the "gilte heer" of the god is "corowned with a sonne / Instede of gold" (F Prologue, ll. 230–31)—a description that recalls Richard's personal appearance and one of his devices.[4]

The Monk of Evesham Abbey describes Richard as having golden hair ("crines glauci"),[5] and Adam of Usk describes him as being as "the fairest of men, like a second Absolom" ("inter omnes mortales ac si secundus Apsalon pulcherimus").[6] Richard's monument in Westminster Abbey, moreover, represents the sun ascending behind clouds—a Ricardian device that

Gower also uses in *Confessio Amantis*.[7] There, however, he gives the clouds a meaning other than death or earthly tribulation, associating them with the blameworthy bad companions and foolish advisers of Richard's youth. He likens Richard, by contrast, to the "hede planete": "Lich to the Sonne in his degree, / Which with the clowdes up alofte / Is derked and bis-chadewed ofte, / But hou so that it trowble in their, / The Sonne is evere briht and feir / Withinne himself and noght empeired" (VIII.3006–11*).

Whereas the sun crown of Cupid recalls Richard's solar cognizance, the gold-fretted crown of pearl "flowrouns" (F Prologue, ll. 220–21) worn by Queen Alceste describes, as many have argued, the ornate lily crown "dec-orated with various gems, including 132 pearls," which was worn by Anne of Bohemia at her wedding.[8] Alceste moreover explicitly identifies Queen Anne as her allegorical double when she first commissions Chaucer to write a "glorious legende / Of goode wymmen, maydenes, and wyves" and then commands him, "And whan this book ys maad, yive it the quene, / On my byhalf, at Eltham or at Sheene" (F Prologue, ll. 483–84, 496–97).

The allegory of personal resemblance between the god and Alceste, on the one hand, and Richard and Anne, on the other—an allegory Chaucer establishes through their royal status, spousal relationship, appearance, de-vices, and place references—is reinforced by parallels in their actions. Many have noted that Alceste makes intercession for the kneeling Chaucer, whom Cupid has condemned as his "foo" and a traitor to Love's cause (F Prologue, ll. 322, 336), even as Queen Anne repeatedly interceded on behalf of oth-ers before King Richard.[9]

The Monk of Westminster emphasizes, in particular, the part that Anne played in reconciling the king with the city of London in 1392: "The queen, more than once, indeed on many occasions, both at Windsor and at Not-tingham, prostrated herself at the King's feet in earnest and tireless en-treaty for the city and the welfare of its citizens, that he would cease to direct his anger against them."[10]

Richard de Maidstone's poem about that same historical reconciliation records a ceremonial public dialogue between Anne and Richard, in which the queen pleads with the king in the language of an Alceste, calling him her "sweet love," without whom life would be death ("Dulcis amor, sine quo vivere fit mihi mors").[11] She pleads for London on her knees ("supplico prostrata") before him, appealing to Richard's mercy, his kingly dignity, his sense of justice, and his love for her. He in turn expresses pleasure at her compassionate entreaty, gladly grants her request—"sumo placenter," ait tunc rex, "carissima conjux"—and raises her to sit beside him on the throne, before turning to address the assembled citizens.[12]

In 1392, then, a kneeling Queen Anne was a popular heroine, whose words and actions belonged to a carefully choreographed script of spectacle and pageantry. In the late 1380s, however, Anne was most famous for her supplication at the feet not of King Richard but of Richard's mortal enemy, Richard of Arundel.

During the course of the Merciless Parliament in 1388, "the Queen was three hours on her knees before the count of Arundel, begging him for the life of one of her knights named Simon Burley, who was nevertheless beheaded. And the said count answered the Queen, 'My friend, it would be more worthwhile for you to pray for yourself and your husband.'"[13] As this report from the *Chronique de la traison et mort de Richart* indicates, in 1397, when King Richard had Arundel beheaded on the charge of treason, he recalled not only Arundel's earlier, unjust beheading of Burley on the same charge, but also his insult to Anne in ridiculing her and refusing her plea.

The F Prologue to Chaucer's *Legend,* then, sets the god of love, as a representation of King Richard, in the very place where Arundel stood during the Merciless Parliament. Before him, Alceste makes her plea, defending the poet in his "latere age," even as Anne pleaded before Arundel for the life of an old Simon Burley, the tutor of Richard's childhood.[14] This double vision of the god, which identifies him allegorically with both Richard and Arundel, is an allegory of opposition that requires us as readers to bridge a gap between and among several different (and apparently mutually exclusive) levels of meaning.

Resisting the idea that Chaucer would even have attempted such a daring double vision of the god as Richard II/Richard of Arundel, David Wallace has argued that the F Prologue must have been composed *before* the Merciless Parliament, and that "the helplessness of king and queen before the events of 1388 [made] the delicate politics and rhetoric of the F *Prologue* seem anachronistic—properly the stuff of dream poetry—almost as soon as they were written."[15] When history caused Anne of Bohemia to kneel before an unrelenting "god," the earl of Arundel, Chaucer's F Prologue was (according to Wallace) transformed retrospectively into a cruelly ironic foreshadowing. Through a change in historical circumstances, its meaning changed, and it became prophetic. Chaucer therefore rewrote the Prologue in the G form in a Petrarchan "attempt to save or withhold the text from history by denying it the force of occasion."[16]

Such an early dating of the F Prologue is, however, highly dubious, given Gower's oblique reference to the unfinished *Legend* in the first recension *Confessio.* The F Prologue is not, as Wallace would have it, an unwitting and completely unintended prophecy of future events; rather, it comments bravely on the recent past and its implications for the political present. Michael Hanrahan has argued that the Prologue to the *Legend of Good Women*—and indeed the *Legend* as a whole—plays upon the common depiction in love poetry of "false lovers . . . as traitors" in order to explore, under the ostensible topic of amatory infidelity, another related matter: the political definition of treason during Richard's reign.[17] The Lords Appellant and King Richard alternately accused their respective opponents of treason and defended themselves against that charge, each side using definitions of the crime that exceeded those in the Great Treason Statute of 1352. Similarly, Cupid accuses the daisy-worshipping Chaucer of having betrayed Love and Love's folk through writing about Criseyde's infidelity to Troilus—a charge against which Chaucer defends himself and is defended by Alceste.

Hanrahan is right in saying that the *Legend* "ultimately opposes *any* sectarian determination of the crime" of treason.[18] Faithless lovers—whether men or women—are all guilty, albeit in varying degrees, of the same crime, and neither side has the right to define infidelity in such a way that it applies only to members of the opposite sex. Indeed, the dark comedy of the *Legend* results precisely from the failed attempt to go from one extreme to the other, to "speke wel of love" while telling of "trewe" women and "of false men that hem bytraien" (F Prologue, ll. 491, 485–86).

The penance that Alceste prescribes actually asks Chaucer to atone for his alleged crime by repeating it in reverse. If men are likely "to wommen lasse triste" (F Prologue, l. 333) after hearing how Criseyde forsook Troilus, women can hardly be expected to trust men more after hearing Chaucer's dreary legends of masculine betrayal. Love's reign is weakened, rather than furthered, by Chaucer's attempt to correct what he has "mysseyde / Or in the Rose or elles in Creseyde" (F Prologue, ll. 440–41). Chaucer, moreover, uncomfortably answers one act of "treason" with another, turning against his own sex by depicting men as villainous.

Chaucer's point, however, is not merely, as Hanrahan says, to enact "the struggle to determine the meaning of treason that characterized Richard's reign."[19] By placing Richard allegorically in the position Arundel held during the Merciless Parliament, Chaucer teaches the king, through the supplication of Alceste/Anne, not to be another Arundel, unyielding to pity and harsh in condemning his enemy. To do so, after all, would be to answer one wrong vengefully with another and thus to threaten the security of the kingdom as a whole, the unity of which is a love dependent on the king's *being* Love, even as God is Love (1 John 4:9). Like Gower's Amans, who turns away from a "blynde" cupidinous love and toward a love that "stant of charite confermed" (*Confessio* VIII.3145, 3164), Alceste instructs Cupid about what it truly means to be a "god of Love": "A god ne sholde nat thus be agreved, / But of hys deitee he shal be stable, / And therto gracious and merciable" (F Prologue, ll. 311, 345–47).

In 1389 Richard declared himself of age and took the government into his own hands. Gower's *Confessio* (1392–93), as we have seen, displays considerable anxiety about whether the king would be "merciable," or whether he would seek "vengaunce" against the Lords Appellant "thurgh cruelte," instead of being grateful for the divine protection and good fortune that had spared his life and kept his own royal "astat . . . / Sauf, as it oghte wel to be" during the course of the Merciless Parliament of 1388 (VIII.2997, 3004–5*). Gower prays on his "bare knees" that God will convey "grace and mercy" to his worthy king, "Richard by name the Secounde," in order that the king, in turn, might continue to show pity to the "liges of his lond" (VIII.2980–87, 2995*).

Chaucer's *Legend* is fraught with the same worrying concern about a possibly vengeful Richard. There, however, the poet's persona falls "doun on knes anoon-ryght," not before God, but before the daisy, who, for her part, delights "in the brightnesse / Of the sonne" (F Prologue, ll. 115, 64–65). When the daisy reappears in his dream in the form of Alceste, who is dressed "lyk a daysie for to sene" (F Prologue, l. 224), the queen symbolically kneels before the king in the act of interceding for Chaucer. "No cause of deth lyeth in this caas," she insists, and therefore the god "oghte to ben the lyghter merciable" (F Prologue, ll. 409–10).

Chaucer's use of Alceste as an allegory of Anne allows him to be more direct than Gower in his address to the king. Gower uses Genius' Aristotelian instruction of Amans in order to teach Richard about political virtues, the practice of which will "make his regne stable" and unite his people in "love and accord" (*Confessio* VIII.3036, 3018*). Chaucer's Alceste, by way of contrast, pointedly warns Cupid about the possibility of false accusation in a court where envy is rampant and where there "ys many a losengeour, / And many a queynte totelere accusour" (F Prologue, ll. 352–53). She pleads with him to be slow in passing judgment and quick to forgive offenses, lest he "be lyk tirauntz of Lumbardye" (F Prologue, l. 374). The king should be particularly concerned, she says, to uphold his liege lords, "For they ben half-goddes in this world here" (F Prologue, l. 387).

In 1389 the king was certainly in need of such advice. As John Capgrave relates, the king removed two of the Appellants, the duke of Gloucester and the earl of Warwick, from his council and replaced them with "othir þat plesed bettir his y3e":

In þis same tyme flatereres þat were aboute þe King told þe King þat þe duke of Gloucetir had gadered a gret hoost to destruccioun of þe kyng and his frendis. The Kyng sent aftir þe duke, and þere was prouyd fals al þat euir was seyd. And whan þe duke began to declare his innocens, to confusion and schame of hem þat stood in þe kyngis presens, þe Kyng prayed þe duke for al þe loue þat was betwix hem þat he schuld hold his pes.[20]

On this occasion in 1389, when Richard's uncle and (former?) enemy stood before him, falsely accused of treason, Richard exercised the kind of restraint to which John of Gaunt and Queen Anne frequently exhorted him. Gaunt's influence, as Anthony Tuck relates, effected Gloucester's restoration to the council in 1390 and helped to bring about a promising period of reconcilation between Richard and the Appellants, among whom "only Arundel remained disaffected" and "failed to make his peace with the king."[21]

When Chaucer cast Anne of Bohemia in the role of Alceste in the F Prologue to the *Legend,* he made a natural and rhetorically effective choice, for the queen was one of those who counseled reconciliation to whom Richard listened. The choice of Anne proved double-edged, however, when she died suddenly in 1394. Wild with grief, Richard ordered Sheen Manor, the place where Anne died, to be destroyed. The King's bereavement also apparently prompted changes in both Gower's *Confessio* and Chaucer's *Legend.* Hans-Jürgen Diller notes that the second recension of *Confessio Amantis* omits Gower's original, concluding "prayer for those who strive after true love" and his acknowledgment of happy lovers (VIII.2967–70, 3078–83*)—a quiet but compelling indication "that the happy lovers of the earlier version were a complimentary reference to Richard and his queen."[22] Similarly, the G Prologue to *The Legend of Good Women* tactfully leaves out the earlier Prologue's explicit mention of Anne and Sheen (F Prologue, ll. 496–97).[23] Despite his revision of the Prologue, Chaucer seems to have abandoned (if he ever had) the intention to write any more legends.[24]

With Anne's passing died also the hope both for a harmonious extension of the king's affection for the queen into his relationship with his lieges and for Anne's mediation between and among them. Indeed, on the occasion of Anne's funeral, Richard dramatically renewed his quarrel with Arundel, striking him a sacrilegious blow within the very walls of Westminster Abbey and then imprisoning him in the Tower of London, on account of the apparent disrespect for the queen that the earl had shown in arriving late.[25] The incident gives vivid proof that, without the intercession of an Alceste-like Anne, and indeed partly because of his memory of her, Richard could become as merciless as Arundel had been. In the words of Wallace, "Richard without Anne is a Melibee without Prudence: outrage and insult to a much-loved wife, in that wife's absence, [are] doomed to lead to a renewal of violence."[26]

Allegories of *Occultatio:* The Tales of "Melibee," the Monk, and the Nun's Priest

Whereas Chaucer's Ricardian allegories in the *Parliament of Fowls* and the *Legend of Good Women* make a fairly obvious use of narrative arguments deriving from similarity and difference, his allegories of the king in the *Canterbury Tales* are considerably more veiled, to the point of escaping modern notice. The complexity of the multilayered narratives that Chaucer constructs attests both to his increasing sophistication as an allegorist and to the high degree of political tension in the late 1390s, when the tales in Fragment VII were linked together.

That fragment, as I have argued elsewhere, is marked by a specific concern with literary issues and structured according to the four Aristotelian causes of books.[27] At the center of the fragment, we find the two tales of Chaucer the Pilgrim. As both C. David Benson and Lee Patterson have observed, these tales are important for our understanding of Chaucer's authorial self-definition.[28] Most obviously, Chaucer adopts different poetic personae in these tales and uses their generic limitations to develop his own self-image. In the "Tale of Sir Thopas," on the one hand, Chaucer aims to delight his auditors by assuming (albeit in parody) the traditional role of a minstrel romancer. In the sententious "Tale of Melibee," on the other hand, Chaucer plays the part of another traditional poet-persona, that of a wise counselor of kings. Chaucer the Pilgrim's dramatized, literal failure when he pursues the ends of delight and instruction in isolation from each other sets the stage for Chaucer the poet's successful combination of them via allegorical composition in the linked tales of the Monk and the Nun's Priest.

Chaucerians have long suspected that the "Melibee" is some sort of topical allegory.[29] In the "Melibee" Chaucer develops relentlessly the Solomonic theme oft repeated by Prudence: "Werk alle thy thynges by conseil" (VII. 1002). At the end of the tale, after much seeking of advice from foolish and wise counselors, Melibee, who has been grievously wronged by his three mortal enemies, is finally persuaded to renounce taking a too hasty vengeance against them and to be reconciled with them. The tale thus concerns itself literally with issues that were important throughout Richard II's reign: the king's need for counsel, the principles guiding the selection of royal counselors, the degree of their proper or improper influence over the king, his receptivity to their advice, and the questions of taking revenge against, or seeking reconciliation with, one's enemies. Like Melibee, after all, Richard II also had three enemies, the senior Lords Appellant—enemies whom he never really forgave, as the events of 1397 bear witness.

There are, in addition to these circumstantial proofs, direct signs of topicality in the tale. Chaucer deleted the proverb in his French source about how troublesome it is to have a child as a king—a deletion which, Judith Ferster and others have observed, "shows that Chaucer knew that the tale could be taken as a reference to Richard II's accession to the throne when he was still a young boy."[30] At the same time, as Helen Cooper has emphasized, Chaucer expanded the closing section on the virtue of mercy in a ruler and added, in direct conjunction with each other, proverbial mentions of a "wilde hert" (l. 1325) and a vulnerable king, thus evoking the image of the white hart, which King Richard had adopted as his badge in 1390. According to Cooper, these additions suggest "that the tract was indeed written for Richard II, but the wayward king of the early 1390s rather than the child."[31]

The allegorical message of the "Melibee" is nonetheless obscured by its literal concern with the giving and receiving of advice. Indeed, the text of the tale is composed largely of multiple and self-contradictory *sententiae*. Patterson sees in the contradictions and paradoxes of the "Melibee" Chaucer's conscious rejection of the role of court poet; Ferster views the tale somewhat similarly, as a deconstructive "attack on the efficacy of advice," but she interprets this attack as Chaucer's timely critique of the king's appointed advisers rather than his poetic withdrawal from social concerns.[32] Like Ferster, I view the tale as participating in a critical discourse about Richard's counselors and the failure of those closest to him (including his own conscience) to direct him well. In particular, Chaucer questions the value of a certain mode of giving advice: the *sententia,* or wise saying. Chaucer's own way of giving the king advice is not direct but indirect; not the writing of philosophical prose about statecraft, not the compilation of prudential *sententiae,* not even the spelling out of a *moralité,* but rather the telling of stories that provide an occasion for Richard to see and know himself before it is too late.

"The Tale of Melibee," I would suggest, serves to introduce the next two tales in which Chaucer gives the good counsel to Richard that the "Melibee" only promises. Taken together, the tales of the Monk and the Nun's Priest actually tell the story of Richard's life, using an artificial order that begins in the middle. The interruption of "The Monk's Tale" by the Knight leaves Richard's soon-to-be-tragic story open-ended, whereas "The Nun's Priest's Tale" narrates the events of Richard's youth. The Ricardian allegory that is veiled in the tales of the Monk and the Nun's Priest thus defines the proper context within which the lessons of counsel and reconciliation announced in Chaucer's "Tale of Melibee" become meaningful.

The Monk's Tragical "Seint Edward"

In the headlink to "The Monk's Tale," the Monk answers to Harry Bailly's jibes by offering to tell "a tale, or two, or three. / And if yow list to herkene hyderward, / I wol yow seyn the lyf of Seint Edward; / Or ellis, first, tragedies wol I telle / Of whiche I have an hundred in my cell" (VII. 1968–72). The passage raises various questions. The choice of Saint Edward, rather than any other saint, is apparently purposeful. Nowhere else in the *Canterbury Tales* does Chaucer mention him. The awkward position of his name at the end of the line calls special attention to it. The appropriateness of the Monk's choice is puzzling. The logical relationship between the "lyf of Seint Edward" and the Monk's "tragedies" is unclear and somewhat jarring. The Monk's motivation for postponing his rendition of Edward's life is unspecified. Most important, the promised "lyf of Seint Edward" is never (literally) told and is permanently withheld through the Knight's interruption.

The Monk's unfulfilled Edwardian promise is best understood in rhetorical terms as an instance of *praecisio* or *occultatio*. It illustrates *praecisio* because the speaker literally begins to say something—"the lyf of Seint Edward" (VII.1920)—that he then leaves untold. As the Ciceronian *Rhetorica ad Herennium* notes, the figure effectively arouses suspicion through a conspicuous silence ("suspicio tacita").[33] It also illustrates *occultatio*, however, for while the Monk literally passes by the saint's life through postponing it, he actually tells it allegorically. This figure, sometimes called *praeteritio*, resembles *praecisio* in that it effectively creates a suspicion in the auditor through an overt omission ("ut utilius sit occulte fecisse suspicionem").[34]

Chaucer uses the initial mention of Edward as an *occultatio* to move his audience to seek for and to discover the political allegory he has hidden beneath the letter of the Monk's and the Nun's Priest's tales. Who is the "Seint Edward" whose story is Chaucer's occult subject matter? The footnote in the *Riverside Chaucer* boldly identifies him as Edward the Confessor. Susan H. Cavanaugh's explanatory note in the same edition is less bold, identifying him "probably" as "Edward the Confessor (c.1004–66), King of England," a saint to whom "Richard II had a special devotion."[35]

The note correctly points us in the direction of King Richard, whose "special devotion" to the Confessor amounted to a virtual identification with him. As Dillian Gordon notes, the Confessor "died on 5 January, the eve of Richard II's birthday," and Richard consciously endeavored to make his life a continuation of Edward's.[36] In so doing, moreover, he also chose a more immediate and unfortunate model, Edward II, his deposed and murdered great-grandfather, whose canonization as a martyr Richard eagerly supported. The "lyf of Seint Edward" to which the Monk refers is, simply put, a recognizable code for the life of Richard.

When the eleven-year-old Richard was crowned king at Westminster on July 16, 1377, the solemn liturgy for the coronation literally fashioned him into an "alter Edwardus." The rite called for Richard to be crowned with Saint Edward's own crown and robed in the clothes of the Confessor: his "tunica, supertunica, armil, girdle, and embroidered pall," as well as his buskins, gloves, and shoes.[37] Richard may have received the Blood of Christ from a "chalice of onyx stone" and the Eucharistic Host from a "paten of the best gold"—precious relics that Saint Edward had bequeathed to Westminster Abbey "for the communion of the lord king, on the day of his coronation."[38] Richard's oath of office obliged him "to grant and keep and by his oath confirm to the people of England the laws and customs granted by the ancient kings of England, his lawful and religious predecessors, and namely the laws, customs, and franchises granted to the clergy and people of the said kingdom by the glorious king Saint Edward."[39]

As the *Liber Regalis* prescribes, at the end of the ceremony, Richard was to go to the Chapel of St. Edward, in order to leave the relics of the saint—his vestments and regalia—on the altar there and to receive, in their stead, a parliament robe and an imperial crown to wear.[40] The Monk of Westminster laments that this custom was not observed strictly on Richard's coronation day. When the exhausted boy king left the Abbey, still wearing the Edwardian vestments, and was carried through the crowd in the arms of Simon Burley, one of the Confessor's "consecrated shoes" fell from Richard's feet and was lost.[41]

Four years later Richard knelt in tears in the Chapel of St. Edward before riding out to meet the peasants at Smithfield in 1381. Accompanied by a body of mounted citizens, the king stopped at Westminster, as the chronicler relates, "to supplicate at the shrine of the sainted king for divine aid where human counsel was altogether wanting."[42] Earlier that same day, a mob had forcibly dragged Richard Imworth out of Westminster Abbey, in violation of sanctuary, and beheaded him. The Monk of Westminster notes that "St. Edward, to the exaltation of his sainthood and the comfort of the realm, was swift indeed to avenge the wrong offered to him."[43] The saint, we are told, inspired the suppliant King Richard, and those who had prayerfully accompanied him, with "fresh heart and fresh hope of a happy outcome"—a hope that proved true in the surprising turn of events that followed.[44]

The *Westminster Chronicle* includes other signs of Richard's devotion to Saint Edward, a devotion that surely increased when the peasants at Smithfield were dispersed. In 1390, immediately after a three-day tournament held at Smithfield, the king solemnly observed the feast of the Translation of St. Edward (October 13): "The king, accompanied by his entire chapel, attended Prime, Vespers, and Compline at Westminster Abbey; with his chapel he was also present for Matins at midnight and at the procession during the day. At High Mass he sat in the choir with his chapel, wearing his crown."[45] In 1392, Richard similarly observed Saint Edward's feast day at Westminster, participating in Vespers and Matins, and attending the procession and High Mass on October 13.[46] Earlier that same year, when the king celebrated his formal reconciliation with the city of London, the public ceremony concluded at the Shrine of Saint Edward in Westminster Abbey: "When the collect for the king had been said, the convent went into St. Edward's shrine to the accompaniment of the antiphon 'Ave, Sancte rex Edwarde.'"[47]

There is speculation whether Richard II also emulated the Confessor in the practice of marital continence. The *Lives* of St. Edward all indicate that he and his wife, Queen Edith, maintained their virginity in marriage.[48] Although Richard's marriage with Anne of Bohemia was companionable, and his affection for her intense, she died childless in 1394 after twelve years of marriage. Richard's politic remarriage in 1396 to the child bride Isabelle of France was certainly not consummated, and as Caroline M. Barron suggests, Richard may have chosen her partly as security for his own chastity.[49]

The beautiful Wilton Diptych, which was probably commissioned by the king for use in Westminster Abbey, shows a kneeling Richard being presented to the Virgin and Child by his three patron saints, Edmund, Edward the Confessor, and John the Baptist.[50] Dillian Gordon argues for an association of the diptych with the events surrounding the Parliament of 1397, at which the three senior Appellants, who had opposed Richard in 1386–88, were condemned. At the conclusion of that parliament, Richard renewed his own coronation oath and required the members of parliament to swear an oath of loyalty to the king at the shrine of Edward the Confessor.[51] Beginning in 1395 or 1397, Richard started to impale his coat of arms with those of Edward the Confessor, setting them side by side, as if (in the words of Caroline Barron) Richard and Edward were "husband and wife."[52] As Gordon notes, Richard's will invokes Edward the Confessor, and "the pouncing on the canopy above Richard's head in the tomb at Westminster Abbey show[s] the royal arms impaled" with the Confessor's.[53]

Richard's last will and testament, which adds the invocation of the Confessor and John the Baptist, follows in other respects the will of King Edward II, the other "Seint Edward" to whom Richard was devoted, for as Anthony Goodman puts it, "Richard II regarded Edward II as a saint."[54] Chaucer's Monk's failure to name the Confessor specifically thus allows for a purposeful ambiguity between the two Edwards who were Richard's chosen models in statecraft and sanctity.

Anthony Tuck voices the consensus of English historians when he points to a conscious early decision on Richard's part to adopt his great-grandfather's "methods of government and . . . rhetoric of political argument": "Richard's attitude to kingship in its governmental aspect bears many marks of reflection upon the reign of Edward II—his use of the chamber, its close connection with the secret seal, and his realization of the ability and administrative potential of the clerks of the chapel royal."[55] Like Edward II, Richard was repeatedly accused by his enemies of listening to bad advisers and of showing favoritism. His friendship with Robert de Vere, in particular, was likened to Edward II's relationship with Gaveston and Hugh Despenser, and it was much resented by the Gloucester party.[56]

The association of Richard II with Edward II gained explicit expression in 1386, when the "Wonderful Parliament," citing a statute of 1310, threatened Richard by asserting its right to depose an unruly king.[57] In response, in 1387 Richard posed to Robert Tresilian and other justices a series of constitutional questions, including the proper punishment for the traitors who had recalled "that statute . . . whereby King Edward [II], son of King Edward and great-grandfather of the present King, was in time past adjudged in parliament."[58]

Richard defended himself and his philosophy of government by enshrining the memory of Edward II as a martyr and working for his canonization.[59] In the words of David Wallace, "Richard's championing of Edward suggests an attempt to find religious sanction for behavior that has, in medieval and modern times, been deemed tyrannical."[60] Richard ensured the proper observances of Edward II's anniversaries at the Abbey of St. Peter in Gloucester, where he was buried.[61] As early as 1385 he wrote to Pope Urban VI, asking him to open Edward's canonization process "propter crebra miraculorum insignia" that Almighty God was working through his apparent intercession.[62] The Monk of Westminster records that Richard traveled to Gloucester in 1390 in order to consult with the archbishop of Canterbury, the bishop of London, and other bishops about "dispatching to the pope testimony about miracles."[63] In 1395 such a "Book of Miracles" was sent to Pope Boniface IX.[64] As Barron notes, "The Exchequer records bear witness to the considerable sums which Richard spent in pursuing the canonisation at the Papal Curia."[65]

Given Richard's own subsequent deposition and murder, his devotion to Edward II and his choice of him as a model seem a sadly self-fulfilling prophecy. Indeed, Richard must have been conscious early in his reign that his fate might well be a "martyrdom" like Edward's, should he insist, in theory and practice, on the royal prerogative of the king as God's anointed. His experience of the parliaments of 1386 and 1388 confirmed him in this belief, as did the reports of assassinations abroad.

The *Westminster Chronicle* curiously links such a report with Richard's concern for Edward's canonization. Marginal notes on the same page record mention both of the king's "special letter to the pope" in 1385 and of the supposed murder of Barnabò Visconti, lord of Milan, in that same year: "Barnabò died in prison, but the manner of his death, whether by cold steel, by starvation, or by poison, is not known."[66] The coincidence of the notations suggests an association in the chronicler's mind of Edward II, Barnabò, and Richard himself.

Chaucer's "Monk's Tale" also tells the story of the murder in prison "off Melan grete Barnabo Viscounte" (VII.2399) at the hands of his nephew and son-in-law. Like the Monk of Westminster, Chaucer's Monk declares himself ignorant about why and how Barnabò was slain (VII.2406). The brief, one-stanza "tragedie" of Barnabò appears in third position in a grouping of four "Modern Instances" of lordly misfortune: those of Peter of Spain (d. 1369), Peter of Cyprus (d. 1369), Barnabò Visconti (d. 1385), and Ugolino of Pisa (d. 1289). As Susan Cavanaugh notes, "Like the two Peters, Barnabò was a figure of special interest to Chaucer and the English court. His niece, Violanta, married Chaucer's first patron, Lionel, duke of Clarence; his daughter Caterina had been offered in marriage to Richard II; and his daughter Donnina married the English condottiere, Sir John Hawkwood."[67]

All four of the Monk's recent examples had been murdered. Unlike virtually all of the other unfortunates whose downfall the Monk relates, their deaths apparently resulted not from their own pride and tyrannical acts but rather from the envy and ambition of their enemies. The Monk compares Peter of Spain, who was betrayed by his own brother, to the virtuous Roland, betrayed by Ganelon (VII.2387–90). Similarly, he declares that the crusader-king Peter of Cyprus was killed by his own lieges "for no thyng but for [his] chivalrie" (VII.2395). Barnabò's murder, too, was an impious act committed by his "double allye" (VII.2403). Finally, Ugolino's death by starvation, and that of his innocent children, resulted from the "fals suggestioun" raised against him by an ambitious prelate, "Roger, which that bisshop was of Pize" (VII.2416–17). The imagery of Ugolino's story contrasts the impiety of the bishop, Ugolino's spiritual father, with the piety of Ugolino's children, who offer their starving father their own flesh to eat.[68] All four stories are "pitous" (VII.2377) both in their affecting woefulness and in their evocation of pious victims and impious murderers. They are, in short, told in a way that reflects Richard's parallel attempt to canonize Edward II as a martyr. As Wallace has remarked, the "modern instances" in Chaucer's "Monk's Tale" make it "a book of grim *Realpolitik* to put beside the book of 'miracles' ascribed to a deposed king of England."[69]

In fifteen manuscripts of the *Canterbury Tales*, including the authoritative Ellesmere manuscript, these four tragedies appear in final position in "The Monk's Tale," whereas in twenty-nine manuscripts they appear between the tragedies of Cenobia and Nero. Donald K. Fry has argued convincingly that the final position reflects Chaucer's own revision of "The Monk's Tale" and offers a double motivation for the Knight's interruption. Not only is the Knight, as a member of the ruling estate, understandably ill at ease to hear of the "sodeyn fal" of lords who had been "in greet welthe and ese" (VII.2772–73), but also he had a personal, historical connection with Peter of Cyprus, having fought under his command at Alexandria, Ayas, and Attalia.[70]

The arguments I have been advancing in this chapter affirm Fry's thesis from another perspective: that of Ricardian political allegory. The Monk's pointed comments in the headlink about his misordering of the tragedies should alert us to Chaucer's use of artificial, rather than natural, order. The Monk apologizes in advance, saying that he will not arrange his tales "of popes, emperours, or kynges" chronologically, "by ordre . . . / Aftir hir ages," but rather "tellen hem som bifore and som bihynde" (VII.1985–88). Such an admission invites and challenges his audience to rearrange in historical sequence what the Monk has misordered.

The Monk begins, however, at the beginning, with the falls of Lucifer and Adam, followed by those of the Old Testament figures Samson, Nebuchadnezzar, and Belshazzar. He pairs the tale of Hercules with that of Samson (a traditional pairing of muscular heroes) and appropriately links the tragedy of Belshazzar, who lost his kingdom "to Medes and to Perses" (VII. 2235), with that of the Persian warrior-queen Cenobia.

Chaucer's original plan was to interrupt this logical and chronological sequence by inserting the "Modern Instances" after Cenobia's tragedy, in the middle of "The Monk's Tale," thereby calling attention to them and expecting his auditors to correct the Monk's mistake by moving them into last position. Through that mental movement, prompted by the Host's or the Knight's interruption of the Monk,[71] Chaucer's late fourteenth-century audience would be forced to supply other "Modern Instances" to complete what the Monk had begun; they would be forced, in short, to think of Edward II and to wonder about the fate of Richard II. Chaucer revised this original plan so as to adopt a natural order in "The Monk's Tale" and place the "Modern Instances" literally in last position. Doing so, and having the Knight (rather than Harry Bailly) interrupt the Monk, solved several artistic problems and offered a greater assurance that his audience would grasp his allegory of the king as a "Seint Edward."

Chaucer nonetheless retained in the headlink to the tale the Monk's apology about chronological disorder. This apology still applies to minor discrepancies, such as placing Ugolino's tragedy after Barnabò's. More important, however, it refers to a large pattern of artificial order that extends beyond the Monk's tragedies to the deliberate pairing of "The Monk's Tale" with "The Nun's Priest's Tale."[72] Whereas "The Monk's Tale" presents an allegory of the end of Richard's reign, "The Nun's Priest's Tale" offers an allegory of its beginning.

The tale of the Nun's Priest, as the "contrarie" of the Monk's tragedies (VII.2774), either completes the turn of Fortune's wheel or reverses it, telling a comic beast fable of "joye and greet solas" about a hero who, caught in dire straits, nevertheless "clymbeth up and wexeth fortunat" (VII.2774–76). The ambiguity of the wheel's upward turn—whether as completion or reversal—derives from placing the allegory of Richard's youth in second position, thus leaving open the possibility that Richard in 1398–99 will somehow escape death a second time, even as he did in 1381.

"The Nun's Priest's Tale" of Chauntecleer, Saint Kenelm, and Richard II

"The Nun's Priest's Tale" is the only place in Chaucer's writings where the name "kyng Richard" appears (VII.3348). The tale also includes a unique Chaucerian reference to the Peasants' Revolt (VII.3393–97).[73] Chaucer's narrator, moreover, ironically compares his "storie . . . trewe" to what a "rethor" might compose for a king: "He in a cronycle saufly myghte it write / As for a sovereyn notabilitee" (VII.3211, 3207–9). This broad hint strongly indicates that the real matter of Chaucer's tale is historical and political (that is, the subject of chronicles), but that Chaucer can write "saufly" for a court audience only if he presents it under the veil of allegory.[74]

That allegory is double-layered. Chauntecleer is represented as a royal figure who listens to flattery and takes wommanish counsel—charges that were frequently directed against Richard II—and, as we shall see, Chauntecleer's story parallels Richard's in important ways. What most effectively bridges the distance between the "tale . . . of a cok" (VII.3252) and the early history of Richard's reign, however, is Chaucer's amazingly sophisticated use of yet another narrative *materia:* the legend of "Seint Kenelm" (VII.3110), whose life story, like that of "Seint Edward," Chaucer retells as the life of Richard II.

Chauntecleer describes himself as having read "the lyf of Seint Kenelm," and he exclaims to Pertelote, "By God! I hadde levere than my sherte / That ye hadde rad his legende, as have I" (VII.3110, 3120–21). The emphasis on the importance of having read Kenelm's *Life,* coupled with the brevity with which Chauntecleer himself retells it in the space of twelve lines, suggests to the reader that the wholeness of Chaucer's tale depends on the discovery of something left unstated. As Robert A. Pratt has shown, moreover, the example of Saint Kenelm's dream does not appear in Robert Holcot's *Super Sapientiam Salomonis* (*lectio* 103 and 202), from which Chaucer drew almost all of his other examples, and thus its addition represents a conscious and purposeful choice on Chaucer's part.[75]

Chaucer's purpose becomes clear from the viewpoint of political allegory when we recall that Richard II was crowned king, as Adam of Usk relates, "on the feast of St. Kenelm" ("in festo Sancti Kenelmi corona-tus").[76] Thomas Walsingham similarly records that Richard's coronation took place on July 16, 1377, the eve of Kenelm's feast ("vigilia Sancti Ken-elmi Regis.")[77] The chroniclers thus strongly associate Richard, the eleven-year-old boy king, with Kenelm, the boy king of Mercia, who succeeded his father on the throne in 821, when he was, as Chauntecleer observes, "but seven yeer oold" (VII.3117). Chaucer's logical association of Richard II with Saint Kenelm was, then, something Chaucer would have shared with his contemporary audience. Indeed, he counts on their knowledge of Ken-elm's *Life* and calls on them to observe parallels between Kenelm's legend and the tale of Chauntecleer, on the one hand, and between the adven-tures of Chauntecleer and Richard, on the other.

Chaucer carefully assimilates the literal, hagiographic, and historical narratives and invites comparison between and among them. Like Chaunte-cleer, Saint Kenelm dreams a prophetic dream that predicts his murder. Despite the wise counsel of his nurse, who correctly interprets the dream and warns Kenelm "to kepe hym weel / For traisoun" (VII.3116–17), Chaucer's Kenelm takes little account of the dream. In "The Nun's Priest's Tale" Kenelm's heedlessness is due to his extreme youth and his inno-cence—"so hooly was his herte" (VII.3119)—whereas Chauntecleer's im-prudence results (in part) from Pertelote's bad counsel about dreams and her exhortation to manly courage and (in greater measure) from his own sensuality.

As *The Early South-English Legendary* records, in the sweet dream ("swete sweuene") of the "ӡong child," Kenelm sees a beautiful tree, full of blos-soms and fruit, growing at the foot of his bed and reaching up to the stars. He climbs the tree and, full of wonder, looks down from its height to see "al þe world" below. Suddenly a close and trusted "frend" of his appears on the ground next to the tree and chops it down. At that moment Kenelm himself becomes a little bird that flies joyfully into heaven.[78] Chaucer's tale turns Kenelm literally into a bird, the "gentil cok" (VII.2865) Chaunte-cleer, who makes his escape from the fox at the end of the tale by flying "heighe upon a tree" (VII.3417), and who looks down from its branches upon his enemy below.

At first sight, Chauntecleer's ominous dream bears little resemblance to Kenelm's. In it he sees himself roaming up and down the barnyard, when a houndlike beast, with a reddish body and black-tipped ears and tail, attacks him with intent to kill. Says Chauntecleer, "[he] wolde han had me deed" (VII.2901). Both dreams, however, portend the dreamer's death, and the waking actions that bring them to fulfillment have definite parallels.

As Pratt has observed, Kenelm's sister feeds her younger brother strong poisons that miraculously have no effect, even as Pertelote, Chauntecleer's "sustre," offers to prepare laxatives for him, which Chauntecleer rejects as "venymes" (VII.2867, 3155).[79] Whereas Pertelote's bad advice makes her an unwitting accomplice of the fox, however, Kenelm's sister Qwendrith actively plots her brother's murder with the aid of his guardian and tutor, Askebert.

Like Kenelm's attendant, whom the boy regards and trusts as his "nexte frend,"[80] the fox approaches Chauntecleer as his "freend" (VII.3285). He claims, moreover, to have played the ambiguous part of a host to both of Chauntecleer's parents: "My lord youre fader—God his soule blesse!—/ And eek youre mooder, of hire gentilesse, / Han in myn hous ybeen to my greet ese" (VII.3295–97). Thus, by extension, the seemingly friendly foes are both household intimates.

In the *Life* of Saint Kenelm, the tutor takes the boy king alone into the wooded valley of Klent. Knowing Askebert's intent, the holy child prepares for his death by naively singing the hymn "Te Deum laudamus." As he sings the line "þe faire compaygnie of Martyrs, louerd, herieth þe," Askebert beheads the boy beneath a hawthorn tree, and Kenelm's soul flies to heaven in the visible form of a white dove.[81] Chaucer assimilates this part of the saint's legend to the crowing of Chauntecleer, who beats his wings, closes his eyes, and stretches out his neck to sing in answer to the fox's flattering request. At that very moment, the fox seizes Chauntecleer "by the gargat" and carries him off "toward the wode" (VII.3335–36).

Although both Chauntecleer and Saint Kenelm sing and are struck in the neck mid-song, the differences between them are striking. Kenelm faces his "frend," knowing him to be an enemy, whereas Chauntecleer sings blindly, deceived by the fox's flattery as one who "koude his traysoun nat espie" (VII.3323). Kenelm raises his voice in praise of God, while Chauntecleer sings out of pride, in order to merit the fox's adulation.

In "The Nun's Priest's Tale," the widow, her daughters, and an assortment of other frenzied people and animals chase after the fox as he runs with a captive Chauntecleer "unto the wodes syde" (VII.3411). In the legend of Saint Kenelm, by contrast, no one dares to search for the boy or to inquire into his sudden disappearance for fear of his sister, who has seized the throne. Only a white cow, the prized possession of a poor widow, makes regular pilgrimages into the woods to the unmarked grave of the boy king and is rewarded for its devotion by a miraculous ability to give a super abundance of milk. Later, through the "tokning" of the widow's cow and a message sent to the pope in Rome through a dove, people learn the secret of Kenelm's martyrdom, find his body, and enshrine it in Winchcombe Abbey.[82]

Chaucer's desire for us to recall the homely end of Kenelm's legend is made obvious by his lengthy description at the beginning of "The Nun's Priest's Tale" of the "povre wydwe," who is a dairywoman ("a maner deye"), and of the barnyard animals in her keeping: "Thre large sowes hadde she, and namo, / Three keen, and eek a sheep that highte Malle" (VII.2821, 2846, 2830–31). The widow is Chauncer's creation. As Kate Oelzner Petersen has shown, all the known analogues to the tale make the rooster's owner a rich farmer.[83] As a part of the *materia* of the saint's life, however, the widow became part of Chaucer's tale.

Both the saint's legend and Chaucer's "Nun's Priest's Tale" employ a beast fable in order to instruct their human audiences. In the legend of Kenelm, the widow's white cow, "a doumb best, þat is with-oute witt," has an unnatural ("aʒein kuynd") knowledge and devotion that surpasses that of "witti" humans.[84] In Chaucer's tale, Chauntecleer and Pertelote are similarly endowed with gifts of language and reason, but the example they set is more ambiguously positive, to say the least, for we must learn (as they do) from their mistakes. Positioned between hagiography and history, the figure of Chauntecleer, as the literal subject of the tale, mediates between the "lyf of Seint Kenelm" (VII.3110), on the one hand, and the life of Richard II, on the other, and thus suggests critical differences between the characters and the fates of the two boy kings.

Crowned in 1377 on the eve of Saint Kenelm's feast, King Richard strikingly resembled Kenelm in his youth, his kingship, his vulnerability, and his need for wise counsel. From early on in his reign, as Louisa D. Duls observes, Richard's "choice of advisers was a favorite target of his critics."[85] In *Vox Clamantis*, for instance, John Gower calls Richard a "puer indoctus," an undisciplined boy, who chooses to be guided by his equally young and foolish companions.[86] Indeed, the chroniclers regularly reproach him for having favorites, for listening to flatterers, and for being vulnerable to various forms of seduction. In "The Nun's Priest's Tale," the household advisers of Richard appear in the form of the "sevene hennes" under Chauntecleer's "governance," among which Pertelote is the acknowledged favorite (VII.2865–66). Chauntecleer enjoys himself among his "wyves alle" in the barnyard, "thus roial, as a prince is in his halle" (VII.3184). From them, the narrator tells us, he receives "wommenes conseils" (VII.3256), but Chauntecleer is clearly susceptible to misleading advice because of his own self-deceiving "pryde" and sensuality, which liken him to the "mermayde in the see" (VII.3191, 3270).

When the fox, the arch-flatterer, appears, and Chauntecleer falls victim to his treacherous deceit, the Nun's Priest breaks into an address to a courtly audience, which is not identical with his fictive audience of Canterbury pilgrims: "Allas, ye lordes, many a fals flatour / Is in youre courtes, and many a losengeour" (VII.3325–26). As Michael Hanrahan observes, the language recalls Alceste's words to the Ricardian god of Love in the *Legend of Good Women:* "For in youre court ys many a losengeour" (F Prologue, l. 352).[87]

The fox's appearance, moreover, occurs at the very moment when the imagery of the tale most closely approaches that of Ricardian devices. First, Chauntecleer is compared to a "grym leoun" (VII.3179), reminiscent of the royal lion or griffon.[88] Then, after casting up "his eyen to the brighte sonne" and pointing to the sun's climb (VII.3191, 3198), Chauntecleer compares the fullness of his bliss to the sun at its height: "Ful is myn herte of revel and solas!" (VII.3203).

When the fox seizes Chauntecleer, the narrator breaks into a series of apostrophic laments, addressing Destiny, Venus, and "Gaufred" (VII.3347). This mock-heroic reference to Geoffrey of Vinsauf and his *Poetria Nova* (ca. 1210) has often been taken as a sign that Chaucer found little of value in the *artes poetriae*.[89] Whether or not this is true (and this book clearly argues the contrary), the immediate purpose of the allusion here is to allow Chaucer to compare Chauntecleer's fate explicitly to that of "worthy kyng Richard" (VII.3348). Geoffrey of Vinsauf's lament for Richard I gives Geoffrey Chaucer an opportunity to seal his allegory of Richard II with Richard's own name, even as he literally offers a plaint "For Chauntecleres drede and for his peyne" (VII.3354).

The chase scene that follows first compares the outcry of the hens to the lamentation of the Trojan women at the fall of Troy (VII.3355–61) and then the general hubbub in the barnyard to the "noyse" in London when "Jakke Straw and his meynee" (VII.3393–94) beheaded the Flemish immigrants, looted their homes and stores, and left their bodies piled up in the streets. This reference to the Peasants' Revolt of 1381 is, as many have noted, one of Chaucer's very few explicit references to contemporary events. Its purpose, like the naming of "kyng Richard," is to offer a key for the discovery of Chaucer's carefully constructed allegory of the king.

In combining images of animals with Graeco-Roman allusions in his treatment of the Peasants' Revolt, Chaucer echoes and creatively alters the lamentatious language of Book I of Gower's *Vox Clamantis*. In that work, as I have remarked, Gower describes a terrifying dream-vision of wild beasts.[90] Among them he sees criminals who have been transformed into doglike, ravenous foxes (pp. 60–61) and cocks, no longer crowing but shouting hellishly (p. 62). The whole troop, moreover, is commanded by "a certain Jackdaw" (p. 65), a "Wat" who announces murder, looting, and mayhem with the words "Now the day has come when the peasantry will triumph."

Gower, too, compares London during the revolt to Troy at its fall: "Just as Troy was once pillaged, so this city remained almost destitute of all consolation for the time being," standing "powerless as a widow" (p. 69). As Gower recalls it, beginning on Thursday, the Feast of Corpus Christi, and continuing with greater intensity on Friday, the peasant hordes raged in the city. In Gower's allusive language, "The Trojan victory was lost in defeat, and Troy became a prey to the wild beast, just like a lamb to the wolf. The peasant attacked and the knight in the city did not resist; Troy was without a Hector, Argos without its Achilles" (pp. 71–72). The powers of hell were unleashed in the form of "wild men . . . deserving of eternal fire" (p. 72), and "there was frequent wailing everywhere, and fresh sorrow" (p. 79).[91] Gower depicts the king as a "Priam" utterly lacking in counsel and courage and virtually defenseless, even when he and his family sought refuge within Ilion's "lofty towers," the Tower of London (p. 72).

Like Chauntecleer, carried "upon the foxes bak" and fearing for his life (VII.3405), the frightened fourteen-year-old King Richard stood among the peasants at Mile End like "a lamb among wolves," as the Monk of Evesham relates ("quasi agnus inter lupos apparuit").[92] He yielded to their demands, while back in London a mob broke into the Tower of London, invaded the quarters of the royal family, and seized and beheaded Archbishop Simon Sudbury, among others. According to Charles Oman, on that same day, June 14, "some 150 or 160 unhappy [Flemish] foreigners were murdered."[93]

The following morning a desperate Richard II asked to meet again with the peasants, this time at Smithfield. That afternoon he prayed at the Shrine of St. Edward, and shortly thereafter the historic meeting took place. Wat Tyler confronted the king with further demands and unsheathed a dagger in his presence. In a sudden turn of events, Mayor William Walworth defended the king, and Tyler was mortally wounded. The fall of Tyler in full view of the assembled peasants precipitated what Oman calls "the most critical moment of the whole rebellion," a moment when "there seemed every probability that Richard and all of his followers would be massacred."[94] The people cried, "Our captain is dead," and raised their bows to shoot arrows at Richard's party.

Just then, as Thomas Walsingham relates, "the king with marvellous presence of mind and courage for so young a man, spurred his horse towards the commons and rode around them, saying, 'What is this, my men? What are you doing? Surely you do not wish to fire on your own king? Do not attack me and do not regret the death of that traitor and ruffian. For I will be your king, your captain, and your leader. Follow me."[95] Miraculously the peasants did just that, and the rebellion was quickly and brutally quelled.

In "The Nun's Priest's Tale," Chaucer offers a parody of this famous speech of King Richard's and of the turn of events it produced in the boastful speech that Chauntecleer formulates and proposes to his captor, the fox: "Turneth agayn, ye proude cherles alle!" (VII.3409). The fox's assent to utter the boast enables Chauntecleer to make his sudden escape, even as Richard's inspired words saved his life at Smithfield.

By moving the rebuke of "proude cherles" from Chauntecleer's mouth to the fox's and by making the poor widow and the others Chauntecleer's friends and benefactors, Chaucer manages to refashion the matter of history in a way that avoids a simple coincidence of social class and political parties with categories of praise and blame. Chaucer's portrayal of Richard in Chauntecleer offers a critique of the king's pride, sensuality, and susceptibility to bad counsel and flattery. At the same time, however, the tale affirms Richard's abilities to learn from his mistakes, as Chauntecleer does. The affectionate regard of the poor and virtuous widow for her prized rooster, and the loyalty to him that she and her companions display in the chase, also serve to soften the poet's implied critique of kings and peasants alike. Finally, the sustained intertextual use of narrative parallels to the *Life* of Saint Kenelm shows not only how far Richard's life has fallen short of Kenelm's innocence, but also how redeemable it is.

Chaucer's tales by the Monk and the Nun's Priest stop short of any prophecy that Richard, like Saint Kenelm and "Seint Edward," will be deposed and murdered. "The Monk's Tale," which moves gloomily in that direction, is forcibly broken off. "The Nun's Priest's Tale," moreover, questions the truth of prophetic dreams and the meaning of destiny in a way that affirms the possibility of free choice, creative intervention, surprise, and sudden reversal. Using an artificial order that begins in the middle of his Ricardian material, Chaucer attaches perhaps a greater allegorical weight to the dark foreshadowing in "The Monk's Tale." Nonetheless, the natural order of the pilgrimage, which allows the Nun's Priest to speak after, and to compete with, the Monk, gives the last word *ad litteram* to one who offers an optimistic remembrance of Richard's youthful escape from the jaws of death.

Judith Ferster has taught us that the 1352 Statute of Treasons explicitly prohibited not only "making war on the king, aiding his enemies, counterfeiting the currency, or killing high government officials," but also imagining "the death of our lord the king or our lady his consort, or of their eldest son and heir."[96] Since such an act of the imagination was adjudged treasonous, a court poet like Chaucer who foresaw the possibility of the king's deposition, who sought to criticize his unwise actions, and who wished to warn him about the probable consequences of his folly virtually had to use indirect means. In Ferster's words, "If one could not safely imagine the death of one's own king, one might turn to imagining the death of someone else's."[97] "The Monk's Tale" is a collection of such imaginings, and "The Nun's Priest's Tale" unfolds as the realization of a rooster's warning dream.

"The Nun's Priest's Tale" is arguably the finest of Chaucer's tales, perhaps even a signature piece.[98] Chaucer may have consciously formulated his last allegory of Richard II as a "tale . . . of a cok" (VII.3252) in order to occasion a backward look at the *Parliament of Fowls,* the first of his Ricardian allegories. Both poems charmingly depict the king as a bird and offer him instruction. The urgent lesson of warning that Chaucer teaches in "The Monk's Tale" and "The Nun's Priest's Tale" is, however, a much harder lesson addressed to a more difficult, older student. Simple analogies are no longer enough, and in order to write "saufly," Chaucer must proceed with care, constructing a multilayered allegory, using artificial order and *occultatio,* and ending with the overt reminder to the wise ones in his audience that "al that writen is / To oure doctrine it is ywrite, ywis"—including Chaucer's apparently lighthearted "folye, / As of a fox, or of a cok and hen" (VII.3441–42, 3438–39).

5

Penitential Politics in *Sir Gawain and the Green Knight:* Richard II, Richard of Arundel, and Robert de Vere

Shame be to him who evil thinks.

Motto of the Knights of the Garter

Chaucer issued a late warning to King Richard II, and the warning of the *Gawain*-poet was equally belated. *Sir Gawain and the Green Knight,* the greatest of the Middle English Arthurian romances, survives in a single manuscript, Cotton Nero A.x. Copied in a "small sharp hand, which is dated by general consent around 1400,"[1] the poem shows "little sign of textual corruption" and thus evidently "stands at few removes from the original."[2] The poet and his scribe shared the distinct dialect of southeast Cheshire,[3] a region that was outstanding for its loyalty to Richard II throughout his troubled reign. Place-names and descriptions show the poet's close familiarity with the area and its Ricardian strongholds.[4] Indeed, after extensive research, historian Michael J. Bennett has concluded that "the household of Richard II is the most likely milieu for the work of the *Gawain*-poet."[5] More recently, John M. Bowers has shown the poet to be "steadily and specifically royalist" in his "obsessive recourse to regalian themes and images."[6]

Despite these strong indications of the poem's particular social context, however, *Sir Gawain and the Green Knight* has seldom been interpreted from the perspective of Ricardian politics.[7] This essay places *Sir Gawain* within a cultural setting similar to that which Bowers has brilliantly elucidated for *Pearl.*[8] As I hope to show, what Lee Patterson has called "the subject of history" is a major concern of, and inspiration for, the *Gawain*-poet and an all-pervasive intertextual component of his romance. The adventures that occur in the long ago land of his "laye" (l. 30) are never too far removed from recent events in late fourteenth-century England. In fact, the poet's additions to his literary sources—additions that are "themselves . . . of an unusual nature" (to echo Larry Benson)—are best understood in terms of their systematic, contemporary historical reference and political motivation.[9]

At the violent close of Richard's reign, *Sir Gawain* bespeaks the poet's desire to use art and legend to imagine a world less tragic than his own, a "variant" world with a fuller range of possibilities.[10] That alternative world, however, refashions an existing one, calling attention to the personal and partisan choices that have been made. In the first three sections of this chapter I trace the hitherto unnoticed pattern of political reference in the romance; in the fourth I explore the indispensable role of hagiography in the poet's vision and revision of Ricardian politics.

Trials for Treason

The opening stanza of the poem leads us directly into the fused realms of legend and politics. After the fall of Troy, we are told, "Þe tulk þat þe trammes of tresoun þer wroȝt / Watz tried for his tricherie, þe trewest on erthe" (ll. 3–4). The emphasis placed on the trial for treason is unusual within the tight economy of the stanza. The syntax leaves in question the identity of the traitor, whether the infamous Antenor or the noble Aeneas, and the oxymoron of a true treason or a true traitor—in a reversal of the formulaic "false traitor" of accusation ("falsus proditor")—is startling.

The open questions of the first stanza parallel the chief enigmas of Ricardian history, enigmas that inform the whole argument of the romance. Viewed in retrospect, Richard II's reign can be seen to circle around two poles: the parliamentary trials of 1388 and 1397, which gave opposed definitions of treason. Extending the explicit criteria given in the 1352 Statute of Treasons, Richard sought in 1387 to indict as traitors the lords who infringed upon the royal prerogative in the Parliament of 1386 through the dismissal of Michael de la Pole and the establishment of the Council of Governance.[11] The senior Lords Appellant—Thomas of Woodstock, duke of Gloucester; Thomas Beauchamp, earl of Warwick; and Richard Fitzalan, earl of Arundel—accused Richard's friends and advisers, in turn, of treason. At their urging, the Merciless Parliament of 1388 issued sentence of death on at least seventeen persons, all of whom maintained their innocence, and many of whom—notably Simon Burley and Nicholas Brembre—were defended as loyal subjects (albeit to no avail) by Richard himself.[12] In a final move, the king summoned the Parliament of 1397, at which the members of the Gloucester party were condemned to death or exile.[13] With the exception of Warwick, who confessed to wrongdoing, the accused lords claimed to be loyal English subjects, indeed, "the trewest on erthe" (l. 4).

The poem's evocation of these contemporary trials for treason in the explicit context of Trojan and British myth is all the more auspicious, given Richard's special alliance with the outlying regions of Cheshire and Wales and the general uneasiness it provoked in the Gloucester party. The specific charge brought against Nicholas Brembre, former mayor of London, in 1388 was that he had endeavored to have London renamed "New Troy" (*Troynovant*) or "Little Troy" ("parue Troie").[14] (Apparently only poets, especially Gloucester sympathizers such as John Gower, who regularly allegorizes London as Troy in his *Vox Clamantis,* could accomplish such a renaming with impunity.)[15]

Arthur's Camelot recalls both Troy and London, and *Sir Gawain* describes the person of Arthur in unusual ways that liken him to Richard II. The poet insists on the youth of Arthur and his courtiers, who are "al . . . fayre folk in her first age" (l. 54), and whom the Green Knight calls "berdlez chylder" (l. 280). This youthfulness, however, which is to be expected of squires and untried knights, accords ill with the many supposed "conquestes" (l. 311) of Arthur's knights, their past achievements and reputation for greatness, and the great "renoun of þe Rounde Table" (l. 313).

This incongruity of youth and fame suggests the political intertext, which is confirmed by Arthur's rash personal acceptance of the Green Knight's challenge. In this important addition to the opening scene, the poet (in the words of Benson) "presents the King in a rather unflattering and definitely unconventional role."[16] The youth of Arthur; his impetuous response to the Green Knight's insults; his reliance on the advice of Gawain and of his courtiers, who "redden alle same" (l. 363); and the subsequent criticism of Arthur voiced by his own men (ll. 682–83; "Who knew euer any king such counsel to take / As knyȝtez in cauelaciounz on Crystmasse gomnez!"): all these traits forcefully recall features common in fourteenth-century portraits of Richard II.

Raised to the throne at age eleven in 1377, Richard inspired William Langland's recitation of the proverb "Ve terre vbi puer Rex etc."[17] Adam of Usk echoes the same proverb: "In keeping with the saying of Solomon: 'Woe to the land whose king is a child,' during the time of this Richard's youth, both because of it and because of what resulted from it, numerous misfortunes continued to plague the English kingdom."[18] John Gower complains that Richard "took the base, immature counsel of fools to himself, and caused the principles of older men to be rejected."[19] *Richard the Redeless* also speaks of the king's youthful folly and childish advisers: "The cheuyteyns cheef þat ȝe chesse euere, / Were all to yonge of ȝeris to yeme swyche a rewme."[20]

The unfolding pattern of historical allusion, which likens Trojan treachery to English treason, Troy to London, and Arthur to Richard, centers on the beheading scene in Fitt I. As Benson has shown, the scene contains details to be found in none of the poet's known sources.[21] Gawain, acting as the agent of King Arthur, accepts the challenge of the strange intruder—green of hue and mounted on a green horse—to offer him a blow in exchange for a blow. The Green Knight kneels down and calmly bares his neck, and Gawain beheads him. The Knight then stands, picks up his "lufly hed" (l. 432), mounts his horse, and lifts his own head threateningly by the hair. In a gruesome manner, the head speaks, reminding Gawain of the terms of the covenant, and the Knight rides away, still holding "his hed in his hande" (l. 458).

Although it may be true, as Benson suggests, that legends of talking heads (such as that of Saint Winifred) were "widespread" in the Middle Ages,[22] only one such fantasy was significant enough to enter the chronicles of England during Richard's reign. King Richard, the chroniclers relate, was haunted by the sensational reports surrounding the death and burial of Richard, earl of Arundel. Despite his protestations of innocence, and in violation of a royal pardon previously granted to him in 1394, Parliament adjudged Arundel in September 1397 to be guilty of treason and ordered him to be beheaded on Tower Hill, at the very site where Richard's beloved chamberlain, Sir Simon Burley, had been beheaded in 1388. As Louisa Duls notes, the parallel action—a beheading for a beheading—and the mention of Burley's name make "Richard's acts of 1397 appear to be a deliberate piece of revenge."[23]

The chronicles emphasize Arundel's courage in facing his execution. According to John Capgrave, "Whan he cam to þe place þere he schuld deye, he chaunged no chere, but took þe swerd fro him that schuld smyte, and felt if it were scharp, and seyde, 'It is scharp inow. Do þi dede. I forgyve þe my deth.' With o strok his hed went of, and a frere Augustin, cleped Fekenham, Maystir of Diuinité, bare it hom in his làp."[24] Similarly, the *Annales Ricardi* reports that the earl acted fearlessly and did not flinch, "but, keeping always a uniform color of face, he paled no more than if he had been invited to feasts."[25] The *Annales* goes on to relate that a miracle occurred at the moment of decapitation: "The headless body erected itself and stood alone long enough for the Lord's Prayer to be said."[26]

The saintly manner of Arundel's death and the miracle it occasioned inspired an immediate cult.[27] Adam of Usk expresses his faith that Arundel "has been admitted to the fellowship of the saints" and reports that his body, which was initially buried without honors in the church of the Austin friars, came to be "venerated with great reverence and glory, and people continually make offerings there."[28] John Gower describes Arundel's death in hagiographic terms as a martyrdom: "With palms outstretched and psalms sounding on all sides, thus did he undergo his final suffering."[29]

Both the *Annales* chronicler and Capgrave indicate that the report spread among the commons that the earl's head had miraculously grown back to his body.[30]

Troubled by these reports, affected by "dredful dremes" that kept him from sleeping at night, and haunted by "a schadow of a man" who constantly "walkid before him," Richard took desperate measures. According to Capgrave, on the tenth day after Arundel's burial, he ordered the body to be exhumed: "at þe x houre at euen, þe kyng sent certeyn dukes and erles to delue up þe body, and make a frere for to go betwyx þe hed and þe body, and with þis dede þe kyng was more quiet, but, for al þis, he comaunded þe wax aboute his graue, and the clothis, and oþir aray, for to be take away, and to leue þe graue desolate."[31] The *Annales* chronicler gives a similar account, adding only that Arundel's head was actually found to be sewn to his body, and that Richard's men separated them again before reburying Arundel and removing the markers, in order to hide the grave from the people.[32]

Positing a pattern of systematic allusion to the Arundel affair helps to account for a whole set of details in *Sir Gawain* for which there is no known literary source. The Green Knight, like the Arundel of the chronicles, is an outspoken, provocative person, who taunts the king and dares to insult the queen, "þe derrest on þe dece" (l. 445).[33] The duality of his attitude toward Arthur and his court, as symbolized by the holly branch of peace, which he carries in one hand, and by the warlike "ax in his oþer" (ll. 206–8), represents the doubleness exhibited by the Lords Appellant, who repeatedly threatened Richard with deposition, even as they professed their loyalty to him. The characterization of the Green Knight thus reiterates the paradox of the true traitor and the loyal conspirator. The ax-carrying Green Knight claims, "I passe as in pes, and no plyȝt seche" (l. 266), even as Arundel, on trial before Parliament, testified on his own behalf, "I was never a traitor!"[34]

The battle-ax with which Gawain beheads the Green Knight with a single stroke is, like the instrument of Arundel's execution, "As wel schapen to schere as scharp rasores" (l. 213). Like Arundel, the Green Knight speaks reassuringly to the one who is about to strike him, and he awaits the blow courageously. The poet dwells upon the bloody horror of the beheading: the rolling of the head "on þe grene" (l. 429), the gruesome standing erect and lurching movements of the headless trunk, the lifting of the head's eyelids, and the final, ominous speech from the Knight's mouth, in which he promises to render a blow in return for Gawain's and identifies himself as "þe knyȝt of þe grene chapel" (l. 454). The realism of the scene and the poet's explicit evocation of supernatural and preternatural forces recall the world of Richard's nightmarish fear. Thus the hidden, desolate grave of Arundel foreshadows the burial mound that proves to be the Knight's "grene chapel" and the destination of Gawain's quest.[35]

Naming the Players

The narrative parallels between the beheading scenes in the chronicles and in the poem provide the salient links between Arundel and the Green Knight. Even before the Green Knight utters a word, however, details in his description—his horse, his hue, and his beard—point to Arundel when they are interpreted in the context of contemporary political writings. Indeed, these texts provide us with a code that enables us to interpret the *Gawain*-poet's work and to measure his achievement.

In his *Cronica Tripertita*, John Gower refers to the three senior Lords Appellant "disguisedly, in hidden form," according to their heraldic devices, naming Arundel in particular as the Horse: "The King, seething in his evil heart, sought to capture the Horse."[36] Quoting the words of Bridlington's prophecy, the *Annales* chronicler also refers to Arundel's arrest as the capture of the Horse.[37] *Richard the Redeless* bewails Arundel's fall, lamenting "þe hirte þat þe hors hadde" (III.89).

The *Gawain*-poet identifies the Green Knight with Arundel in part through a creative use of Arundel's heraldic cognizance, the Horse. He transforms the familiar equestrian emblem in such a way that it assumes symbolic force and plays an integral part within his narrative argument. The poet pictures the Green Knight as mounted on a "grene hors gret and þikke," that was "To the gome . . . ful gayn" (ll. 175, 178). The green hair of the Knight's head matches that of his horse, and they are similarly well groomed: "þe mane of þat mayn hors much to hit lyke" (ll. 179–80, 187). Indeed, the "haþel and [his] horse" (l. 234) are so united as to form a single memorable image: "Such a fole vpon folde, ne freke þat hym rydes, / Watz neuer sene in þat sele wyth syȝt er þat tyme" (ll. 196–97).

In addition to heraldic emblems such as the Horse, the coded language of contemporary political texts also makes use of puns. One such poem, "On King Richard's Ministers," plays on the surnames of Richard's chief supporters in 1397: John Bushy, Henry Green, William Bagot, and William Le Scrope.[38] Similarly, *Richard the Redeless* combines an emblematic reference to the earl of Derby as the Eagle with an account of the Eagle's brood of followers, who complain "on the grene," batter "on busshes abouȝte," and gather "gomes on grene / þer as þey walkyd" (II.152–53).

This paranomastic political code contributes to the *Gawain*-poet's characterization of the Green Knight. While, as Benson has shown, the poet could and did draw on the literary types of the Green Man and the Wild Man, neither of those types, taken singly or in combination, explains the "strange green skin" of the Knight, which is "not a conventional feature."[39] The poet lets the Green Knight, as an apparition of Arundel, appear in the very color of the man responsible for his demise, Sir Henry Green.[40] In this way he incorporates a pun into the rich color symbolism that the "enker-grene" (l. 150) hue and attire of the Knight undoubtedly possess—a primarily vegetative symbolism of life, death, and seasonality. He equips the Green Knight, moreover, with an extraordinarily bushy beard (l. 182: "A much berd as a busk"), in token of Arundel's accuser, Sir John Bushy, who served as Speaker of the Commons in 1397.

The broad outline of plot and the details of description thus establish analogies between Arthur and Richard II, on the one hand, and the Green Knight and Richard of Arundel, on the other. Who, then, does Gawain represent? The argument of the romance, as well as key features in Gawain's depiction, point unmistakebly to Robert de Vere—an identification that the poet confirms through a bold pun on de Vere's name.

As Benson has shown, the *Gawain*-poet departs from his sources through additions that make Sir Gawain "explicitly the surrogate for the King."[41] After Arthur has first personally accepted the Green Knight's challenge, Gawain fulfills it in Arthur's stead, actually receiving the battle-ax from Arthur's hand. In that intimate exchange, the king names Gawain as his "cosyn," blesses him, encourages him, and advises him to strike hard against the Green Knight ("þat þou on kyrf sette"), the better to abide "þe bur þat he schal bede after" (ll. 372–74).

Among Richard's close friends, Robert de Vere, earl of Oxford, is the only one whose relationship to the young king approximates that between the poet's Gawain and Arthur. De Vere was Richard's "cosyn," not by blood but by his marriage to Philippa de Coucy, the daughter of Richard's aunt Isabella, and thus the granddaughter of Edward III. More important, de Vere enjoyed Richard's manifest affection and extravagant favor—so much so that some of their detractors compared their friendship to that between Edward II and the infamous Gaveston.

It was de Vere who acted as the king's surrogate in the critical confrontation between Richard and the Gloucester party in 1387. In November of that year, Gloucester, Warwick, and Arundel appeared before the king at Westminster to appeal of treason five members of Richard's own circle: Michael de la Pole, earl of Suffolk; Robert de Vere, earl of Oxford; Alexander Neville, archbishop of York; Sir Robert Tresilian, Chief Justice of England; and Sir Nicholas Brembre, former mayor of London.[42] Under duress, Richard agreed to summon Parliament. Immediately afterwards, however, he authorized de Vere to leave London in order to gather forces against the Appellants. As Adam of Usk relates, "The earl of Oxford made his way into the Chester region bearing royal letters, and summoned a great crowd of armed Cheshiremen to join him."[43] Gower reports that "the King's banner foolishly authorized him" to muster troops in Cheshire.[44]

In response, Henry Bolingbroke, earl of Derby, and Thomas Mowbray, earl of Nottingham, joined their forces to those of the three senior Appellants. The armies met in battle near Radcot Bridge on December 20, 1387, at which time de Vere's Cheshiremen were soundly defeated.[45] De Vere himself escaped, fled the country, was convicted in absentia of treason by the Merciless Parliament of 1388, and died an exile in Louvain in 1392.[46] In defiance of the nobility, who boycotted the memorial services, Richard had de Vere's body brought back to England for reburial at Colne Priory, Essex, in 1395. In a touching gesture, noted by the *Annales* chronicler and others, Richard opened the coffin to gaze on the features of his dead friend.[47]

Gawain, then, resembles de Vere in his function as the king's surrogate and alter ego in a "Crystemas gomen" (l. 283),[48] especially if the Green Knight is seen as an apparition of Arundel. Arthur's courtiers suggest that the king should have honored Gawain with the title of duke as a reward for his gallant bravery, rather than allow him to be destroyed by "an aluisch man, for angarde3 pryde" (l. 681). Yonder "dere" is worthy "a duk to haue worþed," they say: "A lowande leder of ledez in londe hym wel semez" (ll. 678–79).

The *Gawain*-poet uses the word "duk" only twice, in this telling reference to Gawain and as part of the title "Duk of Clarence" (l. 552). The word is a loaded one in the context of Ricardian politics, and its use strengthens the analogy between Gawain and de Vere. As Anthony Tuck explains, "The rank of duke was . . . jealously guarded, and before 1337 only the King as duke of Aquitaine had borne the title."[49] In 1337 Edward III created the Black Prince duke of Cornwall. Later two of Edward's other sons, John of Gaunt and Lionel, became the dukes of Lancaster and of Clarence, respectively. In 1385 Richard II granted the title to two more of Edward's sons, creating them the dukes of York and Gloucester.[50] The rank had thus been restricted (with one exception) to men of royal blood until 1386, when Richard—in a move that inspired great and lasting resentment among the nobles—widened the *cursus honorum* to confer the novel title "duke of Ireland" upon his young favorite, Robert de Vere. The entitlement made de Vere "by virtue of royal favour, the equal in status of the duke of Lancaster."[51]

The bestowal of dukedoms became a Ricardian hallmark. To humiliate his enemies and to reward his supporters, Richard conferred the title in 1397 (after the beheading of Arundel) on five persons in one day, creating Nottingham duke of Norfolk; Kent duke of Surrey; Rutland duke of

Aumerle; Huntingdon duke of Exeter; and Derby duke of Hereford.[52] Sir Charles Oman remarks, "For the first time in English history the title of duke was made almost vulgar."[53] The common people derided the new dukes as "duketti,"[54] and *Richard the Redeless* uses the title in complaint: "non of ӡoure peple durste pleyne of here wrongis, / For drede of ӡoure dukys and of here double harmes" (I.56–57).

Although dukes proliferated at the end of Richard's reign, Robert de Vere, duke of Ireland, remains the prototypical Ricardian duke, "the brightest of jewels in the royal diadem."[55] Richard's love for de Vere is communicated allegorically in *Sir Gawain,* especially in the scene of Gawain's departure from Camelot. In observance of the Feast of All Saints, Arthur, we are told, "made a fare on þat fest for þe frekez sake / With much reuel and ryche of þe Rounde Table" (ll. 537–38). Gawain uses the occasion to bid an emotional farewell to the king and his court, and on All Souls' Day he arms himself for his journey.

Among Gawain's accoutrements, the shield "þat was of schyr goulez / þe pentangle depaynt of pure golde hwez" (ll. 619–20) represents Gawain in a special way: "Forþy hit acordez to þis knyӡt" (l. 631). The narrator tarries, pausing to explicate the symbolism of the pentangle and to show its appropriateness to Gawain as a knight "ay faythful in fyue and sere fyue syþez" (l. 632).[56] The passage is unusual in its use of the word "pentangle,"[57] and, as Henry L. Savage noted long ago, "no mention of Sir Gawain's bearing of the Pentangle is to be found in any of the Arthurian stories."[58]

Savage's own attempt to trace the pentangle's association "amid courtly circles . . . with a particular knight" failed, partly because he assumed its association with the French Order of the Star.[59] To my knowledge, only William McColly has previously recognized that the poet's pentangle (l. 627: "a figure that haldez fyue poyntez") elaborates the five-pointed mullet argent found on the first quarter of the quartered shield of gules and or (that is, gold) that distinguished the coat of arms of the de Veres.[60] The poet has, to be sure, adapted the English mullet (or Scottish star) that was the badge of the Vere family,[61] transforming it into an "endeles knot" (l. 630) and hiding it under the unusual word "pentangle," a term unknown in English heraldry. The five points that form its basic outline, however, remain unchanged, as do the "rede gowlez" (l. 663) of the field. The shield of Gawain, in short, is a variation on the well-known shield of Robert de Vere, earl of Oxford—the shield that he bore into battle at Radcot Bridge.

Gawain carries the pentangle shield as he makes his lonely journey north through a western countryside with which de Vere was intimately familiar. On September 8, 1387, Richard appointed de Vere the sole justice of

Chester.[62] From Cheshire, North Wales, and Lancashire, he drew the ill-fated army that he led against the Appellants.[63]

The *Gawain*-poet cannot, however, resist sealing the analogy between Gawain and de Vere with a pun on the latter's name, a pun that extends into, and participates in, the color symbolism of the poem as a whole. When Gawain finally arrives safely at Bertilak's castle, he receives a warm welcome from "þe lorde of the lede," who provides his guest with a "bryʒt boure," a personal attendant, and a set of "ryche robes" to wear (ll. 833, 853, 862). When Gawain dons the fine garments, his appearance is transformed, and an epiphany takes place: "Sone as he on hent, and happed þerinne, / Þat sete on hym semly wyth saylande skyrtez, / Þe ver by his uisage *ver*ayly hit semed / Welneʒ to vche haþel" ll. 864–67; emphasis added).

The word "ver," which J. R. R. Tolkien and E. V. Gordon gloss awkwardly as "springtime," is rare and appears only once in the poem. The passage, as they acknowledge in a long note, "is difficult, and much disputed."[64] The poet, I would suggest, is dramatizing his own auditors' shock of recognition of the "truth" (*ver*ayly) of his allegory, boldly likening Gawain's appearance to that of De Vere / Þe ver, playing at the start of a line on both the homonym "ver" and on the paleographic resemblance of a capital thorn to a capital *D*, and thus making an in-house joke for the benefit of a Cheshire audience well acquainted with the visage of the exiled earl. At the same time, however, the pun on the name "Vere" exposes its association with springtime verdure, and thus foreshadows the "greening" of Gawain at the poem's end, when the green girdle of Bertilak's Lady makes possible Gawain's participation in the greenness of the Green Knight himself.

How is it that Gawain, as an allegory of de Vere, is so well known and warmly received in the castle of Bertilak, who appears elsewhere as the Green Knight, and who, I have been arguing, represents Arundel? Why does Bertilak's castle mirror Arthur's Camelot, so much so that it functions as Gawain's home away from home? Part of the answer to that question (I reserve the rest for later) lies in locating Bertilak's castle as a common ground, or point of convergence, between historical opponents.

In his final encounter with Gawain, the Green Knight identifies himself as the lord who has been Gawain's host, calling himself "Bertilak de Hautdesert" (l. 2445). Tolkien and Gordon rightly gloss "Hautdesert" as a "high, deserted place" and note that "the name evidently applies to the castle."[65] Bertilak's castle is, I would suggest, a representation of one of the properties in or near Cheshire that Arundel forfeited to Richard in 1397.

According to Goodman, "apart from [his] Sussex estates, the bulk of Arundel's properties lay in the northern Marches. . . . The Lordship of Bromfield and Yale, protected by Holt Castle, lay adjacent to the county palatine of Chester."[66] From nearby Holt Castle, Arundel's men conducted raids into Cheshire in 1387, shortly before de Vere's defeat at Radcot Bridge.[67] In 1393, during the rebellion of the Cheshiremen, Arundel provisioned Holt Castle and stationed himself there with an armed retinue.[68] Goodman observes that Arundel exercised so much "influence in the King's cherished county of Cheshire" that "if Arundel stayed often at Shrawardine with his wife, Richard may have been disquieted rather than reassured, viewing the earl as a malignant spirit in the part of the realm where he most sought support."[69] After Arundel's execution, Richard annexed to Chester the Arundel lordships in Shropshire and North Wales, forming a new principality that was to serve (in the words of Anthony Tuck) as "a military bastion for the King."[70] Richard saw to it, in particular, that the castles of Chester and Holt were well provisioned and "stuffed with weapons and large garrisons."[71] Haunted by the absent presence of Arundel, Holt Castle may be the "Hautdesert" to which the pun-loving poet alludes, and which Gawain suddenly comes across (albeit in the variant form of romance) in the midst of a forest: "Hiȝe hillez on vche a halue, and holtwodez vnder / Of hore okez" (ll. 742–43).[72]

Hunting, Wooing, and Lancing

The castle becomes the scene of Gawain's second test of "trawþe" as he, on his way to keep his appointment with the Green Knight, enters into a "forwarde" with his host to exchange their daily winnings with each other (ll. 1105–12). The parallels between the hunting scenes outside the castle and the wooing scenes within it have been explored by numerous scholars.[73] Their political signification has eluded us, however, despite Savage's important, ground-breaking research into "the attitude of the medieval hunter and herald toward the several beasts whose chase the poem records."[74]

Once again, the language of political writers provides us with a key for deciphering the poet's code. The logic of the narrative likens Gawain, tempted in his bedchamber by the lovely lady, to the beasts of the hunt, pursued by the lord of the castle. If Gawain represents de Vere, then the three days of the hunt reenact his pursuit by the Lords Appellant, represented by Bertilak/Arundel. On the first day Bertilak hunts the deer that "drof in þe dale, doted for drede" (l. 1151), sparing the harts and bucks as out of season but slaughtering the hinds and does.

While a deer hunt in an Arthurian romance is not in itself unusual, it clearly fits the pattern of the political allegory. Debra Hassig notes, "The white hart was the personal device of Richard II from about 1390,"[75] and the poet of *Richard the Redeles* indicates that Richard marked his lieges with his livery of hertis or hyndis on hassellis brestis" (II.25). He then extends that device into an allegory wherein Richard's "bestis" are frightened by his enemies "And flowen into forest and feldis abouȝte, / All þe hoole herde þat helde so to-gedir" (II.13–16). In the context of this deer chase, *Richard the Redeles* introduces the image of the "greehonde" whom the king has aggrieved, as a result of which Richard must suffer the loss of his many "hertis" (II.113–15). Similarly, Adam of Usk refers to the junior Appellant, Henry Bolingbroke, as "the dog, because of his livery of linked collars of greyhounds, . . . and because he drove utterly from the kingdom countless numbers of harts—the hart being the livery of King Richard."[76]

It was the genius of the *Gawain*-poet to absorb this pattern of heraldic reference into the plot of his romance, turning sign into symbol. He melds the Ricardian livery into the realism of Bertilak's boisterous opening hunt, in which he describes so vividly the barking of the dogs, the chase and flight of the deer, and the cruel work of "þe grehoundez so grete, þat geten hym hem bylyue" (ll. 1171–72).

The second day of the hunt reiterates, in the coded language of contemporary politics, the narrative of the Appellants' opposition to Richard's party. This time the lord chases and kills a wild boar, the "bor alþergrattest" of a herd of "þe sellokest swyn" (ll. 1441, 1439). The beast is so ferocious at bay that he "hurtez of þe houndez" (l. 1453), maiming the hunting pack, until Bertilak himself dismounts from his horse and slays him in a watery fight at a ford. Gower's *Cronica Tripertita* refers to de Vere using the badge of the Boar: "The Boar sought for ruses, tricks, and deadly lurking places, in order that the realm might perish."[77] Gower, too, mentions that the "fleeing Boar . . . crossed the shallows," alluding to de Vere's escape from the Appellants in 1397, when, on horseback, he crossed the Thames at Radcot Bridge.[78]

Although the political parallels of the first and second hunts could be mere coincidence, given the frequency of deer and boar hunts in aristocratic society and Arthurian romance, the fox hunt of the third day can be explained satisfactorily only in terms of this overarching pattern. John A. Burrow has observed that the fox is introduced (at l. 1699) "as if he were inevitable," which is extremely puzzling, given that "foxes were considered 'vermin,' and fox hunts are very rare indeed in the romances—if indeed there are any at all."[79] Moreover, as Savage, echoing Woodward and Burnett, notes, "The fox is an animal seldom met in British Heraldry," owing to its unsavory reputation.[80] Bertilak himself treats his catch as worthless: "For I haf hunted al þis day, and noȝt haf I geten / Bot þis foule fox felle— þe fende haf þe godez!" (ll. 1943–44).

The appearance of the fox on the third day of the hunt is, nonetheless, "inevitable" from the perspective of the political allegory that is unfolding, because Thomas of Woodstock, duke of Gloucester, the third of the senior Appellants, had as his device the fox's tail.[81] The chronicler of the *Annales Ricardi* reports that "a fox's tail was always borne upon a spear in Gloucester's presence."[82] Gower, too, indicates that de Vere, "together with his followers, turned in flight near Oxford at the sign of the duke of Gloucester, who at that time was carrying a fox's tail on his lance."[83] Thus Gloucester, the hunter of foxes, caught the tail of de Vere at Radcot Bridge.

How, then, do the wooing scenes relate to the political allegory of the hunts? Here, in accord with his regular practice of varying the events of history, the poet recalls, through the lady's adulterous seduction of Gawain, the historical adultery committed by Robert de Vere. With King Richard's implicit support, de Vere divorced Philippa de Coucy in 1387 in order to marry a Bohemian woman, Agnes Lancecrona, who was a member of Queen Anne's retinue. De Vere remarried in Chester. According to Anthony Tuck, "The divorce gave great offense to the nobility, especially the duke of Gloucester, who felt very strongly that his niece had been slighted and the royal family insulted."[84] Gloucester vowed revenge. The affair aroused "bitter animosity toward de Vere in 1387 and 1388"—so much so that the author of the *Dieulacres Chronicle* attributes "the whole episode of Radcot Bridge" to de Vere's adultery, divorce, and remarriage.[85]

Had Bertilak returned home from the hunt early one day to find Gawain enjoying his wife's proffered "cors" (l. 1236), the Green Knight would no doubt have repaid him with more than a "tappe" (ll. 2357). Gawain, however, unlike the earl of Oxford, was able to resist his temptation against chastity. The beautiful lady of the castle who seduces Gawain is, nonetheless, a recognizable allegory of de Vere's Lancecrona, whose powers of attraction the chroniclers attributed to magic.[86] Ever accompanied by Morgan le Fey, who appears at her left side as a "crone" figure—ancient, ugly, and wrinkled (ll. 947–69)—Bertilak's wife personifies a "lance" in her symbolic castration of Gawain, whom she reproaches for his lack of virility; in tempting him to save himself through the girdle and thus dash away from death; and, most important, in her verbal duel with him.

The chroniclers all comment on "Lancecrona," the name of de Vere's Bohemian paramour, which seems to have struck them as peculiar. Thomas Walsingham even suggests a pun on it when he complains that de Vere and Richard II's other friends were stronger in the bedchamber than on the battle field, and armed more with words than with lances ("plus valentes in thalamo quam in campo, plus *lingua* quam *lancea* praemuniti").[87] That same pun serves to encode the poet's allegory. On the first day, the narrator relates, "Al laȝande þe lady *lanced* þo bourdez" (l. 1212; emphasis added). And on the third day the lady and Gawain "*lanced* wordez gode, / Much wele þen watz þerinne; / Gret perile betwene hem stod, / Nif Maré of hir knyȝt mynne" (ll. 1766–69; emphasis added).

The moral and physical danger in their amorous conversation is symbolized in the action of the hunt, as the hunters "lance" the bodies of the slain deer (ll. 1343, 1350), and "þe lorde ouer þe londez launce[z] ful ofte" (l. 1561), riding on horseback in the woods near the castle. Gawain, however—unlike the historical de Vere, who died as an exile in a hunting accident—passes the test of his chastity, refusing to "make synne" and be an adulterous "traytor" to his host (ll. 1774–75). He performs his religious duties devoutly, purifying himself through the sacramental confession of his sins and the absolution of a priest in preparation for his personal "domezday . . . on þe morn" (l. 1884), which Gawain clearly expects to be his last, despite the desperate hope raised in him by the reputed magical qualities of the lady's "grene lace" (l. 1858).[88] Indeed, until he hears the Green Knight's revelations, Gawain apparently remains in his own eyes the virtuous Knight of the Pentangle.

When Gawain faces the Green Knight's razor-sharp Danish ax, "fyled in a fylor" (l. 2225), his words and actions match those not only of the Green Knight himself in the initial beheading scene, but also of Richard, earl of Arundel, at his execution. Like Arundel, Gawain notices the sharpness of the blade. Like Arundel, too, Gawain invokes the name of God and forgives his executioner in advance: "I schal gruch þe no grwe for grem þat fallez. / Bot styȝtel þe vpon on strok, and I schal stonde stylle / And warp þe no wernyng to worch as þe lykez" (ll. 2251–53). In a gesture that duplicates the previous actions of the Green Knight and the historical Arundel, he bows down courageously, baring his neck to receive the blow: "He lened with þe neck, and lutte, / And schewed þat schyre al bare, / And lette as he noȝt dutte; / For drede he wolde not dare" (ll. 2255–58). Finally, like the Green Knight and the Arundel of legend, Gawain experiences a miracle of sorts at the very moment when, after two feints, the blade finally falls. He sees droplets of his own blood on the snow and springs, alive, to his feet: "He sprit forth spenne-fote more þen a spere lenþe" (l. 2316).

The Green Knight then confronts Gawain with his hidden fault, the "lewtée" he lacked in withholding from Bertilak the "wouen girdel" that was rightfully his (ll. 2358, 2366); and Gawain, in turn, accuses himself bitterly of having committed the very "trecherye and vntrawþe" (l. 2382) he had always sought to avoid. Donning the green girdle as a gift from the Green Knight, Gawain returns to Arthur's court as the alter ego of his nemesis, and he is received there with great joy.

Sir Gawain thus brings us at its ending back to the themes, images, and setting with which it began. Given the politics of the poem, however, we must ask: How is this possible? Through what means, and with what mo-

tive, has the poet imaged Richard as Arthur, recreated Arundel as the beheaded Green Knight, represented de Vere (as a surrogate for Richard) in
the likeness of Gawain, and then finally imagined an identification of, and
even a reconciliation between, these historical opponents? Like Bertilak's
castle, which stands between Camelot and the Green Chapel and mediates
between them, there must be a *tertium quid* that mediates between the worlds
of Ricardian politics and Arthurian romance and that stands as a common
ground between them. That point of intersection, I would argue, is religious and hagiographic.

Hagiography and the Politics of Penitence

Richard II and Richard, earl of Arundel, had at least one thing in
common: they were both religious men. Richard was generous in his support of Westminster Abbey and devoted to its saints, especially Saint Edward the Confessor, whom he sought to emulate. He founded the Carthu-
sian monastery near Coventry and a Dominican house near his manor at
Langley to ensure prayers for the repose of the soul of his beloved wife,
Queen Anne. As one contemporary of his remarked, "He loved religion
and the clergy."[89] Similarly, Arundel lavished care and expense on religious
foundations, including a college and a hospice in honor of the Holy Trinity
"to house twenty poor men, aged and infirm."[90] He supported the Cluniac
priory of St. Pancras at Lewes, where he wished to be buried quietly. His
will, Goodman observes, "is pervaded by strong religious emotions," bearing witness to his "family feeling and piety."[91]

As I noted as the start of this chapter, a spontaneous popular cult arose
at the time of Arundel's death. People honored him as a saint and a martyr, enumerating his good works and praying at the site of his grave. There
were also reports of miracles.[92] These reports deeply troubled Richard's
conscience, for he was a religious man, and the thought that he might unwittingly have killed a saint, a "trewe" traitor, gave him sleepless nights, driv-
ing him (the chroniclers say) to the point of madness. The sin that haunted
Richard was the beheading of Arundel, who (unlike Warwick) passionately
maintained his innocence to the last.

Richard's sin, the poem suggests, is the sin of King Arthur and Gawain,
who, aroused by anger, make the deliberate choice to behead the Green
Knight, rather than either refusing to play his game or choosing to deal
him a lesser blow. As Victoria Weiss and Sheri Ann Strite have argued, the
Green Knight's game is not necessarily a "beheading" game.[93] The Green
Knight's own restrained and merciful manner of returning Gawain's stroke
and his refusal "to haf . . . wroзt anger" (l. 2344) make it clear, in retrospect,

that Arthur and Gawain could have acted differently than they did, could in fact have practiced Christian charity and the love of one's enemies that it entails rather than beheading an unarmed man. This is the murderous secret sin that Gawain refuses to admit, but which the poem discloses, and which alone explains the vehemence of Gawain's self-accusation at the end of the poem. Gawain has unknowingly committed treason against his host in more ways than one.

The Green Knight, however, kindly forgives Gawain, acknowledging that he acted as he did in ignorance and out of fear for his life. He adjudges Gawain, moreover, to have been thoroughly cleansed by his ordeal: "I halde þe polysed of þat plyȝt, and pured as clene / As þou hadez neuer forfeted syþen þou watz fyrst borne" (ll. 2393–94). Were Arundel in fact a saint and not a "false" traitor, he could be expected to forgive Richard, even as the Green Knight forgives Gawain and as Arundel himself forgave his executioner. Accepting such forgiveness from a saint and martyr would, however, require Richard too to become a saint—a saint in the order of penitents.

Sir Gawain and the Green Knight is permeated with invocations of the saints. As Ronald Tamplin remarks, moreover, the "poet's choice of these saints—the Virgin Mary, St. John the Evangelist, St. Peter, St. Giles Aegidius, and St. Julian the Hospitaller—is not casual, but determined by the requirements of the poem's contexts and atmospheres."[94] What has not been remarked is that these saints are noticeably Ricardian saints, indeed, the saints of Westminster Abbey.

Richard II's devotion to Saint Edward the Confessor, the great king and saint of Westminster Abbey, is well known.[95] The Confessor, in turn, had special devotions—to Saint Peter, Saint John the Evangelist, and the Virgin Mary—which are reflected in Westminster Abbey itself. He first built Westminster as the Abbey of Saint Peter.[96] Saint John the Evangelist figures prominently in the *legenda* of the Confessor as "the special friend of Edward."[97] When the holy king died, we are told, "St. Peter, his friend, opened the gate of Paradise, and St. John, his own dear one, led him before the Divine Majesty."[98] Edward was buried with the legendary ring that he had given to a beggar and received back from Saint John the Evangelist, a ring that was later depicted in the Wilton Diptych and venerated at Westminster as a relic of the Confessor.[99] Also numbered among the most precious of the Abbey's relics was the girdle of the Virgin Mary, which she dropped down to Saint Thomas the Apostle to convince him of the truth of her Assumption.[100]

"A peculiarly Westminster King," Richard II clothed himself in Edward the Confessor's garments on his coronation day, and he took it upon himself to support the rebuilding of the Abbey.[101] Through the installation of his portrait and the use of his personal device, the white hart, Richard made the Abbey his own.[102] The northern entrance, known as Solomon's Porch, which was rebuilt during his reign, "once contained his well-known badge of the White Hart, which still remains, in colossal proportions," painted on the partition between the Muniment Room and the nave.[103] A painted white hart also appears above the altar in the tiny side chapel dedicated to Saint Mary de la Pew, where Richard had his private devotions and where he reportedly consecrated himself in 1381 to the Blessed Virgin.[104] In the Wilton Diptych, which Richard may have commissioned for this chapel, Saint Edmund, Saint Edward the Confessor, and Saint John the Baptist present the kneeling king to the Virgin and Child, who are surrounded by eleven angels, each of whom wears a Plantagenet necklace of broomcods and the badge of the white hart upon her gown.[105]

When Richard introduced the white hart into Westminster Abbey, he not only included himself thereby in the company of Edward the Confessor, John the Evangelist, Peter, John the Baptist, and the Virgin Mary, but also associated himself with those saints who are represented iconographically with harts and hinds. Two such saints appear in *Sir Gawain*: Saint Julian the Hospitaller, the "gentyl" saint of hospitality, whom Gawain invokes as his guide as he approaches the castle (ll. 7774–75), and Saint Giles Aegidius, on whom Bertilak calls at the payment of one of Gawain's kisses (l. 1644). These saints, so to speak, wear Richard's badge. Their *legenda* function intertextually to connect the poem's beginning with its end and to meld the worlds of politics and romance. The "saynt" (from Old French *saint*) is, as it were, literally the "saynt" (ll. 589, 243; from Old French *ceint*, meaning "girdle") that encircles the poem and makes possible its unity.

Sir Gawain points to, and participates in, the legend of "Sayn Gilyan" (l. 774). A nobleman, Julian is a hunter who one day pursues a hart in a forest. After a long chase, the hart suddenly turns around and speaks "wiþ him as God it wolde," reproaching Julian for his bloodlust and prophesying that he will kill not only animals but also his own parents.[106] The haunting specter of the talking hart in the legend resembles that of the talking head in *Sir Gawain*. Terrified, Julian leaves his own country in order to avoid committing the awful impiety "þat he ssolde fader & moder sle," even as Gawain departs from Camelot, lest he be guilty of "untrawþe." Both Julian and Gawain journey "into a uer contreie," where they find shelter at a distant court. Julian distinguishes himself in arms and eventually marries a beautiful "leuedi of a castel gret," even as Gawain is honored by Bertilak and enjoys his lady's favor.

One day, when Julian is out hunting, his own parents arrive at the castle, seeking him.[107] Julian's wife welcomes them and lets them sleep in her and Julian's own bed. When Julian arrives shortly before dawn, he enters the bedchamber. Noticing a man and a woman in the bed, he believes his wife to be an adulteress, and he kills them both in a fit of jealousy, only to discover later that the prophecy of the hart has been fulfilled: "He slou is fader and is moder mid is swerd riȝt þere." From that day on, Julian and his wife embrace a life of penance, extending hospitality to poor travelers and ferrying them across "a dep water perilous," in atonement for Julian's sin against his parents, who had been his guests and travelers in a strange land.

Sir Gawain may be seen as a variation of this legend in its remarkable combination of the hunting and wooing scenes, in its evocation of danger, in the belated discovery of Gawain's sin, in Gawain's repentance, and in the life of penance he embraces when he accepts the girdle as an outward reminder of his "faut" (l. 2435).[108] More important, perhaps, the dual persona of Julian, who seeks to avoid but ultimately fulfills the prophecy, killing his father as an extension of himself, has its complex counterpart in the poem in the relationship between Bertilak the hunter and Gawain the hunted.

Whereas the iconography of the hart and the hunter predominates in the Julian legend, the image of the hind and the hunted comes to the fore in the life of Saint Giles. Unlike the talking hart in the Julian legend, which serves, in Ronald Tamplin's memorable words, as "the voice of his sin,"[109] the hind in the legend of "saynt Gile" (l. 1644) is a sign of his virtue. Not surprisingly, therefore, the legend of Giles overlaps in its bearing on *Sir Gawain* with that of Julian in Fitt III, where the hunts take place.

Giles is not a hunter but a hermit, who is regularly nourished in the wilderness by the milk of a doe. After some time passes, the king's men come into the woods with their hounds and hunt the doe on three successive days. Each time the doe runs and takes refuge at the feet of the hermit, whom the dogs dare not approach. On the third day an archer accidentally wounds the holy man. Finding the old hermit with the hind at his knee, the hunters marvel. The archer begs Giles's forgiveness, and the king offers Giles the care of physicians, but the hermit refuses medicine, preferring to suffer from a wound that never heals as a reminder of his dependence on "Goddes grace."[110]

The legend of Giles reinforces the political allegory of the three-day hunt by placing the persecuted Ricardian hind under the protection of the saint. It aligns the saint's wound, moreover, both with Gawain's nick in the neck and with his decision to wear the girdle in token of his moral and physical frailty and as a stimulus to humility (l. 2435). Thus the girdle as a sign unites Gawain as a penitent with both Julian the hunter and Giles the hunted.

Giles, unlike Julian, however, suffers and offers atonement primarily for the sins of others rather than his own. When King Charles of France comes to the hermit, he begs Saint Giles to pray for him to God for forgiveness of a sin so terrible that he cannot bear to confess it, even to Giles, because he is so ashamed: "Ich habbe he sede a sunne ido þat i nemai for ssame telle." A week later, as Giles celebrates Mass, an angel brings a scroll to him on which the king's unconfessed sin is written, along with the heavenly notice that Charles has been forgiven for it through the prayers of Giles, provided that he believe it, repent, and confess. At the sight of the miraculous scroll, the king, "sore wepinge," confesses to Giles, gives thanks to God, and begins a new life.

Only a little less clearly than the angelic scroll of Saint Giles, *Sir Gawain and the Green Knight* spells out the unconfessed sin of a king: Richard's vengeful beheading of Arundel. It comforts him with the promise of forgiveness and calls him to penitence as a way of sanctity. When the shoeless Green Knight (l. 160) finally names himself "Bertilak de Hautdesert" (l. 2445), the beheaded Arundel takes the form of Richard's own beloved, ax-wielding (cf. Matthew 3:10), and beheaded patron saint, John the Baptist.[111] Pictured shoeless in the Wilton Diptych, John the desert prophet firmly but gently preaches the baptism of repentance (on which Bertilak's name puns) to Richard, his spiritual son.[112]

As the Wilton Diptych and a stained-glass window at Winchester College (ca. 1393) suggest, Richard was intimately attached to John.[113] The king possessed and treasured relics of the Baptist, including the plate on which John's severed head had supposedly rested.[114] Key events in Richard's life coincided, moreover, with Johannine feasts. According to the *Annales,* Richard was born on January 6, the Feast of Christ's Baptism. The anxious midwives who delivered the sickly baby, and who feared for his life, baptized him hurriedly with the name John ("obstetrices, turbatae, baptizaverunt eum in camera, vocantes eum, pro temporis districtione, 'Johannem'").[115] Later, when the infant's health improved at the arrival of his godfather, King Richard of Majorca, he was christened "per Episcopum . . . 'Ricardus.'" Richard acceded to the throne, moreover, on June 22, 1377, "circa Natiuitatem Sancti Johannis."[116]

Not unlike the pageant of Saint John the Baptist with which the city of London celebrated its reconciliation with King Richard in August 1392,[117] *Sir Gawain* transposes scenes from the life of the Baptist in order to convey its penitential message. Picture cycles of the life and execution of John the Baptist, such as that on the north wall of St. Hubert's in Idsworth, Hampshire, correspond in a remarkable fashion to the images used by both the *Gawain*-poet and the illustrator of Cotton Nero A.x.[118] Dated circa 1330, the Idsworth wall painting is divided by a decorative horizontal bar. The top half depicts the arrest of John the Baptist as an elaborate hunting scene, where hunters, on foot and mounted on horseback, accompanied by their dogs, corner a "weird, shaggy coated animal," whose "bearded human head" is surrounded by a nimbus.[119] At the top right, the longhaired, bare-footed Baptist appears in human form, his wrist grasped by his abductor. The bottom half of the wall painting shows, to the left, a menacing man lurking behind a wall, holding an ax; to the right, a royal banqueting scene, in which the king and queen are prominent. In the foreground, in front of the banquet table, Salome dances a sword dance. Above her head a figure holds the head of John the Baptist on a plate.

The parallels between the array of images in *Sir Gawain and the Green Knight* and those in the picture cycle are breathtakingly obvious. Like the *Gawain*-poet, who first images the Green Knight and then gradually establishes a series of parallels between him and Gawain, the painter first depicts the Baptist as a wild man, whose desert habitat and biblical clothing in camel's hair (Matthew 1:6) liken him to a beast to be hunted. Like the poet, too, who traces Gawain's path to the Green Chapel, the painter shows the Baptist as a human being on his lonely way to meet his death at the hand of a cruel executioner.[120] Both works establish a parallel between a hunting and a seduction scene, combine a banquet with a beheading, and link a seduction (by Salome, acting for Herodias, and by Bertilak's lady, acting as a surrogate for Morgan le Fey) with a deadly blade stroke.

As a retelling of John's life, *Sir Gawain* could hope for a favorable reception from the king. Richard remained devoutly attached to his patron saint until the last, invoking Saint John in his will of 1399 and in the inscription on his tomb.[121] There are strong indications, however, that after the beheading of Arundel, Richard was regarded (and perhaps regarded himself) not as another John the Baptist but rather as John's antitype, Herod.

According to the *Annales* chronicler, Richard began to take his cruel revenge on the Lords Appellant in 1397 "post festum Sancti Johannis Baptistae."[122] After Gloucester's arrest, Thomas Arundel, the archbishop of Canterbury, naively encouraged his brother Richard to turn himself in, assuring him "per Sanctum Johannem Baptistam" that he would go unharmed if he cooperated peacefully with the king.[123] In 1398, Henry Bolingbroke, earl of Derby, offered Richard an ambiguous, if not ominous, New Year's gift: a gold tablet with an image of the Baptist.[124] One year later, in 1399, Richard imprisoned in the Tower a hermit who, in imitation of the Baptist, dared to preach to the king, claiming he had been sent by God to call him to repentance ("ut moneret eum de vita correctiori summenda").[125] Finally, in 1399, on the eve of Derby's invasion, Richard was deeply troubled by the widely circulated prophecy "Vix binis annis durabit pompa Johannis." Discounting John of Gaunt, who was already dead and buried,

Richard concluded that he himself must be the arrogant "John" whose im-
minent downfall was predicted ("quod ipse foret Johannes").[126]

The evidence collected in this chapter indicates that *Sir Gawain and the Green
Knight* must have been written between 1397 and 1400. The humble response of Arthur, who consoles Gawain and who enjoins upon his courtiers
the wearing of a bright green "bauderyk" in Gawain's honor (l. 2516), both
mirrors and models the response that the Cheshire poet desired from
Richard. As a mirror, it reflects the Ricardian livery with which the king in
1397 and 1398 gratefully and lavishly distinguished his loyal Cheshiremen,
especially those who had served in de Vere's army at Radcot Bridge.[127] As
a model, it images Richard as a latter-day Arthur, who pursues a penitent's
path, welcomes reconciliation with his enemies, and draws spiritual benefit from the memory of his suffering and his sin.

What we do not know is whether the poem was written shortly before or
immediately after Richard's deposition. Given the careful path the poet
walks throughout the poem on politically explosive turf, the epilogue's admonition to refrain from thinking bad thoughts (*mal pence*) can only be
regarded as an urgent plea, perhaps from one Knight of the Garter to
another.

6

Joan of Arc, Margaret of Anjou, and Malory's Guenevere at the Stake

"For wyte you well," seyde sir Gawayne, "my harte woll nat serve me for
to se her dye, and hit shall never be seyde that ever I was of youre
counceyle for her deth."

Sir Thomas Malory, *Morte Darthur*

Like the *Gawain*-poet, Sir Thomas Malory used Arthurian materials to comment in a veiled way on the troubled reign of an English king.
In 1468–69, Edward IV was facing a threat of deposition akin to that
Richard II had faced in 1398–1400. Edward IV, moreover, regarded himself as Richard's heir by right of his ancestral ties, via Edmund Mortimer,
to Roger Mortimer, earl of March, who was Richard II's appointed successor and the descendant of King Arthur's heir, Cadwalader.

Whereas the political allegory in *Sir Gawain and the Green Knight* is enormously artful, codified, and complex, the allegory in Malory's *Morte Darthur*
(1469) is relatively simple and typological—so much so that even scholars
who admit its political significance hesitate to call the *Morte* "allegorical."
Typology, understood as a historical foreshadowing, and oracular prophecy
are, however, fundamental and enduring modes of allegory that are common to biblical, legendary, and political history. We err if we underestimate
their importance in the composition and reception of Malory's work in
the mid-fifteenth century, when Edward IV was being heralded as a new
Arthur and when Merlin's prophecies, reinforced by the prophecies of living visionaries, were announcing French victories abroad and the advent
of civil war in England. Whereas the *Gawain*-poet used the lives of saints—
Giles, Julian, and John the Baptist—to imagine a happier alternative history (via conversion) for Richard II, Malory was forced to deal with the
more difficult hagiography of a contemporary martyr, Joan of Arc (1412–
31), whose life and death had literally altered English history. In order to
imagine a different history for Edward IV, Malory first had to reinvent hers
as a romance.

Historians have long been puzzled by the lack of reference to Joan of Arc in fifteenth-century English texts. As W. T. Waugh observes, "When one begins to seek contemporary English allusions to Joan, one is immediately struck by their rarity."[1] This is all the more surprising, given the Maid's prominence in Continental sources, some of them written by leading Englishmen. Notable among these are circular letters, dispatched from Rouen in June 1431 by the duke of Bedford, who wrote in the name of King Henry VI (in Latin) to the emperor and to the kings and princes of Europe and (in French) to all the prelates, nobles, and cities of France, in order to explain and justify Joan's death at the stake on May 30. In Waugh's words, "The silence of the [English] . . . chronicles concerning Joan's trial and execution" cannot be "simply explained."[2]

Waugh infers from this lack of contemporary mention "that Joan made no great impression on the popular mind in England," and V. J. Scattergood similarly asserts that Joan of Arc does not "appear to have impressed her [English] contemporaries."[3] James Darmesteter, however, reaches the opposite conclusion. The "English conscience," he writes, "was ill at ease" with the official pronouncements concerning Joan, and "no small section of the English public misdoubted the version of the government."[4] The relative silence of the English chroniclers results, in Darmesteter's view, from a combination of doubt, shame, and fear. The consequences of questioning the official English-Burgundian verdict on the Maid's person and mission might well be, after all, to share her fate.

In this chapter I suggest that the most important fifteenth-century English reference to Joan of Arc occurs not in any chronicle, but rather in Thomas Malory's *Morte Darthur*, where the figure of Joan of Arc at the stake, which is suppressed in the histories, returns imaginatively recast in the form of Queen Guenevere. As Deborah Fraioli has maintained, "Literature offers . . . what history often does not: the *image* of Joan of Arc in her own time."[5] This dictum holds true also with regard to allegorical representations of Joan. If twentieth-century readers, such as Nellie Slayton Aurner, are apt to remember "the burning of Jeanne d'Arc" when they think of Guenevere's "threatened punishment," we may well assume that Malory and his audience also associated the two women and their sentences.[6] This bold (and superficially fanciful) claim has, as I hope to show, much evidence in its support.

There are significant narrative parallels between Guenevere and Joan of Arc, and Malory's treatment of Guenevere's rescue departs from his known sources in a way that answers directly to William Caxton's contemporary account of Joan's life. Fifteenth-century historical sources explicitly liken Margaret of Anjou, Henry VI's adulterous queen (and Edward IV's powerful French foe), to Joan of Arc; and Malory's Guenevere, in turn, resembles both Margaret and Joan. Another set of associations links Joan of Arc to Edward IV. The Maid died in Rouen, the city of Edward's birth. In addition, both Joan of Arc and Edward IV were frequently associated with the Arthurian legend through prophecy and genealogy, respectively. Indeed, a prophecy of Merlin directly connects the Maid with the English king. A definable rationale, in short, exists for Malory's use of Arthurian material to comment on events in England and France at a time when the matter of the Hundred Years' War was inextricably linked with that of the War of the Roses.

Richard R. Griffith's careful work on the question of authorship has brought us to a point where we can and must specify the rhetorical *circumstantiae* surrounding the composition of the *Morte Darthur*.[7] Indeed, the timely rhetorical dimension of Malory's work remains largely lost to us if we fail to take seriously the possibility—even the probability—of topical allusion and political allegory in his Arthuriad. As Griffith has demonstrated, Malory's work as a whole evinces a definite pro-Edwardian "political bias."[8] Viewed in this context, the figure of Guenevere permits a focused exploration of Malory's historical imagination in relation to the unsettling contemporary hagiography of Joan of Arc—a hagiography invested with compelling proofs not only for divine intervention in human affairs, but also for the power of human sanctity and sin to effect history.

Malory's Guenevere and Joan of Arc

In Malory's "Most Piteous Tale of the Morte Arthur Saunz Guerdon," Queen Guenevere and her lover, Sir Lancelot, are surprised together one night in the queen's chamber by Aggravayne, Mordred, and company. Lancelot escapes after killing Aggravayne and twelve other knights, but Guenevere is arrested, and King Arthur renders a "hasty jougement," condemning her without trial to be burned at the stake in keeping with the statutory punishment for treason: "And the law was such in tho dayes that whatsomever they were, of what astate or degré, if they were founden gylty of treson there shuld be none other remedy but deth."[9] Despite his own affection for Guenevere and Lancelot, and in the face of Gawain's protest that there was no incontrovertible proof of the queen's adultery (and thus of treason), Arthur takes the firm position, "She shall have the law" (p. 1175), and he sentences "the quene to the fyre and there to be brent" (p. 1174).[10] "Dispoyled into her smok and shryvyn" of her sins, Guenevere mounts the scaffold, from which Lancelot valiantly rescues her, killing Gaheris, Gareth, and others in the process.

Malory's treatment of Guenevere's judgment and rescue differs from his known sources, the Old French *Mort le Roi Artu* and the stanzaic Middle English *Morte Arthur*, in two important respects: legal and deliberative.[11] First of all, Malory adds the sentence referring to the statute on which Arthur bases his decision. As Ernest C. York observes, "Malory very explicitly points out that this is a case of treason" and thus distinguishes it from adultery per se, an offense that fell under the jurisdiction of the ecclesiastical courts, and which was not punishable in Malory's time by burning.[12] Whereas the romance tradition that is continued in the *Mort Artu* insists that "it was a *crime passionnel* which brought Guenevere within sight of the stake and the waiting faggots" (to echo J. H. Reinhard), Malory underscores the political dimension of Guenevere's infidelity to the king and carefully matches her crime to her punishment.[13]

When Guenevere receives her death sentence, she becomes the last of four women in Malory's Arthuriad to be condemned to be burned at the stake. "What seems strange in Malory's treatment of these legal cases," York notes, "is that burning at the stake is the only type of death depicted, and exile is the only type of non-capital punishment." Nowhere does Malory mention "such regular forms of death as hanging, drawing, quartering, or flaying."[14] According to Barbara Hanawalt, felons of both sexes were regularly hanged; "only if they had committed treason . . . were the punishments differentiated: the treasonous man was drawn and quartered, and the woman was burned at the stake."[15] In late medieval England burning was also the regular punishment for women who had murdered their husbands and for heretics of both sexes.[16]

When Joan of Arc was burned at the stake on May 30, 1431, the charges against her were manifold. Condemned by church authorities for heresy and idolatry and reviled by her English captors as a witch and a whore, Joan was also implicitly (and more fundamentally) charged with treason in the form of sedition, armed revolt, and allegiance to Charles VII in his claim to the throne of France. In justification of her death, the duke of Bedford wrote in 1431 in the name of Henry VI of England to the duke of Burgundy: "She cam into the field and guided men of war, and gathred companies, & assembled hostes . . . stirring sedicions, and commocions emongest the people, inducing them to . . . rebellion . . . in disturbyng of peace and quietnes and renewyng of mortal warre."[17]

As the ecclesiastical Rehabilitation of Joan in 1449–56 was to make clear, the trial at Rouen in 1431 was a horrific miscarriage of justice. Although charges of heresy were leveled against her, Joan actually suffered as a political prisoner and died for having been England's enemy on the battlefield. In the words of the first article of the "Second Interrogatory," "because she had come to the aid of the most Christian King of France and fought with the army against the English, Joan was pursued by a mortal hatred and was hated by the English, and . . . they sought her death by every means."[18]

Other French soldiers, by way of contrast, were treated honorably by the English as prisoners of war and offered for ransom, not burned as traitors. It is precisely this difference in the case of Joan that seems to have troubled William Caxton (b. 1412), Joan's exact contemporary and Malory's publisher. In his 1480 edition and continuation of Ralph Higden's *Polychronicon*, Caxton first celebrates the deeds and accomplishments of Joan of Arc, "La pucell de dieu": "This mayde roode lyke a man, and was a valyaunt capytayne among them, and toke vpon her many and grete enterpryses, in soo moche that they had a byleve to have recoverd al theyr losses by her."[19] Then Caxton records her capture at Compiègne on May 23, 1429, and her subsequent death by burning:

> The sayd Pucelle was taken in the felde armed lyke a man, and many other capytayns with her, and all brought to Roan, and there she was putte in prysonne, and there she was iuged by the lawe to be brente. And then she sayde that she was with childe, wherby she was respyted a whyle; but in conclusion it was founde that she was not with childe, and thenne she was brente in Roan. And the other capytaynes were putte to raunsonne, and entreated as men of warre ben acustommed.[20]

Caxton's account in noteworthy for several reasons. It provides us with one of the earliest English references to Joan's death by burning. It makes no mention of any charge of heresy or witchcraft against her. Caxton instead pictures Joan as a brave captain among captains who, unlike the other prisoners of war, and contrary to military custom, fails to be ransomed and suffers death at the stake.

Caxton is also the first chronicler to include the story of Joan's plea of pregnancy. Waugh speculates that the story may have been circulated early on by the English authorities, in order to explain and justify the lengthy period between Joan's capture and execution. In his view, however, the pregnancy tale "more probably . . . grew up as a retort to the Rehabilitation," in order to counter the testimonies to Joan's sanctity with a tale of her deceitfulness and whoredom.[21] A third explanation, it seems to me, is more likely and more consistent with other details in Caxton's account—in particular, his praise of Joan's military valor and his evident embarrassment about her singular mistreatment as a prisoner of war.

As Barbara Hanawalt instructs us, male and female felons in English prisons were housed together, and "mixed prison conditions" made pregnancy and repeated pregnancy not only possible but "almost impossible to avoid," as women were subject to rape by their fellow prisoners, guards, and other peace officers.[22] Joan of Arc was chained and guarded during the five months of her trial at Rouen by as many as five men at a time, and these English guards occupied her cell with her.[23] They were, by all accounts, ruffians. According to the testimony of Guillaume Manchon, a sleep-deprived Joan complained to her judges that she had had to defend her-self against her guards at night; and she insisted that, given her situation, it clearly behooved her to continue wearing male attire in prison as a pro-tection for her virginity.[24]

When Joan's report about attacks against her reached the earl of War-wick, he ordered an immediate change of guards.[25] His response, however, cannot simply be explained as the outrage of a Christian gentleman. While a rape would end Joan's mystique as the Maid, it could also forestall or even prevent her execution, should she be impregnated, and it would certainly impugn the already highly questionable proceedings. Since Joan's com-plaints were known to the authorities at Rouen, and since testimony given at the Rehabilitation by Martin Ladvenu and Isambart de la Pierre includes mention of a final rape attempt virtually on the eve of her death,[26] these public and private reports of her mistreatment (and the stories presum-ably circulated by the guards themselves) would have provided ample grounds for Caxton's mention of a possible pregnancy (albeit not a preg-nancy plea)—a pregnancy that would have been caused, however, not by Joan's whoredom among soldiers, but by the criminal violence of her English guards.

The strangeness of Caxton's account signals by its gaps and omissions considerable anxiety about the English treatment of Joan of Arc, the ex-traordinary maiden-warrior whom the French, the Scots, and virtually all of Europe acclaimed as a virgin, saint, and prophetess. Knowing Joan's fame, the English leaders had sought to reverse her reputation through her offical condemnation as a heretic. In so doing, they only added mar-tyrdom to her glory. The Rehabilitation succeeded effectively in exoner-ating and elevating Joan and thus in reinforcing Charles VII's claim to France—a claim he had by then made secure through successive military victories, treaties, and powerful alliances, especially with England's former ally, the Duke of Burgundy. Accordign to J. R. Lander, "By mid-August 1450 all was over."[27]

By 1469, when Malory completed his *Morte Darthur*, the English, looking back to 1431, no doubt wished that history could be rewritten and the guilt for Joan's death removed from them, or at least shared with Charles VII himself. Was not the Dauphin to blame for having abandoned the Maid of Orléans, who had led him to his coronation at Rheims? Had Charles VII offered a suitable ransom for Joan, proposed a tempting exchange of pris-oners—John Talbot, for instance, for Joan of Arc—or forcibly rescued her,

then the English would not have burned a saint.[28] Was not his abandon-
ment of the Maid, his refusal to rescue her, an awful act of ingratitude, as
well as a form of passive aggression against the English? Caxton's reference
to the ransom suggests that even during Joan's lifetime, the English may
have hoped for an alternative to killing her, an alternative that Charles VII
might have given them.

Malory's King Arthur faces a similar dilemma with regard to Guenevere.
He makes the difficult and generally unpopular decision to have her burned,
knowing that Lancelot will probably attempt to save her. Lancelot does so,
riding into the press and carrying Guenevere off to Joyous Guard. In order to call attention to the cause for, and the consequences of, Lancelot's
rescue of the queen, however, Malory adds to his source material a deliberative passage in which Lancelot first talks at length with Sir Bors and his
kin about what he should do. The king, Lancelot relates, has "by evyll
counceile" decided to "put my lady the quene unto the fyre and there to
be brente." Asked for their advice, his relatives and friends "seyde all at
onys with one voice, 'Sir, us thynkis beste that ye knyghtly rescow the quene.
Insomuch as she shall be brente, *hit ys for youre sake*. . . . [Y]e have rescowed
her frome her deth many tymys for other mennes quarels; therefore us
semyth hit ys more youre worshyp that ye rescow the quene from thys
quarell, insomuch that she hath hit *for your sake*'" (p. 1172; emphasis
added). Hearing this unanimous opinion, Malory's Lancelot still has questions and carefully counts the cost to himself and others of a rescue attempt.

In the *Mort Artu,* by contrast, Lancelot simply cries, "Gentlemen, . . . to
horse!" ("Seigneur, fet il or del monter!") and immediately rides to Guenevere's rescue after hearing from a messenger the news: "Our lady the queen
is sentenced to death, and there is the fire in which they are preparing to
burn her" ("madame la reïne est jugiee a mort, et veez le feu que l'en
apareille por li ardoir").[29] Similarly, in the stanzaic *Morte Arthur,* Lancelot
responds instantaneously to the messenger's report:

> A squeer gonne tho tythandes lythe,
>   That launcelot to courte had sente;
> To the foreste he wente as swithe
>   There launcelot and hys folke was lente,
> Bad hem come and haste blythe,
>   The quene is ledde to be brente;
> And they to hors and Armes swythe
>   And Iche one be-fore other sprente.
>   (stanza 244, ll. 1942–49)[30]

When the French knight Lancelot rescues from the flames the queen,
who is about to die at the stake because of her involvement with him ("for

[his] sake"), he saves her life, preserves the noble Arthur from acting cruelly, and precipitates the strife that leads not only to the end of the Round
Table but also to the hagiographic conclusion of the Arthuriad. Guenevere
and Lancelot become penitent saints, but only after (and in part because)
Lancelot rescues the lady he loves. Joan of Arc, in contrast, becomes a saint
because she dies a martyr's death.[31] When Lancelot rides to Guenevere's
rescue, he does for her what Charles VII failed to do for Joan of Arc. Although Joan's "Voices" prophesied to her in prison that she would "be delivered by a great victory,"[32] she received no earthly rescue from a cruel
death. Her deliverance from suffering took instead, as her Voices had in-
timated to her, the form of "martyrdom" (*martyrium*), and the "great victory" that won her that release was a moral one.

The witnesses to Joan's last day report that a large crowd was present, including as many as eight hundred English soldiers, the earl of Warwick, the
duke of Bedford, and Cardinal Beaufort.[33] Joan's piety, as she forgave her
tormentors and asked their forgiveness and God's, was such that many people were moved to tears by her final speeches. According to Isambart de la
Pierre, "The words she uttered were so devout, pious, and Christian that all
who watched her—and they were a great multitude—wept warm tears. Even
the Cardinal of England (the Bishop of Winchester) and several other Englishmen were constrained to weep and were moved to compassion."[34]

Similarly Jean Massieu attests, "The judges who were present, and even
several of the English, were moved . . . to great tears and weeping, and indeed they wept most bitterly. Some, and several of these same English, recognized God's hand and made profession of faith when they saw her make
so remarkable an end."[35] Guillaume de la Chambre remarks, "The wood
was already prepared for her burning, and she uttered such pious lamen-
tations and prayers that many wept."[36] According to Pierre Cusquel, "Master Jean Tressard, the King of England's secretary, wept and groaned with
sorrow on his way back from Joan's execution. He shed tears of grief . . .
and said: 'We are all lost, for it is a good and saintly person that has been
burnt.'"[37]

Others in Rouen shared Tressard's view. Indeed, "it was common report
and almost all the people protested that a great wrong and injustice had
been done to Joan."[38] In a calculated effort to prevent the emergence of
her posthumous cult, the English had her ashes collected and thrown into
the Seine.[39] Bedford also moved quickly, as we have seen, to write circular
letters, asserting that the English had taken just action against a person
whom ecclesiastical judges, under the leadership of Bishop Cauchon of
Beauvais, had condemned as a "supersticious sorceresse, and a diabolical
blasphemeresse of God, and his sainctes, and a persone scismatike and er-
ronious, in the lawe of Iesu Christe."[40] If some believed Bedford in 1431,
fewer did so in 1456, at the conclusion of the Rehabilitation.

When Malory writes about Guenevere's condemnation and approach to the stake, he departs from his French source, deleting passages that accuse the king of committing treason against his own wife, that impute holiness to Guenevere, and that register popular outcry against her burning. In *Mort Artu,* the people of the city, "weeping and crying as if out of their minds" ("plorant et criant aussi com s'il fussent hors del sens"), follow the queen as she goes to the stake, praising her pity to the poor and objecting to Arthur's heartless disloyalty: "Ah, lady, gracious above all other ladies, more courteous than any other, where will the poor ever again find pity? Ah, King Arthur, who have brought her to her death by your disloyalty, may you yet repent, and may the traitors who have accomplished this die a shameful death!" ("Ha! dame debonere seur toutes autres dames et plus cortoise que nule autre, ou trouveront jamés povre gent pitié? Ha! rois Artus, qui as porchaciee sa mort par ta desloiauté, encor t'en puisses tu repentir, et li traïteur qui ce ont porchacié puissent morir a honte!").[41] The deletion of such passages, perhaps too reminiscent of the crowd's tearful and critical response at Rouen to Joan's execution, is easily explicable if we imagine an aristocratic English audience for Malory's *Morte Darthur,* an audience inclusive, perhaps, of Edward IV himself, "the Rose of Rouen."[42]

Apart, however, from their shared sentence of death by burning, their ambiguous condemnation for treason, the pity their fate evoked in bystanders, and their right to expect rescue by a French noble, Joan of Arc and Guenevere would seem to have little in common. Joan was a shepherdess, Guenevere a queen. Joan led armies, whereas Guenevere inspired from a courtly distance the chivalrous deeds of her knights. Joan hoped to go on crusade, but Guenevere opposed the quest for the Holy Grail. Accused of whoredom, Joan was a saintly virgin, whereas Guenevere was in fact Lancelot's lover, however delicately Malory handles the affair. Joan died a martyr, whereas Guenevere escaped the flames. Guenevere was to achieve holiness only later, as a penitent adulteress. The differences are indeed marked.

The imaginative association between the two, however, is not simple and direct, except perhaps in the moment when they stand at the stake. The allegory is rather a decidedly mediated one, which connects Joan of Arc first with Queen Margaret of Anjou and then, through her, with Malory's Queen Guenevere.

Joan of Arc, Margaret of Anjou, and Guenevere

Joan of Arc and Margaret of Anjou famously appear as doubles in William Shakespeare's *I Henry VI* (ca. 1590). In that play, as Phyllis Rackin notes, Joan's "sexual promiscuity associates her with . . . Margaret of An-jou, soon to become the adulterous queen of Henry VI."[43] In a single scene (V.iii) York exits with Joan, the "ugly witch" whom he has captured, just as Suffolk enters with his enchanting young captive, Margaret. The onstage substitution for Joan by her "direct successor," Margaret, is, Andrew S. Cairncross remarks, "no accident."[44] Margaret's royal father, René, then appears in order to "ransom" her by promising her in marriage to Henry VI, a marriage to be arranged by Margaret's conspiratorial lover, Suffolk. The parallel between Joan and Margaret is reinforced in the following scene (V.iv), where Joan's poor father enters and attempts in vain to save his captive daughter's life. Joan, however, denies his paternity, claims to be of royal blood, and seeks to forestall her execution by entering a plea of pregnancy, naming as the father of her unborn and illegitimate child ei-ther the Dauphin himself, or the duke of Alençon, or Margaret's own fa-ther, René, the king of Naples. As the play ends, Joan goes to the stake as a witch, while a betrothed Margaret approaches the throne from which she will reign as Henry's spouse: "Margaret shall now be Queen, and rule the King" (V.v.107).

When Shakespeare likens Joan the Maid to the princess Margaret, he builds upon a traditional association of the two. In support of this thesis, Patricia-Ann Lee cites the fifteenth-century *Commentaries* of Pope Pius II, which record a speech by Queen Margaret to her French troops in which she explicitly compares herself to Joan: "You who once followed a peasant girl, follow now a queen!"[45] According to Pius II, the French captains "all marvelled at such boldness in a woman, at a man's courage in a woman's breast, and at her reasonable arguments. They said that the spirit of the Maid, who had raised Charles to the throne, was renewed in the Queen."[46]

Married on April 23, 1445, at age sixteen to Henry VI, Margaret in many ways continued the work that the Maid had begun. Lee observes, "Almost from the beginning she attempted to press forward the interests of her French relatives. On behalf of Charles VII and her father, she used her wifely influence to secure the surrender of Maine and Anjou."[47] Charles sent advisers to his niece Margaret, and he sheltered her followers during the War of the Roses, siding with the House of Lancaster against York.[48] When a weak and demented Henry VI became incapable of rule, Margaret gained recognition as the leader of the Lancastrian party. From 1459 on, Lee notes, Margaret's image in contemporary sources is increasingly that of "the ambitious woman, the virago with the spirit of a man," and "the adulterous queen."[49]

The composition of Malory's Arthuriad (1469) dates from the troubled years of Edward IV's reign, when the earl of Warwick was working to engi-neer his deposition and Henry VI's return to power. In October 1462, and again in 1465, Margaret was in Paris, seeking French support for Henry's restoration.[50] In 1467 Charles's successor, Louis XI, helped to effect an agreement between Warwick and Margaret.[51] Soon thereafter Edward IV threatened an invasion of France, in response to rumors that Margaret was preparing a fleet with plans to invade England in October 1468.[52]

According to Charles Ross, in the latter half of 1468, "Edward's troubles again multiplied. The realm was filled with reports of intrigue, disaffection, and Lancastrian conspiracies."[53] Many were accused of treason, including Henry Courtenay and Thomas Hungerford, who were executed in January 1469 for having "plotted, in league with Margaret of Anjou, the 'final death and final destruction . . . of the Most Christian Prince, Edward IV.'"[54] Between June 1469 and May 1471, the control of England's government "changed hands three times," going from Edward IV to Warwick, from Warwick to Henry VI, and from Henry VI back to Edward IV.[55] When Edward IV entered London in triumph in April 1471, Margaret of Anjou was among his prisoners of war.

In 1469, therefore, Malory's "ninth yere of the reygne of Kyng Edward the Fourth" (p. 1260), the story of an adulterous queen's trial for treason, her rescue by a French noble, and the destructive threat it posed to Arthur's kingdom at home and abroad would almost certainly have recalled Margaret of Anjou to a Yorkist audience. As Nellie Slayton Aurner wrote long ago, "The character of Guenevere, in its main features, parallels that of Margaret of Anjou as preserved in the chronicles."[56]

The direct association of Margaret of Anjou with Guenevere is, moreover, historically grounded. Larry D. Benson relates, "In 1446 King René of Anjou . . . celebrated the departure of his daughter, Marguerite of Anjou, to marry Henry VI of England by staging the magnificent *Pas de la joyeuse garde*."[57] This *pas d'armes* was a particularly elaborate reenactment of the romance motif wherein a "knight sets himself up at a given spot, often on or near a main highway (hence *pas*) and offers joust to all comers."[58] René had a castle constructed as an exotic replica of Joyous Guard, the castle to which Lancelot carried Guenevere after he had rescued her from death at the stake. In disguise René himself played the part of Lancelot, jousting oncomers in defense of the castle, wherein his wife stood as an *altera*-Guenevere. Many English knights participated, including William de la Pole, duke of Suffolk, who was later in real life to play the adulterous part of a Lancelot opposite Margaret's Guenevere.[59]

In constructing Guenevere as an allegory (in the typological sense) of Margaret of Anjou and Joan of Arc, then, Malory accomplishes in a vertical and hidden fashion what Shakespeare's *I Henry IV* achieves literally through an anachronistic juxtaposition of Joan and Margaret. Shakespeare, in effect, literalizes Malory's historical allegory, placing on one level what

Malory had arranged hierarchically on two different levels. What Judson B. Allen has observed about Shakespeare's doublings in *King Lear* applies equally well to his pairing of Joan and Margaret in Part I of the Henriad: "The difference between *Lear* and most late medieval poetry is that the cosmos is larger. For *Lear,* the analogies work within the world of the play; for medieval poetry, they work for the world as a whole. Thus, for any given late medieval poem, one must expect parallels which exist outside the poem but are no less present to it than Gloucester is to Lear."[60]

Joan and Margaret stand as present to Malory's Guenevere, as Shakespeare's Joan stands to his Margaret. In pairing them, moreover, Shakespeare establishes a literary precedent for other anachronistic Jehannine doublings, as, for example, the contrastive pairing of Joan of Arc with Charles VII's mistress Agnes Sorel (1422–50) in Friedrich Schiller's *Die Jungfrau von Orléans* (1801) and Jean Anouilh's *L'alouette* (1953).[61] Only eight years older than Margaret of Anjou, Agnes had belonged to the household of Isabel of Lorraine, the wife of René of Anjou and Margaret's mother. Like Margaret, Agnes became a beautiful courtly seductress. Like Margaret, too, she exerted influence on the French monarch whose cause Joan of Arc had championed and whose coronation she had achieved. The literary pairings of Joan with Margaret and Agnes, respectively, effectively refract the historical English view of the Maid as the Dauphin's whore.

If Guenevere in the last books of the *Morte Darthur* may be identified with Margaret of Anjou and (at a further remove) with Joan of Arc, who then does Arthur represent? Richard Griffith notes that, "for more than half a century," Malory scholars have accepted the view that "the author of *Le Morte Darthur* supported the Lancastrian cause," and that King Arthur—in his youth, at his prime, and in his tragic end—is a composite allegory of the three Lancastrian kings, Henry IV, Henry V, and Henry VI, respectively.[62] Such a view permits a logical pairing of Henry VI (as Arthur) with an adulterous Margaret (as Guenevere). Arthur, even in his downfall and defeat, however, bears virtually no resemblance to the pious, weak, and occasionally demented Henry VI. The assumption that Malory had Lancastrian leanings is, moreover, as Griffith and others have shown, extremely questionable.

Convinced as I am by Griffith's identification of Arthur with Edward IV (an identification to which I will return), I would argue that Arthur's condemnation of Guenevere reflects Edward's emnity against Margaret, whereas Arthur's ardent, youthful choice of Guenevere recalls Edward's marriage to Elizabeth Wydville in 1464. Edward IV, after all, had to contend with two queens of England and France: his own wife, Elizabeth, and Henry VI's wife, Margaret. Distinguishing these two queens in relation to a single king helps to address a problem that has long troubled Malory's readers, namely, the rigor with which King Arthur condemns to death the queen to whom he was so passionately attached in his youth.

Like Griffith, Edward D. Kennedy notes a contrast between "Arthur's attitude [toward the queen] in the first tale" and his "attitude in the later ones." Rejecting the view that Malory intended from the beginning "to show Arthur maturing from a private individual to a king who is aware of his responsibilities as a ruler," Kennedy argues that the "events following Edward's marriage in 1464" to Elizabeth Wydville (against the wishes of Richard Neville, earl of Warwick) "would have clearly shown" the disastrous effects of a king's undue concern for his wife, and that "these events may have caused Malory to consider the proper relationship between a king and his wife."[63]

Although his whole argument depends on an identification between Edward IV and Arthur, Kennedy nonetheless insists that Malory's Arthuriad is not a "political allegory," and that "Arthur was surely not intended to represent Edward IV"—disclaimers that reflect not only a critical bias against political allegory, but also an understandable inability on Kennedy's part to see the Guenevere of the last books as an adulterous Elizabeth sacrificed by Edward IV for the good of the kingdom.[64] Unlike Kennedy, Griffith is unafraid to assert a (broadly defined) Edwardian allegory in the Arthuriad, but even he decides that the distance between Arthur and Guenevere in the later books is "motivated, not by political bias at all, but by artistic considerations" that seek "to make less personal, and less heinous, Arthur's . . . betrayal by Lancelot (the author's favorite) through his affair with the queen."[65]

The difficulties raised by Kennedy and Griffith largely fall away, however, if we remember that, in constructing his political allegory, Malory was not creating a new story that corresponded exactly to the events of Edward IV's life and reign; rather, he was "inventing" or "discovering" preexistent *materia* at two levels. At the literal level, he was compiling the Arthurian legend in its various versions, as he found it in his English and French sources; at the allegorical level, he was considering the *materia* of recent history, which also existed in various versions and genres, some of them hagiographic. Once he had gathered these two sets of *materia* together, he was dividing each of them mentally into discrete, logical, and movable parts, which he could then rearrange, amplify, and abridge in order to effect a discoverable, unitary correspondence between the "said" and the "unsaid."

The notion of a *unitary* correspondence—that is, the matching of this part of one story to that part of another through similarity or ironic dissimilarity—is crucial to our understanding. It allows for the allegorical material either to be substituted occasionally for the literal material with which it has been matched or to intrude into the ongoing narrative in some other way (for example, through a pun, an allusion, a digression, or a direct address to the audience), thus creating gaps and disjunctures in the literal narrative that mark its status as a part of a whole, which comprises literal and allegorical elements artfully set in relation to one another. Since the history of Edward IV's reign included his dealings with two English queens, Elizabeth and Margaret, those separate parts of Malory's historical *materia* could be aligned allegorically with appropriate, separable parts of the legend of Arthur and Guenevere and thus affect Malory's rendition of key episodes, such as Arthur's dispassionate and strict sentencing of the queen.

Arthur and Edward IV

Such an analysis presupposes and depends on our ability to identify Malory's political *materia* and perspective as Edwardian and, on that allegorical basis, to understand his literal choice and treatment of Arthurian subject matter. Malory himself defines the *Morte Darthur* as an Edwardian composition, "ended the ninth yere of the reygne of King Edward the Fourth" (p. 1260). Shortly before this *explicit,* in a much noted addition to his sources, Malory breaks into his account of Arthur's war with Mordred to complain about the "new-fangill" ways of the people, who sided with Mordred against the king:

> Lo ye all Englysshemen, se ye nat what a myschyff here was? For he that was the moste kynge and nobelyst knyght of the worlde, and moste loved the felyshyp of noble knyghtes, and by hym they all were upholdyn, and yet myght nat thes Englyshemen holde them contente with hym. Lo thus was the olde custom and usayges of thys londe, and men say that we of thys londe have nat yet loste that custom. Alas! thys ys a great defaughte of us Englysshemen, for there may no thynge us please no terme. (p. 1229)

This direct address to a contemporary audience renders literal, albeit briefly, Malory's political allegory, for it draws an analogy between Arthur and Edward IV, who in the year 1469 was, as we have seen, facing popular unrest, the threat of invasion, and a serious challenge from a Mordred-like earl of Warwick, who had helped to enthrone him only ten years before. Given the obvious appropriateness of Malory's remarks to King Edward's immediate situation, we must agree with Griffith that it makes no sense to see them as referring to King Henry VI's deposition in 1460–61.[66]

In addition to these overt references to Edward IV, Malory characterizes Arthur in a way that accords well with contemporary descriptions and accounts of Edward. Griffith has noted many of these correspondences, many of them remarkably detailed, and he insists that the resemblances between them would have been obvious to a Yorkist audience: "Edward . . . was the most notable warrior and finest commander of his age, with a record of victory equal to Arthur's—more than one Yorkist writer compared his achievements to the British Worthy's."[67] The narrator of "The Battle of Barnet" (1471), for example, declares of Edward IV, "Of a more famous knyght I neuer rad / Syn the tyme of Artors dayes."[68] Similarly, the poet who composed "The Recovery of the Throne by Edward IV" (ca. 1471) sings Edward's praises: "Nothur Alisaunder ne Artur, ne no conquerouere / No better were acompenyd with nobill men."[69]

Following Griffith, Beverly Kennedy argues that Malory "may have modeled his portrait of Arthur upon the Yorkist monarch." Hesitant "to push this highly speculative hypothesis any farther," she nonetheless finds it "significant that the political dimensions of Malory's history are so clear as to suggest" the identification.[70] Indeed, she concludes her book by finding in "Malory's triumvirate of [knightly] types—Arthur, Gawain and Lancelot—a reflection of the triumvirate which dominated the Yorkist court: King Edward IV, his brother Richard, Duke of York, and his brother-in-law, Anthony Wydeville, Earl Rivers."[71]

As Griffith has amply demonstrated, however, the strongest argument for seeing a parallel between King Arthur and Edward IV is genealogical, especially since an Arthurian genealogy played a crucial role in justifying Edward's claim to the throne against that of Henry VI. As Griffith explains, "Through his Mortimer ancestry Edward could trace his descent from Arthur's heir, Cadwalader, and royal pedigrees of the period consistently do so. . . . [T]he first Lancastrian ruler usurped the throne not only from Richard II, but also from Edmund Mortimer (a minor at the time), and Edward IV was Mortimer's heir."[72]

Sidney Anglo details the line of Edward's descent as follows: "His father Richard, Duke of York, was the son of Anne, daughter of Roger Mortimer, Earl of March. The Mortimers could trace their descent to the marriage, in 1230, between Ralph de Mortimer and Gwladys Duy, daughter of Llewellin ap Iorwoeth. This in turn led back to Rhodri Maur who died in 878 and whose descent was traced by medieval authorities to Cadwalader, the last British king."[73] "This Yorkist lineage," Anglo remarks, "was recognized by all genealogists" and was an essential ingredient in Yorkist propaganda, whereas "there was no attempt to connect Henry VI with the British and Trojan kings—for there was no connection that could have been satisfactorily employed."[74]

Indeed, as Griffith notes, poets, heralds, and genealogists hailed Edward, on the one hand, as the Briton "Arthur returned from Avalon, the Red Dragon revived," while Henry, on the other hand, "was thought of as representing the Saxon line, the Albus Draco of Merlin's prophecy, which would be defeated by the heir of Cadwalader, the Red Dragon, Edward IV."[75] Anglo calls attention to fifteen different manuscripts that trace Edward IV's ancestry through the British line of descent back to Cadwalader (d. 689). Three of these genealogies identify Edward specifically with the "Rubius Draco," or Red Dragon, about which Merlin prophesies to King Vortigern in Book VII.3 of Geoffrey of Monmouth's *Historia regum Britanniae,* and four gloss Edward IV's reign as fulfillment of the angelic prophecy to Cadwalader in Book XII.17–18 of Geoffrey's *Historia.*[76]

Given this frame of cultural reference, Malory's *Morte Darthur* had to have been written and received as celebratory of Edward IV. Malory, moreover, certainly counted on his audience's prior association of Arthur and Edward as he constructed his allegory, using Arthurian *materia* as a means of veiling (and thus seeing afresh) the matter of history and allowing for an alchemical change (in them and in his audience) through their combination. Malory, in short, assigned to himself the potent role of a Merlin, voicing in the present the prophecies of the past and seeing them fulfilled. These prophecies were, however, decidedly ambivalent.

Edward IV and Joan of Arc

Even as Merlin's prophecy of the victorious Red Dragon of the Britons had apparently seen a first fulfillment in Edward IV's victory over Henry VI, his prophecy of a victorious virgin had come true in Joan of Arc. At least that was what the French claimed, and the English feared. In her *Ditié de Jehanne D'Arc,* dated July 31, 1429—shortly after the coronation of Charles VII at Rheims and before the Maid's unsuccessful attack on Paris— Christine de Pizan celebrates Joan's divinely inspired career as fulfilling what had been long foretold:

Car Merlin et Sebile et Bede,
Plus de V^c ans a, la virent
En esperit, et por remede
En France en leurs escripz la mirent,
Et leur[s] prophecies en firent,
Disans qu'el pourteroit baniere
Es guerres françoises, et dirent
De son fait toute la maniere. (stanza 31)

[For more than five hundred years ago, Merlin, the Sybil, and Bede foresaw her coming, entered her in their writings as someone who would put an end to France's troubles, made prophecies about her, saying that she would carry the banner in the French wars and describing all that she would achieve.][77]

Nor was Christine the first to see in Joan's advent the fulfillment of Merlin's prophecies. As Joan herself testified during her trial at Rouen, when she first arrived at the Dauphin's court in Chinon, "several people asked her if there were not in her part of the country a wood called the oak-wood; for there was a prophecy which said that out of this wood would come a maid who should work miracles."[78] According to Geoffrey of Monmouth, Merlin had foretold that a virgin would "be sent forth of the city of Canute's Forest to work healing by leechcraft" ("Ad hec ex urbe canuti nemoris eliminabitur puella ut medele curam adhibeat"):

> When she shall have put forth all her arts, by her breath only shall she dry up the hurtful fountains. Thereafter, when she shall have refreshed her with the wholesome water, in her right hand shall she carry the forest of Caledon and in her left the bulwarks of the wall of London. Whithersoever she shall walk, her footsteps shall smoke of brimstone that shall burn with a two-fold flame, and the smoke thereof shall arouse the Flemings, and make meat for them that be under the sea.[79]

The specific references to London and to England's Flemish allies had led the French people to apply Merlin's prophecy to the Hundred Years' War. When the Maid from Domremy in the Lorraine region arrived at the Dauphin's court, claiming to have been sent by God to lift the siege at Orléans and to lead Charles to his coronation, she seemed to many to be the long-awaited virgin.

As Deborah Fraioli observes, Joan "became associated almost immediately with prophecies and prophetic-sounding patriotic literature that had been in circulation before 1429, the year she left Domremy."[80] After the Treaty of Troyes in 1420, it was a commonplace prophecy that even as France had been lost by a woman, Isabeau de Bavière, it would be saved by a woman. The *Sibylla Francica* (1429) shows that this prophecy was current even in Germany. Joan applied it to herself when she asked her uncle Durant Lassois for his help, reminding him, "Was it not said that France would be ruined through a woman, and afterwards restored by a virgin?"[81]

During the Rehabilitation, Jean Barbin testified that "a certain Master Jean Érault, Professor of Theology," had also applied to Joan during the hearings at Poitiers a prophecy by a certain visionary, Marie Robine d'Avignon. Years before, Marie Robine had come to the king and told him "that a Maid . . . would come after her," clad in armor, and "deliver the kingdom of France from its enemies."[82] Marie's prophecy was corroborated, in turn, by that of Merlin, who had foretold in *Historia* VII.iv: "The Virgin shall forget her maiden shame, and climb up on the back of the Sagittary" ("Ascendet uirgo dorsum sagittarii. & flores uirgineos obfuscabit").[83]

Building on this prophetic tradition, as Fraioli relates, "the Dauphin's official propagandists" composed in 1429 a sixteen-line poem in Latin, beginning with the words "Virgo puellares." "Modeled after the Merlin prophecies and capitalizing on the association," she writes "Virgo puellares" served to increase Joan's stature and launch her "as a formidable opponent to the English."[84] Whereas Merlin's prophecies of the *puella* had stressed a campaign into England, this Jehannine prophecy concerned a struggle against the English that was to be conducted by the Maid ("Puella" / "la Pucelle") on French soil. Manuscripts of "Virgo puellares" are extant in Scotland and Germany and attest to its wide dissemination.[85]

Beginning at Orléans, victory after victory proved these prophecies and Joan's own predictions correct. As André Vauchez insists, "It is very important to note that from the start, Joan was considered a prophetess by her contemporaries."[86] She exhibited extraordinary powers of insight and prediction which Anne Llewellyn Barstow has termed "shamanistic," and which inspired tremendous confidence in her followers.[87] Indeed, to echo Vauchez, "Joan's success was undoubtedly due to her gift of prophecy—the sign of her divine election—and even more so to the authenticity of her spiritual life."[88]

The French hailed the Maid as their deliverer, and the English soldiers fled before her.[89] Even in her battle gear, however, she remained an image of maidenly tenderness to many. At the Rehabilitation, witnesses commented on Joan's crying over the wounded and the dead.[90] Her frequent, freely flowing tears, and the pity and kindness that she showed to the French and English soldiers alike, further confirmed the words of Merlin, who had prophesied of the virgin in *Historia* VII.4: "She herself shall overflow with tears of compassion and shall fill the island with the shrieks of her lamenting" ("Lacrimis miserandis manabit ipsa. & clamore horrido replebit insulam").[91]

Even after Joan's execution, people continued to identify her with Merlin's *puella*. Walter Bowmaker's *Scotichronicon* (ca. 1437) links Joan's life and death with Merlin's prophecy of an avenging maiden. As we have seen, testimony given at the Rehabilitation specifically recalls various prophecies, including those of Merlin. In addition, Jean Bréhal's 1456 *Recollectio* of the Rehabilitation includes a version of Merlin's prophecy which has been carefully edited in order to enhance its aptness to Joan and lend credence to her mission.[92]

What has seldom been noted about the prophecy of Merlin in Geoffrey's

Historia, and what is crucial to understanding the relative silence among English commentators about the Maid's execution, is that it also includes a prediction about the Maid's death and the curse it would bring upon her killer:

> He that shall slay her shall be a Stag of ten branches, whereof four shall wear horns of gold, but six shall be turned into horns of wild oxen that shall arouse the three islands of Britain with their accursed bellowing. The Forest of Dean shall awaken, and bursting forth into human speech shall cry aloud: "Hither, thou Wales, and bringing Cornwall with thee at thy side, say unto Winchester . . . 'the day is at hand wherein thy citizens shall perish for their crimes of perjury. . . . Woe unto the perjured race, for by reason of them shall the renowned city fall into ruin.'"[93]

This prophecy of Merlin specifically links the killing of the Maid to a "crime of perjury," even as the Rehabilitation in 1456 adjudged the trial at Rouen to have been "contaminated with fraud, calumny, wickedness, contradictions, and manifest errors of fact and law."[94] The mention, moreover, of a stag whose ten horns divide into sets of four and six eerily suggests the opposition between a crowned Edward IV and a dethroned Henry VI. The oracle of a ruined city and of an English nation divided by war in punishment for its crimes—in particular, for the killing of the Maiden—could easily be interpreted as linking the War of the Roses causally to the war in France and to Joan's trial and execution at Rouen. The well-known prophecy of Merlin and its attested application to Joan during her lifetime provide, in short, a real basis for Darmesteter's speculation that during the War of the Roses "the name of Joan was . . . bandied between the opposing parties and cast in the teeth of those who had burned her."[95]

Joan predicted her own early death on more than one occasion.[96] According to Guillaume de la Chambre, her last speeches on May 30, 1431, included a public lament for the city of Rouen: "Oh, Rouen, I am much afraid that you may suffer for my death."[97] When Rouen, the English capital, fell to Charles VII on October 9, 1449, its citizens may well have remembered the Maid's words.

Born in Rouen in Normandy on April 28, 1442, Edward IV would have been particularly sensitive to reminders of the death of Joan of Arc in that city, by which he was and is frequently named. The poem titled "The Battle of Touton" (1461) celebrates the achievements of Edward IV as "the rose of Rone": "Had not the Rose of Rone be, all England had be shent" (l. 14).[98] Another celebratory poem, "A Political Retrospective" (1462), likens England to a bed of weeds that Edward of Rouen converts into a flourishing garden: "Wherfore all trewe englyssh peuple, pray yn fere / Ffor Kyng Edward of Rouen, oure comfortoure, / That he kepe Iustice and make wedis clere, / Avoydyng the blak cloudys of languore" (ll. 77–80).[99]

Since Edward IV's claim to the throne rested on the double basis of Arthurian genealogy and prophecy (the angel's message to Cadwalader), it was important that the prophecies of Merlin, which pointed to Joan of Arc and French victory over England, be either invalidated or accommodated within another, larger prophetic frame. This was doubly so, since in 1399 the genealogical claim to the throne of a previous earl of March, Edmund Mortimer, had been surpassed by the prophetic claim of Henry of Lancaster. Mary Giffin explains that "while Mortimer's lineage made him the true heir to the throne, Henry's accession was [regarded as] predestined."[100] Giffin points to the *Chronicon* of Adam of Usk, wherein he justifies his own switch of allegiance from Roger Mortimer, Edmund's father, to Henry Bolingbroke by setting "Merlin the prophet *versus* Brutus the ancestor": "Their struggle is a lively one in which the prophecies of Bridlington reinforce the prophecies of Merlin against the persuasive force of Mortimer's descent from Brutus."[101]

Malory begins his "Tale of King Arthur" with the book of Merlin, a prophetic book which concludes with an account of Arthur's slaughter of innocent children in an attempt to avert the fulfillment of Merlin's prophecy: "for ye have lyene by youre syster and on hir ye have gotyn a childe that shall destroy you and all the knyghtes of youre realm."[102] Edward IV, as another Arthur, also had to deal with prophecy and the death of an innocent. Facing the troubles that were his in 1468–69, Edward saw Joan of Arc, as it were, both rehabilitated by the church as a saint and reincarnated in Margaret of Anjou as a battle leader. Even as her life had been a fulfillment of Merlin's prophecy, so now her afterlife seemed a fulfillment of his curse. Even as at the start of Joan's career her actual sword, unearthed (as she had predicted) in the chapel of Sainte-Catherine-de-Fierbois, had mysteriously resembled the mythic sword that Arthur drew from the stone,[103] so now after her death she was, like King Arthur himself, "once and future": "REX QUONDAM REXQUE FUTURUS" (p. 1242).

From the very beginning of the Hundred Years' War, the struggle between the English and the French had been inextricably linked to a contest over the ownership of the legend of King Arthur. John Capgrave's entry for the year 1344 is a telling and characteristic one: "This ȝere þe kyng renewed þe Round Tabil at Wyndesore, whech was first mad by Arthure. That aspied, þe kyng of Frauns mad a Round Tabil in Frauns, to drawe þe knytehod of Almayn fro þe kyng of Ynglond."[104] Both sides appropriated the myth and applied its history in a prophetic (and propagandistic) sense to themselves.[105] As the conflict between the warring parties drew to its close a century later, the claiming of prophecy was decidedly two-edged, involving, as it did, both blessing and curse.

Saint Joan and Malory's Saint Guenevere

When Thomas Malory writes his *Morte Darthur* in English in 1469, drawing upon many a "Frensshe book" (p. 1256) in order to compile the whole story of the rise and fall of Camelot, he symbolically claims for the English ownership of the Arthurian material. He does so, moreover, at the very time when the English must admit and accept the historic loss of virtually all their former property holdings in France.

If Richard Griffith is right (and I believe he is) in his identification of Thomas Malory with Thomas Malory of Papworth, then Malory's sources were literally loot taken from the French. Among the spoils of war, the royal library of France, which "contained some thirty Arthurian works, including—insofar as they can be identified—every French romance used in composing *Le Morte Darthur*," had come into the possession of John, duke of Bedford.[106] Through his widow, Jacquetta of St. Pol, it is likely to have passed into the hands of Sir Richard Wydville, her second husband, and through him to the Wydville heir, Sir Anthony Wydville, Lord Scales, the eldest brother of Edward IV's queen and the patron of both William Caxton and Thomas Malory. As Griffith has argued, no other library in England could have afforded Malory access to the materials he needed and used in composing the *Morte Darthur*.

The duke of Bedford would have bequeathed yet another legacy, however: the memory of Joan of Arc. It was Bedford, as regent of France, who bore the main responsibility for safeguarding the proceedings at Rouen. During the trial, Bedford's own wife examined Joan physically in prison to test her virginity, and testimony given at the Rehabilitation indicates that Bedford himself watched as she did so.[107] In the name of Henry VI, Bedford in 1431 wrote the circular letters to the civil and ecclesiastical rulers of Europe and to the cities of France which served to justify Joan's execution and to oppose her popular cult as saint ("comme femme sainctifiée").[108]

Confronted with this double Arthurian and Jehannine legacy of Bedford, and with its interwovenness through the prophecies of Merlin, Malory reformulated his English and French source materials in order to create a new prophetic synthesis that combines curse with blessing, even as it subordinates the former to the latter. Malory achieves this mainly through the hagiographic conclusion of the Arthuriad, which answers to the suppressed tale of a real saint's martyrdom with a romance tale of saintly penitence. Rescued from the stake, Guenevere the sinner becomes a saint, even as her rescuer Lancelot does, and their hard-won holiness leads them in the end into a new and eternal fealty to each other and to Arthur.

Discussions of Malory's originality have drawn their main inspiration from the last books of the Arthuriad. There Malory alters his sources in order to highlight the tragic theme of divided loyalties, to explore the meaning of faithful love and infidelity within a Boethian frame of *eternitas* and mutability, and to trace a pattern of spiritual growth in his protagonists.[109] In particular, Malory departs from the *Mort Artu* and develops material found in the Middle English stanzaic *Morte Arthur,* weaving together the strands of earthly and divine love through the mutual achievement of sanctity by Lancelot and Guenevere as penitents.

In the "Frensshe book" (p. 1256), Guenevere withdraws to a convent and dies there before Lancelot arrives to fight a final battle with Mordred's two sons. The account of her conversion and death is brief and totally unconnected to Lancelot's own subsequent embrace of an eremetical life. Lancelot is merely told that "the queen had recently left this world": "But never did a lady of high degree make a finer end or more noble repentance, nor more fervently cry for mercy from our Lord than she did" ("la reine estoit trespassee de cest siecle nouvelement; mes onques haute dame plus bele fin n'ot ne plus bele repentance, ne plus doucement criast merci a Nostre Seigneur du'ele fist").[110] Malory's Guenevere, unlike the Guenevere of the *Mort Artu,* enters the convent at Amesbury as a penitent and lives there for several years after Arthur's death: "And there she lete make herselff a nunne, and wered whyght clothys and blak, and grete penaunce she toke uppon her, as ever ded synfull woman in thys londe. And never creature coude make her myry, but ever she lyved in fastynge, prayers, and almes-dedis, that all maner of people mervayled how vertuously she was chaunged" (p. 1243).

The example of this "saint" Guenevere inspires Lancelot to embrace a similar life of prayer and penance: "But the selff desteny that ye have takyn you to, I woll take me to, for the pleasure of Jesu, and ever for you I caste me specially to pray" (p. 1253). Purified through eremetical withdrawal and heroic austerities, Lancelot perfects his knighthood in priestly orders, even as his faithful love for Guenevere matures in chastity and charity. Lancelot himself celebrates her funeral Mass and sees to her burial at the side of Arthur. Afterwards his compunction intensifies, until finally, his soul accompanied by angels, Malory's Lancelot literally dies in the odor of sanctity: "He laye as he had smyled, and the swettest savour about hym that ever they felte" (p. 1258).

The celebration of penitential sanctity in the *Morte Darthur* answers to the Rehabilitation of Joan of Arc by providing another model of holiness—one that is universally accessible (for anyone with sufficient humility can be a penitent) and that admits the possibility (if not during Edward IV's reign, then in times to come) of a "once and future" king, capable of uniting the knights of England and France in peace around a single table.[111] As a female saint, Guenevere is infinitely more tame and traditional than

Joan of Arc, whose canonization was not declared until centuries after her death, in 1920.[112] In performing penance for their disloyalty to Arthur and in offering atonement for its disastrous effects on the kingdom, moreover, Guenevere and Lancelot suffer willingly what the "seditious" Joan had to have forced upon her during her imprisonment and martyrdom.

A prisoner himself at the time when he completed the *Morte Darthur,* and awaiting execution (as Griffith reconstructs events) at Warwick's orders for having aided the Wydvilles, Malory prays, "God sende me good delyveraunce" (p. 1260). Joan of Arc begged for the same, as did Guenevere at the stake. Having played the part of a latter-day Merlin for Edward IV by showing the events of his troubled reign to have been prefigured, albeit in bits and pieces, in the episodes of Arthurian legend, Malory stops short of declaring every prophecy fulfilled. Were it fulfilled, after all, prophecy would cease to be prophecy, its deliberate obscurity and ambiguity resolved through a particular historical reference, its future tense rendered present and past. Rather, every prophecy even in its fulfillment must become yet another prophecy or typological foreshadowing of what is yet to come, and thus the vehicle of an ever mediated "once and future" historical allegory.

Conclusion

The defense of poetry depends not on what its works do directly, but on what they do indirectly.

Walter J. Ong, S.J., "The Province of Rhetoric and Poetic"

Those who write about political allegory often start on the defensive, in an almost apologetic attempt to differentiate their interpretations from the "fanciful" readings of other critics. David Bevington's pathbreaking study of topical meaning in Tudor drama, for instance, begins by referring to an "inglorious history" of scholarly articles "of the lock-picking type," which have endeavored in unconvincing ways to decode medieval poetry in terms of its covert reference to particular individuals and events.[1] John M. Bowers worries that his New Historicist essay on *Pearl*, which unveils political allusions that are "hidden in plain sight, as it were," will appear to resemble "an antiquarian historicism of the most old-fashioned kind."[2] Judith Ferster, too, sounds a note of caution at the start of her study, when she admits that "historicizing literary works is always tricky" because "it is difficult to define the context in which the work resonates," all the more so if we lack basic information about authorship, audience, dating, and provenance.[3]

Bevington, Bowers, and Ferster defend their approaches to topical meaning in different but related ways. Bevington uses both diachronic and synchronic evidence in support of his thesis about the topical meaning of Tudor drama. "During the formative midcentury years," he writes, "religious politics was virtually the whole substance of drama, inevitably creating a tradition both of political commentary in the drama and of various dramaturgic techniques by which ideology could be given maximum propagandistic effect."[4] As a writer of history plays, Shakespeare drew on the same materials that were "habitually employed in topical controversy comparing Queen Elizabeth with her incompetent predecessors John, Edward II, Richard II, and Henry VI"—a circumstance that obliged him "to be conscious of latent meanings for his audience" (p. 4). External evidence, moreover, strongly supports the thesis that Shakespeare's plays and those of his contemporaries were intentionally used and regularly interpreted as vehicles of social and political commentary. The challenge for playwrights during the period, when "the habit of analogizing . . . was universal" (p. 6), was to work with their twofold material artfully, weaving contemporary debates into the arguments of their plays in order to clarify the basic principles underlying them.

Following Paul Strohm and others, Bowers argues that much of the political meaning of medieval poetry was "hidden in plain sight, as it were," for its contemporary audience, and that we too can see that "hidden" meaning, as soon as we place works within their "textual environment," rather than reading them in "a contextual vacuum." Certain "images and details of fourteenth-century kingship" were in fact so laden with "superficial" and readily evident political meaning that their appearance in poetry necessarily evoked it. Thus "it can no longer be assumed that religious images (Lamb of God), biblical images (the pearl of great price), and specific saints (John the Baptist) floated as free-floating agents in a homogeneous Christian culture and were included in a poem such as *Pearl* for exclusively artistic and moral reasons."[5] Such "artistic and moral reasons" undoubtedly existed, but, Bowers stresses, they must be seen alongside the political motivations that help to explain the use of these images.

Whereas Bowers emphasizes the "openness" of late medieval political allegory, Ferster places the accent on its "hiddenness." Ferster notes that while scholars of the early modern period, such as Bevington, can affirm the existence of topical allegory, both intentional and perceived, by drawing on a wealth of records attesting to the censorship of works and giving other evidence of contemporary responses to publications and performances,[6] medievalists possess a relative dearth of such materials. The evidence we do have, however, suggests (in Ferster's words) that "there were medieval constraints on speech and writing, not officially instituted or announced, but still effective." Moreover, "some of the signs of constraint, are visible in the works themselves—both in what appears to be intentional ambiguity and in devotion to translation and historical examples."[7]

Ferster analyzes "the techniques for criticism used by writers" who seek "to escape punishment or repression" through artworks of public deference that make "oblique references to the hidden transcript" of social and political defiance.[8] In this book, too, I have concerned myself with the poetic and rhetorical techniques used by allegorists in order to comment on the social and political issues of their time. With Ferster I would argue not only that "the separation of historicism from formalism is unnecessary,"[9] but also that the principles of formalism actually provide us with a means to recover, more precisely than we have hitherto dared to believe possible, the audience, occasion, and topical meaning of late medieval texts.

In the opening pages of this book, I recalled how C. S. Lewis distinguished between the "poetic" and the "unpoetic" readers of Spenser's *Faerie Queene*.[10] He attributed to the former an appreciation for artistic form and the ability to recognize moral and philosophical allegories, whereas he accorded to "unpoetic" readers the ability to decipher veiled topical references. What Lewis failed to understand is that no "matter" was "unpoetic" for medieval and early modern authors and their auditors. The stuff of contemporary politics belonged (potentially, if not actually) to the building blocks of poetry, and it was the poet's task to give it form by relating it as a dissimilar similitude to other kinds of matters.

As I have shown, it is a great mistake to view political allegory apart from the moral and philosophical allegory that contextualized it, and vice versa. Moral and philosophical allegory loses its force when it is treated as something "timeless" instead of something appropriated by particular interpreters and interpretive communities and evoked to provide a timely commentary on current events. Whereas some critics are quick to dismiss the allegories of philosophy as mere "external outlines," which are arbitrarily brought to a work by "imaginative" readers, others are just as eager to reject as "fanciful" or "irrelevant" the allegories of topical reference. Both kinds of allegory, however, share a common basis in medieval poetics and rhetoric, which insists that allegorical and literal meaning alike belongs to the *materia* that the poet invents and the audience discovers. Taken together, they exhibit a dialogism not only with each other but also with the complex culture they mirror and (re)form.

From this perspective, allegory is an obvious trope, and arguably the most important, for the heterogeneity of medieval audiences, for whom images and narratives meant different things at different times and places. Its very presence signals a multiplicity of hypothetical, if not actual, audiences and of (at least potentially) controversial issues that require indirect treatment. Its narrative shifts from part to part, from level to level, are carefully controlled in order either to permit or to prevent the discovery of what has been concealed. Its language, moreover, necessarily echoes contemporary watchwords and codes in order to facilitate topical understanding by the intended audience. It thus provides an avenue into what Thomas H. Bestul, echoing Louis Montrose, has termed the "synchronic intertextuality" of medieval narratives as cultural documents.[11]

In this book I have endeavored to trace that intertextuality by comparing literary and historical treatments of key events in fourteenth- and fifteenth-century England and of the issues raised by them. At the level of language alone, we have observed an amazing match of allusions and code words (especially those deriving from puns, titles, heraldic devices, and personal cognizances), as well as repeated proverbs, prophecies, and exempla. We have (to paraphrase Lynn Staley) found poets such as Gower and Chaucer to be "using the language of their day" to write stories from the past as commentaries on the present.[12]

In so doing, we have come to a new practical and theoretical understanding of the rhetorical nature of allegorical poetry in the late Middle Ages. It has been my concern, first of all, to grasp the medieval theory that underlies the poet's step-by-step, intentional composition of allegory; second, to find that theory realized in the practice of poets; and third, to see how that same theory operated in reverse to guide the processes of interpretation by which auditors perceived allegorical meaning and were moved by its discovery.

We have found whole sets of tales to be structured in parallel formation through the horizontal *divisio* and *ordinatio* of their parts. We have seen, moreover, the strategic vertical exchange of literal and allegorical *materia* that has been thus configured. Works that have been previously regarded as only vaguely political in their subject matter—Gowerian exempla; Chaucer's "Melibee," "The Monk's Tale," and "The Nun's Priest's Tale"; *Sir Gawain and the Green Knight;* and Malory's *Morte Darthur*—have been shown to be astoundingly detailed and specific in their veiled historical references, implied audiences, and admonitions.

Their messages are in some cases similar and bespeak the underlying anxieties of the age. Gower, Chaucer, and the *Gawain*-poet, for example, all urge King Richard II to listen to good counsel, to refrain from taking revenge on his enemies, and to repent his own sins humbly. The consummate artistry with which they embed these messages, moreover, serves to enhance their rhetorical appeal and provides us with a sense of the sophisticated decoding abilities that (at least some of) their auditors were expected to possess.

The works we have studied were all produced in England within the rough span of a century, from John Ball's letters of 1381 to Sir Thomas Malory's *Morte Darthur,* published by William Caxton in 1485. Evident in these works is a truly rhetorical *inventio* that conceives of and appeals to the audience as a trusted co-player in a game of hide-and-seek directed by the poet. Indeed, the audience is part of the *materia* that the poet invents.

As we have seen, the very existence of rhetorical invention in medieval poetics has been regularly denied by scholars because of the limited direct references to it in thirteenth-century *artes poetriae*. This study, however, affirms the importance of invention in the *artes*. As an early commentator on Geoffrey of Vinsauf's *Poetria Nova* observed, "invention pervades the entire work," because it includes all five canons of rhetoric, and "all the parts of rhetoric invoke, basically, invention."[13] Indeed, it is to invention, rather than to style alone, that we must look if we want to understand the theoretical influence of the *artes* on the practice of vernacular poets.

Ever since John M. Manly's famous 1926 lecture "Chaucer and the Rhetoricians," Chaucerians have been alerted to Chaucer's undeniable familiarity with Geoffrey of Vinsauf's *Poetria Nova*.[14] The results of this awareness have, however, generally been unsatisfactory. Scholars have often succumbed (in Robert O. Payne's words) to the "danger of a rather sterile circularity in combing through Chaucer's works and tabulating the figures in them that are also listed and described in the manuals."[15] Such inventories, Paul Zumthor remarks, are "without significance," since some of the most frequently found figures of speech "belong either to language (metonymy, metaphor) or to the imagination (hyperbole, antithesis) in their natural forms."[16]

Others, such as Robert M. Jordan, have argued that Chaucer knew but rejected the lore of the *artes* in favor of his own "inchoate poetics," because he found in them "no theory of literature based on rhetorical principles, only prescriptive compositional techniques."[17] Indeed, the best rhetorical studies of Chaucer have found their starting point not in the *artes poetriae* but elsewhere, for example, in medieval preaching, *dictamen*, and memory.[18] As Rita Copeland has asserted, however, and as I have argued, the *artes* appealed to Chaucer and to other vernacular writers of the later Middle Ages on rhetorical and poetic grounds. They discovered in them a powerful fusion of the grammatical and rhetorical traditions whereby invention becomes a "hermeneutical procedure" that values the "ingenuity of the exegetical performance" by author and audience alike and establishes a common ground between them.[19]

Using an intertextual approach to key terms—such as *materia*, invention, division, and *sententia*—in Geoffrey of Vinsauf's *Poetria*, I have bridged the apparent gap between the rhetorical practice of vernacular poets, such as Chaucer, and the compositional theory expressed in the *artes poetriae*. That same intertextual approach, which links the *artes* with the *accessus ad auctores*, on the one hand, and with Ciceronian topical invention, on the other, suggests a basis for a radical reconsideration of grammar and dialectic during the Middle Ages as assembled parts of a rhetorical whole, rather than as separate fragments of a lost classical synthesis. For that medieval wholeness, as Saint Augustine had prescribed, the model is the Incarnate Word of God in his human and divine natures; the scriptural Word of God, in its literal and allegorical *sensus;* and Jerusalem, the temporal and eternal city, to which God speaks his Word.

Notes

Introduction

1. C. S. Lewis, *The Allegory of Love* (Oxford: Oxford University Press, 1936; repr. 1971), p. 321.

2. Anne Middleton, "The Idea of Public Poetry in the Reign of Richard II," *Speculum* 53 (1978): 94. See also her essay, "The Audience and Public of 'Piers Plowman,'" in *Middle English Alliterative Poetry and Its Literary Background. Seven Essays,* ed. David Lawton (Cambridge: D. S. Brewer, 1982), pp. 101–23.

3. Middleton, "Idea of Public Poetry," pp. 112, 101, 113.

4. Ibid., p. 95.

5. Ibid., pp. 107, 112.

6. David Lawton, "Dullness and the Fifteenth Century," *ELH* 54.4 (1987): 762, 793. For a study that emphasizes the "subjection" of fifteenth-century readers, see Seth Lerer, *Chaucer and His Readers: Imagining the Author in Late Medieval England* (Princeton: Princeton University Press, 1993).

7. Middleton, "Idea of Public Poetry," p. 106; emphasis added.

8. Steven Justice, *Writing and Rebellion: England in 1381,* New Historicism Series, no. 27 (Berkeley: University of California Press, 1994), p. 209, n. 64.

9. Judith Ferster, *Fictions of Advice: The Literature and Politics of Counsel in Late Medieval England* (Philadelphia: University of Pennsylvania Press, 1996), p. 15.

10. Ibid., p. 36.

11. Andrew Galloway, "The Rhetoric of Riddling in Late Medieval England: The 'Oxford' Riddles, the *Secretum Philosophorum,* and the Riddles in *Piers Plowman,*" *Speculum* 70 (1995): 96–97.

12. Middleton, "Idea of Public Poetry," p. 94.

13. Lee Patterson, *Chaucer and the Subject of History* (Madison: University of Wisconsin Press, 1991), p. 24.

14. Justice, *Writing and Rebellion,* pp. 230–31.

15. Middleton, "Idea of Public Poetry," p. 95.

16. See Louis Althusser, "Ideology and Ideological State Apparatuses (Notes toward an Investigation)," in *Lenin and Philosophy, and Other Essays,* trans. Ben Brewster (New York: Monthly Review Press, 1971), p. 174.

17. Middleton, "Idea of Public Poetry," pp. 98–99.

18. Ferster, *Fictions of Advice,* p. 4.

19. See Joyce Coleman, *Public Reading and the Reading Public in Late Medieval England and France* (Cambridge: Cambridge University Press, 1996).

20. Harry Caplan, "Memoria: Treasure-House of Eloquence," in *Of Eloquence: Studies in Ancient and Mediaeval Rhetoric,* ed. Anne King and Helen North (Ithaca: Cornell University Press, 1970), p. 239.

21. On memory, see Mary J. Carruthers, *The Book of Memory: A Study of Memory in Medieval Culture* (Cambridge: Cambridge University Press, 1990). On delivery, see Jody Enders, *Rhetoric and the Origins of Medieval Drama* (Ithaca: Cornell University Press, 1992).

22. See Michael Murrin, *The Veil of Allegory: Some Notes toward a Theory of Allegorical Rhetoric in the English Renaissance* (Chicago: University of Chicago Press, 1969).

23. Middleton, "Idea of Public Poetry," pp. 99–100.

24. Saint Augustine, *The City of God against the Pagans,* trans. William M. Green, Loeb Classical Library, 7 vols. (Cambridge: Harvard University Press, 1972), II.2, 1:147; hereafter cited parenthetically in the text.

25. Jon Whitman, *Allegory: The Dynamics of an Ancient and Medieval Technique* (Cambridge: Harvard University Press, 1987), p. 263.

26. Murrin, *Veil of Allegory,* p. 4.

27. Frank Kermode, *The Genesis of Secrecy: On the Interpretation of Narrative* (Cambridge: Harvard University Press, 1979).

28. The Cumaean Sibyl supposedly sold the books, which were collections of oracles, to Tarquin the Proud. Destroyed by fire in 83 B.C., they were collected anew. Augustus ordered their revision in 12 B.C. Now lost, they were still in existence in Rome in A.D. 363. The Sibylline Books inspired imitation by Christians. See *The Sibylline Oracles,* trans. Milton S. Terry (1890; El Paso, Texas: Selene Books, 1991). Saint Augustine refers to Sibylline oracles in *De civitate Dei* XVIII.23.

29. Cicero, "In Catilinam," in *The Speeches,* trans. Louis E. Lord, Loeb Classical Library (Cambridge: Harvard University Press, 1937), III.iv.9, p. 89; hereafter cited parenthetically in the text.

30. Cicero, *De inventione,* trans. H. M. Hubbell, Loeb Classical Library (Cambridge: Harvard University Press, 1949), I.ii.2, pp. 5, 7.

31. Cicero, *De re publica,* trans. Clinton Walker Keyes, Loeb Classical Library (Cambridge: Harvard University Press, 1928; repr. 1952), I.iv.7, p. 23; hereafter cited parenthetically in the text.

32. Livy reports that Romulus was assassinated by members of the Senate (*Historia* I.xvi.4).

33. See Augustine, *City of God,* II.xxi, 1:215–21; XIX.xxi, 6:206–13.

34. Plato, *Gorgias,* trans. Terence Irwin (Oxford: Clarendon Press, 1979), p. 80.

35. Ibid., pp. 94–96.

36. For the latter, see Augustine, *City of God,* XIX.xxiii, 6:214–31.

37. Horace, *Art of Poetry,* in *The Works of Horace,* trans. C. Smart, rev. Theodore A. Buckley (London: Bell and Daldy, 1870), p. 322.

38. Cicero, *De inventione,* I.ii.2, pp. 5, 7.

39. Saint Augustine, *On Christian Doctrine,* trans. D. W. Robertson, Jr. (New York: Macmillan, 1958), III.x.15, p. 88; hereafter cited parenthetically in the text.

40. Saint Augustine, *Confessions,* trans. William Watts, Loeb Classical Library, 2 vols. (Cambridge: Harvard University Press, 1912; repr. 1977), III.v, 1:113; hereafter cited parenthetically in the text.

41. Cassiodorus, *Explanation of the Psalms,* trans. P. G. Walsh, Ancient Christian Writers, no. 51, 3 vols. (New York: Paulist Press, 1990), 1:38–39.

42. James J. Murphy, *Rhetoric in the Middle Ages: A History of Rhetorical Theory from St. Augustine to the Renaissance* (Berkeley: University of California Press, 1974; repr. 1990), pp. 292, 59.

43. See ibid., p. 291; George Kennedy, *Classical Rhetoric in Its Christian and Secular Traditions from Ancient to Modern Times* (Chapel Hill: University of North Carolina Press, 1980), p. 157.

44. Kennedy, *Classical Rhetoric in Its Christian and Secular Tradition*, p. 158.

45. See Augustine's comments on the admissibility of multiple interpretations in *Confessions* XII.xxx–xxxi, 2:364–69.

46. Murrin, *Veil of Allegory*, p. 42.

47. Murphy, *Rhetoric in the Middle Ages*, p. 293.

48. On the resulting "confusion of poetic with rhetoric," see Walter J. Ong, "The Province of Rhetoric and Poetic," in *The Province of Rhetoric*, ed. Joseph Schwartz and John A. Rycenga (New York: Ronald Press, 1965), pp. 48–56.

49. Kennedy, *Classical Rhetoric and Its Christian and Secular Traditions*, p. 158.

50. Coleman, *Public Reading*, p. 90.

51. See my *Chaucer and the Universe of Learning* (Ithaca: Cornell University Press, 1996), esp. chap. 1.

52. Murrin, *Veil of Allegory*, p. 70.

53. Mark Jordan, *Ordering Wisdom: The Hierarchy of Philosophical Discourses in Aquinas* (Notre Dame: University of Notre Dame Press, 1986), p. 61.

1. The *Materia* of Allegorical Invention

1. "Rhetoric and Poetry," in *The New Princeton Encyclopedia of Poetry and Poetics*, ed. Alex Preminger and T. V. F. Brogan (Princeton: Princeton University Press, 1993), p. 1049.

2. Susan Brown Carlton, "Poetics," in *Encyclopedia of Rhetoric and Composition: Communication from Ancient Times to the Information Age*, ed. Theresa Enos (New York: Garland, 1996), p. 532.

3. Robert O. Payne, "Chaucer's Realization of Himself as Rhetor," in *Medieval Eloquence: Studies in the Theory and Practice of Medieval Rhetoric*, ed. James J. Murphy (Berkeley: University of California Press, 1978), p. 272.

4. Paul Zumthor, *Toward a Medieval Poetics*, trans. Philip Bennett (Minneapolis: University of Minnesota Press, 1992), pp. 28–29.

5. Douglas Kelly, "Theory of Composition in Medieval Narrative Poetry and Geoffrey of Vinsauf's *Poetria Nova*," *Mediaeval Studies* 31 (1969): 140.

6. Geoffrey of Vinsauf, *The "Poetria Nova" and Its Sources in Early Rhetorical Doctrine*, ed. and trans. Ernest Gallo (The Hague: Mouton, 1971), p. 17; "Circinus interior mentis praecircinet omne / Materiae spatium. Certus praelimitet ordo / Unde praearripiat cursum stylus, at ubi Gades / Figat" (ll. 55–58, p. 16).

7. See Marjorie Curry Woods, "In a Nutshell: *Verba* and *Sententia* and Matter and Form in Medieval Composition Theory," in *The Uses of Manuscripts in Literary Studies: Essays in Memory of Judson Boyce Allen*, ed. Charlotte Cook Morse, Penelope Reed Doob, and Marjorie Curry Woods, Studies in Medieval Culture 31 (Kalamazoo, Mich.: Medieval Institute Publications, 1992), pp. 19–39; Kelly, "Theory of Composition." See also Douglas Kelly, "Topical Invention in Medieval French Literature," in Murphy, *Medieval Eloquence*, pp. 231–51.

8. Douglas Kelly, "The Scope of the Treatment of Composition in the Twelfth- and Thirteenth-Century Arts of Poetry," *Speculum* 41 (1966): 276. For an introduction to the *accessus* tradition, see Edwin A. Quain, "The Medieval *Accessus ad Auctores*," *Traditio* 3 (1945): 215–64. See also Alastair J. Minnis, *Medieval Theory of Authorship: Scholastic Literary Attitudes in the Later Middle Ages*, 2nd ed. (Philadelphia: University of Pennsylvania Press, 1988).

9. See Cicero, *De inventione,* trans. H. M. Hubbell, Loeb Classical Library (Cambridge: Harvard University Press, 1949; repr. 1960), I.v.7, pp. 14–17.

10. Brunetto Latini, *The Book of the Treasure (Li Livres dou Tresor),* trans. Paul Barrette and Spurgeon Baldwin, Garland Library of Medieval Literature, Series B, vol. 90 (New York: Garland, 1993), III.2, p. 281. Notice the corrected translation of *les maladies* as "illnesses," not "sick people." The original reads: "La matire de retorique est ce de quoi li parliers dist, ausi comme les maladies sont matires dou fisicien." Brunetto Latini, *Li Livres dou Tresor,* ed. Francis J. Carmody (Berkeley: University of California Press, 1948), p. 319. Subsequent citations of the English translation are given parenthetically by page in the text.

11. On the Platonic definition of the subject matter of rhetoric, see Adele Spitzer, "Self-Reference in the *Gorgias," Philosophy and Rhetoric* 8 (1975): 1–22.

12. Michael C. Leff, "The Topics of Argumentative Invention in Latin Rhetorical Theory from Cicero to Boethius," *Rhetorica* 1.1 (1983): 41.

13. Ibid., p. 40.

14. *Boethius's "In Ciceronis Topica,"* trans. Eleonore Stump (Ithaca: Cornell University Press, 1988), p. 26; emphasis added. See also p. 186, nn. 18 and 21. I use this translation throughout, giving citations parenthetically.

15. See James J. Murphy, *Rhetoric in the Middle Ages: A History of Rhetorical Theory from St. Augustine to the Renaissance* (Berkeley: University of California Press, 1974; repr. 1990).

16. Richard McKeon, "Rhetoric in the Middle Ages," *Speculum* 17.1 (1942): 3.

17. See Jody Enders, *Rhetoric and the Origins of Medieval Drama* (Ithaca: Cornell University Press, 1992), esp. pp. 106–8, 114–16, 119–20; Mark Jordan, *Ordering Wisdom: The Hierarchy of Philosophical Discourses in Aquinas* (Notre Dame: University of Notre Dame Press, 1986), pp. 61–67.

18. On the classification of poetry under ethics, see Jordan, *Ordering Wisdom,* p. 44; Philippe Delhage, "*Grammatica* et *ethica* au XIIe siècle," *Recherches de théologie ancienne et médiévale* 25 (1958): 59–110.

19. Richard McKeon, "Poetry and Philosophy in the Twelfth Century: The Renaissance of Rhetoric," *MP* 43.4 (1946): 232–33.

20. Dante Alighieri, "Epistle to Can Grande," in *Medieval Literary Theory and Criticism, ca. 1100–ca. 1375: The Commentary Tradition,* rev. ed., ed. A. J. Minnis and A. B. Scott, with the assistance of David Wallace (Oxford: Clarendon Press, 1988; repr. 1991), p. 460. On the question of the authorship of the letter, see Robert Hollander, *Dante's Epistle to Cangrande* (Ann Arbor: University of Michigan Press, 1993). Hollander forcefully upholds its traditional attribution to Dante.

21. In Minnis and Scott, *Medieval Literary Theory,* pp. 5, 460, 198–203.

22. Eugene Vance, *From Topic to Tale: Logic and Narrativity in the Middle Ages,* Theory and History of Literature 47 (Minneapolis: University of Minnesota Press, 1987).

23. Cicero and Boethius distinguish between intrinsic arguments, which are invented by the rhetor, and extrinsic arguments, which are drawn from external evidence.

24. See my *Job, Boethius, and Epic Truth* (Ithaca: Cornell University Press, 1994), esp. pp. 11–12, 41–69. See also Vance's approach to this definition in *From Topic to Tale,* pp. 53–79.

25. See my "Chaucer's 'Literature Group' and the Medieval Causes of Books," *ELH* 59 (1992): 269–87; *Chaucer and the Universe of Learning* (Ithaca: Cornell University Press, 1996), pp. 179–99.

26. Judson Boyce Allen, *The Ethical Poetic of the Later Middle Ages: A Decorum of Convenient Distinction* (Toronto: University of Toronto Press, 1982), esp. pp. 68, 73, 81.

27. Conrad of Hirsau, "Dialogue on the Authors," in Minnis and Scott, *Medieval Literary Theory,* p. 46. The Latin text reads: "Materia est unde constat quodlibet, unde et vocabulum trahit quasi mater rei. Duobus autem modis dicitur materia, ut, sicut in

edificio sunt ligna et lapides, sicut in vocibus genus et species et cetera quibus opus perficitur quod auctor agendum aggreditur." *Accessus ad auctores,* ed. R. B. C. Huygens (Leiden: E. J. Brill, 1970), p. 78.

28. "Materia est unde constat quidlibet, unde et materia quasi rei mater appellatur. Haec bifaria accipitur, in rebus, ut in domo lignum aut lapides, in vocibus, ut in Porfiro genus, species, differentia, proprium, accidens. Distingunt etiam nonnulli materiam sic, dicentes aliam esse de qua fit, ut litera de incausto, aliam in qua fit, ut pergamenum, aliam per quam fit, ut penna. Et in auctoribus quidem personas agentes, ut in Lucano Pompeium, Cesarum, senatum materiam accipiunt quidam, quidam solas personarum actiones ut civile bellum, secundum quos sententiae a Theodolo collatae vel ipsae certantes personae libri huius materia dici possunt. Duas etiam in operibus materias notant, principalem, de qua maxime tractatur, secundariam, quae incidit." *Accessus ad auctores,* p. 67; the translation is mine.

29. As Porphyry the Phoenician writes, some statements "are said of many things, such as genera, species, differences, properties, and accidents, that occur jointly in many and not uniquely in some one thing. An example of genus is 'animal'; of species, 'man'; of difference, 'rational'; of property, 'capable of laughing'; of accident, 'white,' 'black,' 'sitting.'" Porphyry the Phoenician, *Isagoge,* trans. Edward W. Warren, Mediaeval Sources in Translation, no. 16 (Toronto: Pontifical Institute of Mediaeval Studies, 1975), p. 31.

30. Cicero, *De inventione* I.xxiv.34, p. 71.

31. Geoffrey of Vinsauf, *Poetria Nova,* p. 17; "Si quis habet fundare domum, non currit ad actum / Impetuosa manus: intrinseca linea cordis / Praemetitur opus, seriemque sub ordine certo / Interior praescribit homo, totamque figurat / Ante manus cordis quam corporis; et status ejus / Est prius archetypus quam sensilis" (p. 16).

32. Kelly, "Theory of Composition," p. 126.

33. Gregory the Great, "Ad Leandrum," in *Moralia in Job,* ed. Mark Adriaen (Turnhout: Brepols, 1979), 143:4.

34. *The Didascalicon of Hugh of St. Victor,* trans. Jerome Taylor, Records of Western Civilization (New York: Columbia University Press, 1961; repr. 1991), VI.2, p. 135.

35. Dante, "Epistle to Can Grande," p. 459.

36. Ibid., p. 460.

37. Boccaccio, "Expository Lectures on Dante's *Comedy,*" in Minnis and Scott, *Medieval Literary Theory,* p. 505.

38. Alchemical language makes a striking appearance in another thirteenth-century text, Jacob Anatolio's introduction to his Hebrew translation of Averroes' Arabic *Middle Commentary on Porphyry's Isagogue.* There Jacob defends and urges the study of logic as a means for interpreting scriptural allegory. In answer to those who, following Solomon's advice in Proverbs 2:4–5, "Seek understanding as men seek silver," Jacob presents logic as "a crucible for refining the silver of understanding and a furnace for refining the gold of belief." Since "every word of God is refined" (Proverbs 30:5), it is the task of every philosopher to mine the scriptural *materia* and "extract the hidden meaning of the words of the Torah" through the aid of theoretical science. See Jacob Anatolio, "Introduction," in Averroes, *Middle Commentary on Porphyry's Isagogue,* trans. Herbert A. Davidson (Cambridge, Mass.: Medieval Academy of America, 1969), pp. 3, 5.

39. Dante, *The Banquet,* trans. Christopher Ryan, Stanford French and Italian Studies (Saratoga, Calif.: ANMA Libri, 1989), II. 1, pp. 43–44.

40. In his "Epistle to Can Grande," Dante explicates the fourfold meaning of Psalm 113, verses 1–2, in order to explain what he means when he says that his own *Commedia* is "polysemous."

41. Honorius of Autun, *Expositio in Cantica Canticorum,* PL 172, c349–50. For a more detailed treatment, see my book *The Song of Songs in the Middle Ages* (Ithaca: Cornell University Press, 1990; repr. 1994), pp. 31–33.

42. See the "M" volume of the *Middle English Dictionary*, ed. Sherman M. Kuhn and John Reidy (Ann Arbor: University of Michigan Press, 1968), pp. 213–18.

43. I quote from *The Complete Works of John Gower*, ed. G. C. Macaulay (Oxford: Clarendon Press, 1899–1902), vols. 2 and 3, giving book and line citations parenthetically in the text.

44. See also the exemplum of the poor knight and Julius in *Confessio Amantis* VII. 2079–80.

45. I use William Langland, *Piers Plowman: The B Version*, ed. George Kane and E. Talbot Donaldson (London: Athlone Press, 1975); hereafter cited parenthetically in the text.

46. Here and throughout I use *The Riverside Chaucer*, ed. Larry D. Benson, 3d ed. (Boston: Houghton Mifflin, 1987); hereafter cited parenthetically in the text.

47. Geoffrey of Vinsauf, *Poetria Nova*, p. 19; "cura sequens, qua compensare statera / Pondera, si juste pendet sententia" (p. 18).

48. See Michael Murrin, *The Veil of Allegory: Some Notes Toward a Theory of Allegorical Rhetoric in the English Renaissance* (Chicago: University of Chicago Press, 1969), p. 42.

49. Boccaccio, "Short Treatise in Praise of Dante," in Minnis and Scott, *Medieval Literary Theory*, p. 495.

50. In Minnis and Scott, *Medieval Literary Theory*, p. 26; "Materia sua amici sui sunt, ad quos scribit, mittens singulis singulas epistolas, vel ipsa verba, quibus precatur" (*Accessus ad auctores*, p. 35).

51. In Minnis and Scott, *Medieval Literary Theory*, p. 26; "Materia sua est periculorum descriptio vel ipsi amici quibus singulis mittit epistolas" (*Accessus ad auctores*, p. 35).

52. Allen, *Ethical Poetic*, p. 289.

53. Ibid., p. 263.

54. Ibid., p. 180.

55. David Aers and Lynn Staley, *The Powers of the Holy: Religion, Politics, and Gender in Late Medieval English Culture* (University Park: Pennsylvania State University Press, 1996), p. 180.

2. John Ball's Letters and *Piers Plowman*

1. *The Peasants' Revolt of 1381*, ed. and trans. R. B. Dobson, 2d ed. (London: Macmillan, 1983), pp. 123, 125–26; *The Anonimalle Chronicle, 1333–1381*, ed. V. H. Galbraith (Manchester: Manchester University Press, 1970), pp. 133, 135.

2. The letters have been newly edited by James M. Dean, *Medieval English Political Writings*, TEAMS Middle English Texts Series (Kalamazoo, Mich.: Medieval Institute Publications, 1996), pp. 135–39. I quote from the letters as they appear in Henry Knighton, *Chronicon*, ed. Joseph Rawson Lumby, Rolls Series 92, no. 2 (1895; London: Kraus Reprint, 1965), pp. 138–40; Thomas Walsingham, *Historia Anglicana*, ed. Henry Thomas Riley, Rolls Series 28, no. 1, pt. 2 (1864; London: Kraus Reprint, 1965), pp. 33–34.

3. For a millenarian interpretation of Ball's letters, see Norman Cohn, *The Pursuit of the Millenium* (New York: Oxford University Press, 1970; repr. 1972), pp. 200–204.

4. Walsingham, *Historia Anglicana*, 2:33.

5. Ibid., 2:34.

6. *Peasants' Revolt*, p. 379; see also Richard F. Green, "John Ball's Letters: Literary History and Historical Literature," in *Chaucer's England: Literature in Historical Context*, ed. Barbara Hanawalt, Medieval Studies at Minnesota, no. 4 (Minneapolis: University of Minnesota Press, 1992), p. 182.

7. Steven Justice, *Writing and Rebellion: England in 1381*, New Historicism Series, no. 27 (Berkeley: University of California Press, 1994), p. 23; hereafter cited parenthetically in the text.

8. Walsingham, *Historia Anglicana*, 2:33.

9. V. J. Scattergood, *Politics and Poetry in the Fifteenth Century* (London: Blandford, 1971), p. 354.

10. Knighton, *Chronicon*, p. 140.

11. Siegfried Wenzel, *Preachers, Poets, and the Early English Lyric* (Princeton: Princeton University Press, 1986), pp. 174, 196–98.

12. Green, "John Ball's Letters," p. 187.

13. Rossell Hope Robbins, "Dissent in Middle English Literature: The Spirit of (Thirteen) Seventy-six," *Medievalia et Humanistica*, n.s. 9 (1979): 26.

14. On the rebels' self-definition as the "trewe communes" and their use of the expression in a watchword, see Paul Strohm, *Hochon's Arrow: The Social Imagination of Fourteenth-Century Texts* (Princeton: Princeton University Press, 1992), pp. 41–42.

15. Susan Crane, "The Writing Lesson of 1381," in Hanawatt, *Chaucer's England*, p. 211.

16. Scattergood, *Politics and Poetry*, p. 355.

17. Andrew Galloway, "The Rhetoric of Riddling in Late Medieval England: The 'Oxford' Riddles, the *Secretum philosophorum*, and the Riddles in *Piers Plowman*," *Speculum* 70 (1995): 85.

18. Maureen Quilligan, *The Language of Allegory: Defining the Genre* (Ithaca: Cornell University Press, 1979), pp. 58–79; Mary S. Carruthers, *The Search for St. Truth: A Study of Meaning in "Piers Plowman"* (Evanston, Ill.: Northwestern University Press, 1973), esp. pp. 55–63; Lavinia Griffiths, *Personification in "Piers Plowman,"* Piers Plowman Studies 3 (Cambridge: D. S. Brewer, 1985), esp. pp. 26–40.

19. Quilligan, *Language of Allegory*, pp. 26, 64, 31–32.

20. A. J. Colaianne, *Piers Plowman: An Annotated Bibliography of Editions and Criticism, 1550–1977* (New York: Garland, 1978), p. 170.

21. Morton W. Bloomfield, *Piers Plowman as a Fourteenth-Century Apocalypse* (New Brunswick, N.J.: Rutgers University Press, 1961), p. 32.

22. On the general issue of literacy in relation to the revolt, see Margaret Aston, *Lollards and Reformers: Images and Literacy in Late Medieval Religion* (London: Hambledon Press, 1984); Rosamond Faith, "The 'Great Rumour' of 1377 and Peasant Ideology," in *The English Rising of 1381*, ed. R. H. Hilton and T. H. Aston (Cambridge: Cambridge University Press, 1984), pp. 43–73; Justice, *Writing and Rebellion;* Anne Hudson, "'Laicus litteratus': the Paradox of Lollardy," in *Heresy and Literacy, 1000–1530*, ed. Peter Biller and Anne Hudson, Cambridge Studies in Medieval Literature 23 (Cambridge: Cambridge University Press, 1994), pp. 222–36; M. T. Clanchy, *From Memory to Written Record: England, 1066–1307* (Cambridge: Harvard University Press, 1979).

23. G. R. Owst has emphasized the important use of biblical allegory, such as Matthew 20:1–16, for social commentary by medieval preachers: "A favourite *figure* used by the preachers to set forth their political or social ideal is that of the Vineyard with its three Orders of husbandmen." G. R. Owst, *Literature and Pulpit in Medieval England* (New York: Barnes and Noble, 1966), p. 549.

24. Rodney Hilton, *Bondmen Made Free: Medieval Peasant Movements and the English Rising of 1381* (London: Methuen, 1973; repr. 1980), p. 208.

25. See Green, "John Ball's Letters," pp. 191–92.

26. Hilton, *Bondmen Made Free*, pp. 209–10.

27. *Peasants' Revolt*, p. 378.

28. Ibid., pp. 276, 375.

29. Ibid., p. 374; Walsingham, *Historia Anglicana*, 2:32: "Hic per viginti annos, et amplius, semper praedicans in diversis locis ea quae scivit vulgo placentia, detrahens tam personis ecclesiasticis quam dominis saecularibus. . . . propter quae, prohibitus ab Episcopis in, quorum parochiis haec praesumpsit, ne in ecclesiis de caetero praedicaret, concessit in plateas et vicos, vel in campos, ad praedicandum."

30. *Peasants' Revolt*, p. 374. Russell A. Peck notes that Ball's letters seem self-consciously Pauline in their salutation ("John Balle seynte Marye prist gretes wele alle maner men") and concluding Trinitarian formula and thus invite a comparison of Saint Paul and John Ball as political prisoners. See Russell A. Peck, "Social Conscience and the Poets," in *Social Unrest in the Late Middle Ages*, ed. Francis X. Newman, Medieval and Renaissance Texts and Studies 39 (Binghamton: State University of New York Press, 1986), p. 114.

31. *Peasants' Revolt*, p. 375; Walsingham, *Historia Anglicana*, 2:33.

32. *Peasants' Revolt*, p. 375; Walsingham, *Historia Anglicana*, 2:33: "Monuit ut essent viri cordati, et amore boni patrisfamilias excolentis agrum suum, et extirpantis ac resecantis noxia gramina quae fruges solent opprimere, et ipsi in praesenti facere festinarent."

33. *Peasants' Revolt*, p. 375; Walsingham, *Historia Anglicana*, 2:33: "Primo, majores regni dominos occidendo; deinde, juridicos, justiciarios, et juratores patriae, perimendo; postremo, quoscunque scirent in posterum communitati nocivos."

34. Knighton, *Chronicon*, p. 140. Cf. Green, "John Ball's Letters," pp. 186–87.

35. Walsingham, *Historia Anglicana*, 2:34.

36. *Peasants' Revolt*, p. 375; Walsingham, *Historia Anglicana*, 2:33: "sic demum et pacem sibimet parerent et securitatem in futurum, si, sublatis majoribus, esset inter eos aequa libertas, eadem nobilitas, par dignitas, similisque potestas."

37. Walsingham, *Historia Anglicana*, 2:34.

38. *Peasants' Revolt*, p. 375; Walsingham, *Historia Anglicana*, 2:34. On *Piers Plowman* and the plowman in Ball's sermon, see Justice, *Writing and Rebellion*, pp. 110–11.

39. Wenzel, *Preachers, Poets*, pp. 80–81.

40. Ibid., p. 13.

41. Ibid., p. 175.

42. Thomas L. Kinney, "The Temper of Fourteenth-Century English Verse of Complaint," *Annuale Mediaevali* 7 (1966): 77.

43. Ibid., pp. 82–83.

44. Ibid., p. 89.

45. Anne Middleton, "The Idea of Public Poetry in the Reign of Richard II," *Speculum* 53 (1978): 99.

46. Wenzel, *Preachers, Poets*, p. 185.

47. Ibid., p. 187. The entire text of this poem appears in the Introduction to *Speculum Christiani: A Middle English Religious Treatise of the Fourteenth Century*, ed. Gustaf Holmstedt, EETS o.s. 182 (London: Humphrey Milford, Oxford University Press, 1933), pp. clxxxv–clxxxvii. See V. J. Scattergood, "Political Context, Date, and Composition of 'The Sayings of the Four Philosophers'," *Medium Aevum* 37 (1968): 157–65.

48. Green, "John Ball's Letters," p. 185.

49. Appendix, *Speculum Christiani*, p. 331. Holmstedt includes an edition of the complete text.

50. Wenzel, *Preachers, Poets*, p. 186.

51. Appendix, *Speculum Christiani*, pp. 335–36, 332–33.

52. Ibid., p. 332.

53. *Speculum Christiani*, p. 124. On the date of this work, see Vincent Gillespie, "The Evolution of the *Speculum Christiani*," in *Latin and Vernacular: Studies in Late Medieval Texts and Manuscripts*, ed. A. J. Minnis (Cambridge: Boydell and Brewer, 1989), p. 54, n. 40.

54. *Speculum Christiani*, p. 126.

55. Walsingham, *Historia Anglicana*, 2:34.

56. Knighton, *Chronicon*, p. 140.

57. *The Early English Versions of the "Gesta Romanorum,"* ed. Sidney J. H. Herrtage, EETS e.s. 33 (London: Oxford University Press, 1879; repr. 1962), p. 360.

58. *John Capgrave's Abbreuiacion of Cronicles*, ed. Peter J. Lucas, EETS 285 (Oxford: Oxford University Press, 1983), p. 166.

59. *Early English Versions of the "Gesta Romanorum,"* p. 360.

60. Ibid.

61. Kinney, "Verse of Complaint," p. 77.

62. See Introduction, *Speculum Christiani,* p. clxxxviii.

63. On "Gifte is domesman," see Wenzel, *Preachers, Poets,* p. 189.

64. Ibid., p. 188.

65. Quoted in *Speculum Christiani,* p. clxxxvii.

66. Ibid., p. clxxxviii.

67. Knighton, *Chronicon,* p. 139.

68. See Green, "Letters of John Ball," p. 85.

69. Knighton, *Chronicon,* pp. 138–39.

70. *Speculum Christiani,* p. 142. The couplet appears in the "Septima Tabula," a rhymed sermon that supposedly comments on the "boke of wysdom" and thus continues the moral themes of the "Sayings of the Philosophers" in the "Sexta Tabula."

71. The Four Daughters of God famously meet in the B text of *Piers Plowman,* Passus XVIII, ll. 113–425.

72. Appendix, *Speculum Christiani,* p. 336.

73. Walsingham, *Historia Anglicana,* 2:34.

74. See Green, "John Ball's Letters," p. 183; Dean, *Medieval English Political Writings,* p. 161.

75. Walsingham, *Historia Anglicana,* 2:34. I correct "scharpe" to "schappe." See Dean, *Medieval English Political Writings,* p. 135.

76. *Speculum Christiani,* p. 126.

77. Ibid., p. 124.

78. Walsingham, *Historia Anglicana,* 2:34.

79. *Speculum Christiani,* p. 124.

80. Knighton, *Chronicon,* p. 139. On "si dedero," see Dean, *Medieval English Political Writings,* p. 164.

81. See Siegfried Wenzel, "Medieval Sermons," in *A Companion to "Piers Plowman,"* ed. John A. Alford (Berkeley: University of California Press, 1988), pp. 155–72; Owst, *Literature and Pulpit.*

82. Anne Hudson, "Epilogue: The Legacy of *Piers Plowman,"* in Alford, *A Companion to "Piers Plowman,"* p. 252.

83. Knighton, *Chronicon,* p. 139.

84. Walsingham, *Historia Anglicana,* 2:34.

85. John Gower, *The Voice of One Crying,* in *The Major Latin Works of John Gower,* trans. Eric W. Stockton (Seattle: University of Washington Press, 1962), p. 74; *Vox Clamantis,* in *The Complete Works of John Gower,* ed. G. C. Macaulay, 4 vols. (Oxford: Clarendon Press, 1902), 4:53. See also *Vox Clamantis* VII.1473–74.

86. Dean, *Middle English Political Poetry,* p. 159.

87. Knighton, *Chronicon,* p. 139. A macaronic poem dating from the same time, "On the Times," similarly places the "kattys nek to the bel" and mentions a "John," whom Richard Green has identified as John of Gaunt. See Richard Firth Green, "Jack Philipot, John of Gaunt, and a Poem of 1380," *Speculum* 66 (1991): 330–41; Dean, *Medieval English Political Writings,* pp. 140–46, 168.

88. Here and elsewhere I quote from William Langland, *Piers Plowman: The B Version,* ed. George Kane and E. Talbot Donaldson (London: Athlone Press, 1975), giving Passus and line numbers parenthetically in the text.

89. See Elisabeth M. Orsten, "The Ambiguities in Langland's Rat Parliament," *Medieval Studies* 23 (1961): 216–39; Eleanor H. Kellogg, "Bishop Brunton and the Fable of the Rats," *PMLA* 50.1 (1935): 57–69.

90. Hilton, *Bondmen Made Free,* p. 194.

91. See Dean, *Medieval English Political Writings,* p. 160; *Peasants' Revolt,* p. 379; Hud-

son, "Epilogue," p. 252; Sir Charles Oman, *The Great Revolt of 1381*, ed. E. B. Fryde, 2nd ed. (Oxford: Clarendon Press, 1906; repr. 1969), p. 44.

92. Walsingham, *Historia Anglicana* 2:34.

93. Knighton, *Chronicon*, p. 139.

94. Hilton, *Bondmen Made Free*, p. 194.

95. *Peasants' Revolt*, p. 157; *Anonimalle Chronicle*, p. 141.

96. Knighton, *Chronicon*, p. 139.

97. Dobson, *Peasants' Revolt*, p. 169.

98. Ibid., p. 184.

99. Dean's edition expands "Bathon" to "Banthon" (*Medieval English Political Writings*, p. 164). In his edition, Green notes the suspension over the *a*, but preserves the form "Bathon" ("John Ball's Letters," p. 194). Justice proposes "Bamthon" instead, identifying the figure as "John of Bampton, who along with his fellow Essex justice of the peace John of Gildesburgh appeared at Brentwood to reassess the poll tax in the event that sparked the rising" (*Writing and Rebellion*, p. 133).

100. Knighton, *Chronicon*, p. 139.

101. On the figure of Mede, see John A. Yunck, *The Lineage of Lady Meed: The Development of Mediaeval Venality Satire* (Notre Dame: University of Notre Dame Press, 1963); A. G. Mitchell, "Lady Meed and the Art of *Piers Plowman*," in *Style and Symbolism in "Piers Plowman": A Modern Critical Anthology*, ed. Robert J. Blanch (Knoxville: University of Tennessee Press, 1968), pp. 174–93; Griffiths, *Personification in "Piers Plowman*," pp. 26–40.

102. On Meed and Perrers, see Bernard F. Huppé, "The A-Text of *Piers Plowman* and the Norman Wars," *PMLA* 54.1 (1939): 37–64; J. A. W. Bennett, "The Date of the A-Text of *Piers Plowman*," *PMLA* 58.2 (1943): 566–72; John L. Selzner, "Topical Allegory in *Piers Plowman:* Lady Meed's B Text Debate with Conscience," *PQ* 59.3 (1980): 257–67; Anna Baldwin, *The Theme of Government in "Piers Plowman"* (Cambridge: D. S. Brewer, 1981), p. 34; Justice, *Writing and Rebellion*, p. 133.

103. See Anthony Goodman, *John of Gaunt: The Exercise of Princely Power in Fourteenth-Century Europe* (New York: St. Martin's Press, 1992), pp. 58–59, 72.

104. Knighton, *Chronicon*, p. 139.

105. *Peasants' Revolt*, p. 123.

106. Ibid., p. 133.

107. Ibid., p. 130.

108. See *Chaucer: Life-Records*, ed. Martin M. Crow and Clair C. Olson (Austin: University of Texas Press, 1966).

109. T. H. Lloyd, *The English Wool Trade in the Middle Ages* (Cambridge: Cambridge University Press, 1977), p. 225.

110. Ibid., p. 228. For the chancellor's words, see, *Peasants' Revolt*, p. 113.

111. Lloyd, *English Wool Trade*, p. 225.

112. Hilton, *Bondmen Made Free*, p. 195.

113. Ibid.

114. *Peasants' Revolt*, p. 201.

115. Hilton, *Bondmen Made Free*, p. 197.

116. See David Nicholas, *The Metamorphosis of a Medieval City: Ghent in the Age of the Arteveldes, 1302–1390* (Lincoln: University of Nebraska Press, 1987).

117. Goodman, *John of Gaunt*, p. 29.

118. Ibid.

119. *Anonimalle Chronicle*, pp. 104–5.

120. Geoffrey Chaucer, "Romaunt of the Rose," in *The Riverside Chaucer*, ed. Larry D. Benson, 3rd ed. (Boston: Houghton Mifflin, 1987), A, l. 574. I use this edition of Chaucer's works throughout, giving subsequent citations parenthetically in the text.

121. John Matthews Manly, *Canterbury Tales* (New York: Henry Holt, 1928; repr. 1930), p. 527.

122. Barry Cunliffe, *The City of Bath* (New Haven: Yale University Press, 1987), pp. 8, 90. See also D. W. Robertson, Jr., "'And for my land thus hastow mordred me?': Land Tenure, the Cloth Industry, and the Wife of Bath," *Chaucer Review* 14 (1980): 403–20.

123. Manly, *Canterbury Tales*, p. 527. Manly's view is accepted by Muriel Bowden, *A Commentary on the General Prologue to the Canterbury Tales* (New York: Columbia University Press, 1948; repr. 1967), p. 215.

124. John Matthews Manly, *Some New Light on Chaucer: Lectures Delivered at the Lowell Institute* (1926; Gloucester: Peter Smith, 1959), p. 229; Henry Atton and Henry Hurst Holland, *The King's Customs* (London: Frank Cass, 1967), 1:25–26.

125. Sheila Delany, "Substructure and Superstructure: The Politics of Allegory in the Fourteenth Century," *Science and Society* 38 (1974): 266.

126. Ibid., p. 263.

127. Ibid., p. 277. Delany actually applies the phrase to Chaucer, but she likens him to Langland in her analysis.

128. *The Plowman's Tale: The ca. 1532 and 1606 Editions of a Spurious Canterbury Tale*, ed. Mary Rhinelander McCarl (New York: Garland, 1997), ll. 1373–74, p. 214.

129. "The Testimony of William Thorpe," in *Two Wycliffite Texts: The Sermon of William Taylor 1406, The Testimony of William Thorpe 1407*, ed. Anne Hudson, EETS o.s. 301 (Oxford: Oxford University Press, 1993), p. 61.

130. Ibid., pp. 62–63.

131. Ibid., p. 65.

132. See Justice, *Writing and Rebellion*, p. 124.

133. For the Lollard view of pilgrimages as idolatrous, see Aston, *Lollards and Reformers*, pp. 143, 151–52.

134. See John Burrow, "The Action of Langland's Second Vision," in *Style and Symbolism, in "Piers Plowman": A Modern Critical Anthology*, ed. Robert J. Blanch (Knoxville: University of Tennessee Press, 1968), pp. 209–27.

135. William Langland, *The Vision of William Concerning Piers Plowman*, ed. Walter W. Skeat, EETS o.s. 81 (London: N. Trübner, 1884; repr. 1973), pt. IV, sec. 2, p. xliv.

136. Robbins, "Dissent in Middle English Literature," p. 98.

137. David Aers, *Chaucer, Langland, and the Creative Imagination* (London: Routledge and Kegan Paul, 1980), esp. pp. 10, 16.

138. George B. Kane, "Some Fourteenth-Century 'Political' Poems," in *Medieval English Religious and Ethical Literature: Essays in Honor of G. H. Russell*, ed. Gregory Kratzmann and James Simpson (Cambridge: D. S. Brewer, 1986), p. 90.

139. Peck, "Social Conscience and the Poets"; Green, "John Ball's Letters," pp. 191–92.

140. Anne Middleton, "The Audience and Public of *Piers Plowman*," in *Middle English Alliterative Poetry and Its Literary Background: Seven Essays*, ed. David Lawton (Cambridge: D. S. Brewer, 1982), pp. 108, 119; hereafter cited parenthetically in the text.

141. James Simpson, "The Constraints of Satire in 'Piers Plowman' and 'Mum and the Sothsegger,'" in *Langland, the Mystics, and the Medieval English Religious Tradition: Essays in Honour of S. S. Hussey*, ed. Helen Phillips (Cambridge: D. S. Brewer, 1990), pp. 12–13.

142. Peck, "Social Conscience," pp. 115–16, 118–29.

143. *Peasants' Revolt*, p. 380.

144. Kinney, "Verse of Complaint," p. 89. Cf. Elizabeth D. Kirk, "Langland's Plowman and the Recreation of Fourteenth-Century Religious Metaphor," *YLS* 2 (1988): 1–21.

145. See William Langland, *Piers Plowman: The A Version*, ed. George Kane (London: Athlone Press, 1960), XI.219–31.

146. Anna P. Baldwin, "The Historical Context," in Alford, *A Companion to "Piers Plowman"*, p. 72.

147. See Justice, *Writing and Rebellion*, pp. 231–51.

148. Knighton, *Chronicon*, p. 34.

149. Aers, *Chaucer, Langland, and the Creative Imagination*, p. 23.

150. See Robert W. Frank, "The Pardon Scene in *Piers Plowman*," *Speculum* 26 (1951): 317–31; Mary S. Carruthers, "The Tearing of the Pardon," *Philological Quarterly* 49.1 (1970): 8–18; Susan H. McLeod, "The Tearing of the Pardon in *Piers Plowman*," *Philological Quarterly* 56.1 (1977): 14–26.

151. See Denise N. Baker, "From Plowing to Penitence: *Piers Plowman* and Fourteenth-Century Theology," *Speculum* 55.4 (1980): 715–25; idem, "The Pardons of *Piers Plowman*," *Neuphilologische Mitteilungen* 85.4 (1984): 462–72; Rosemary Woolf, "The Tearing of the Pardon," in *"Piers Plowman": Critical Approaches*, ed. S. S. Hussey (London: Methuen, 1969), pp. 50–75.

152. See John Lawlor, "*Piers Plowman:* The Pardon Reconsidered," *Modern Language Notes* 45.4 (1950): 449–58.

153. For an interpretation of this scene as a turning from the active to the contemplative life, see T. P. Dunning, *"Piers Plowman": An Interpretation of the A Text*, 2nd ed., rev. T. P. Dolan (Oxford: Clarendon Press, 1980), p. 115.

154. David Aers and Lynn Staley, *The Powers of the Holy: Religion, Politics, and Gender in Late Medieval English Culture* (University Park: Pennsylvania State University Press, 1996), p. 63.

155. On pardons *a culpa et a poena*, see Henry Charles Lea, *A History of Auricular Confession and Indulgences in the Latin Church*, 3 vols. (New York: Greenwood, 1968), 3:54–82.

156. Baldwin, *Theme of Government*, pp. 56–63.

157. Ibid., p. 62.

158. Knighton, *Chronicon*, p. 34.

159. As Nikolaus Paulus emphasizes, pardons were regularly attached to an impressive list of public works: the construction and maintenance of churches, schools, hospitals, and other charitable institutions; the building of bridges, dams, roads, harbors, and fortifications; and the stimulation of such important social movements as Crusades and the Truce of God. The rebels' association of a pardon with their work of justice was not, therefore, as anomalous as it may at first seem. See Nikolaus Paulus, *Indulgences as a Social Factor in the Middle Ages*, trans. J. Elliot Ross (New York: Devin-Adair, 1922).

160. Judson Boyce Allen, "Langland's Reading and Writing: *Detractor* and the Pardon Scene," *Speculum* 59 (1984): 358.

161. See Dean, *Medieval English Political Writings*, p. 123; Hudson, "Epilogue," p. 252. Recall here my earlier discussion of Ball's pseudonym "Schep" and his pun on his own name (Ball/bell) as additional intertextual references to *Piers Plowman*.

162. See Colaianne, *Piers Plowman: An Annotated Bibliography*, pp. 168–69; Derek Pearsall, *An Annotated Critical Bibliography of Langland* (Ann Arbor: University of Michigan Press, 1990), pp. 187–99. For exceptions to this rule, see Allen, "Langland's Reading and Writing"; Joan Heiges Blythe, "Sins of the Tongue and Rhetorical Prudence in 'Piers Plowman,'" in *Literature and Religion in the Later Middle Ages: Philological Studies in Honor of Siegfried Wenzel*, ed. Richard G. Newhauser and John A. Alford, Medieval and Renaissance Texts and Studies 118 (Binghamton: State University of New York Press, 1995), pp. 119–42; Galloway, "Rhetoric of Riddling"; Middleton, "Audience and Public."

3. Gower's Arion and "Cithero"

1. John Gower, *The Voice of One Crying*, in *The Major Latin Works of John Gower*, trans. Eric W. Stockton (Seattle: University of Washington Press, 1962), pp. 49–50; *Vox Clamantis*, in *The Complete Works of John Gower*, ed. G. C. Macaulay, 4 vols. (Oxford: Clarendon

Press, 1901), 4:20: "In huis opusculi principio intendit compositor describere qualiter seruiles rustici impetuose contra ungenuos et nobiles regni insurrexerunt . . . narrat se per sompnium videsse diuersas vulgi turmas in diuersas species bestiarum domesticarum transmutatas: dicit tamen quod ille bestie domestice . . . crudelitates ferarum sibi presumpserunt." I use this translation and this edition throughout, giving page references to Stockton's translation parenthetically in the text.

2. See Steven Justice, *Writing and Rebellion: England in 1381* (Berkeley: University of California Press, 1994), pp. 214–18; see also my essay "The Peasants' Revolt: Cock-crow in Gower and Chaucer," in *Four Last Things: Death, Judgment, Heaven, and Hell in the Middle Ages,* ed. Allen J. Frantzen, Essays in Medieval Studies 10, 1993 Proceedings of the Illinois Medieval Association (Chicago: Loyola University Press, 1994), pp. 53–64. I use *The Riverside Chaucer,* ed. Larry D. Benson, 3rd ed. (Boston: Houghton Mifflin, 1987), giving citations parenthetically in the text.

3. John H. Fisher, *John Gower: Moral Philosopher and Friend of Chaucer* (New York: New York University Press, 1964), p. 206.

4. Ibid., p. 185.

5. For Gower's *Confessio Amantis,* I use vols. 2 and 3 of Macaulay's *The Complete Works of John Gower,* giving book and line numbers parenthetically in the text. Following Macaulay's usage, I mark passages that appear only in the first recension with an asterisk.

6. *Complete Works of John Gower,* 2:xxiii.

7. Peter Nicholson, "The Dedications of Gower's *Confessio Amantis,*" *Mediaevalia* 10 (1984): 159.

8. Fisher, *John Gower,* pp. 9–12, 124. He provides convenient charts, based on Macaulay's descriptions, pp. 303–7.

9. Nicholson, "Dedications," p. 174.

10. See A. I. Doyle and M. B. Parkes, "The Production of Copies of the *Canterbury Tales* and the *Confessio Amantis* in the Early Fifteenth Century," in *Medieval Scribes, Manuscripts, and Libraries: Essays Presented to N. R. Ker,* ed. M. B. Parkes and Andrew G. Watson (London: Scolar Press, 1978), pp. 163–210.

11. *Complete Works of John Gower,* 2:cxxviii.

12. Anne Middleton, "The Idea of Public Poetry in the Reign of Richard II," *Speculum* 53 (1978): 98.

13. Ibid., p. 107.

14. Paul Strohm, "Form and Social Statement in *Confessio Amantis* and *The Canterbury Tales,*" *SAC* 1 (1979): 38.

15. Nicholson, "Dedications," p. 174.

16. Larry Scanlon, *Narrative, Authority, and Power: The Medieval Exemplum and the Chaucerian Tradition* (Cambridge: Cambridge University Press, 1994), p. 252.

17. On causality (efficient, material, formal, and final) in medieval *accessus,* see Alastair J. Minnis, *Medieval Theory of Authorship: Scholastic Literary Attitudes in the Later Middle Ages,* 2nd ed. (Philadelphia: University of Pennsylvania Press, 1988), pp. 28–29.

18. Hans-Jürgen Diller, "'For Engelondes sake': Richard II and Henry of Lancaster as Intended Readers of Gower's *Confessio Amantis,*" in *Functions of Literature: Essays Presented to Erwin Wolff on His Sixtieth Birthday,* ed. Ulrich Broich, Theo Stemmler, and Gerd Stratmann (Tübingen: Max Niemeyer, 1984), p. 45.

19. R. F. Yeager, *John Gower's Poetic: The Search for a New Arion* (Cambridge: D. S. Brewer, 1990), p. 268. For another study stressing the importance of Gower's political context, see Russell Peck, *Kingship and Common Profit in Gower's "Confessio Amantis"* (Carbondale: Southern Illinois University Press, 1978).

20. Yeager, *John Gower's Poetic,* p. 265.

21. Ibid., p. 240.

22. Thomas Walsingham, *Historia Anglicana (1381–1422),* ed. Henry Thomas Riley,

Rolls Series 28, no. 1, pt. 2 (London: Her Majesty's Stationery Office, 1864; repr. 1965), p. 204.

23. Ibid., pp. 204, 205.

24. Pliny, *Natural History,* ed. and trans. H. Rackham, Loeb Classical Library, 10 vols. (Cambridge: Haryard University Press, 1940; repr. 1947), IX.viii.28, 3:182–83: "quae faciunt ut credatur Arionem quoque citharoedicae artis, interficere nautis in mari parantibus ad intercipiendos eius quaestus, eblanditum uti prius caneret cithara, congregatis cantu delphinis, cum se iecisset in mare exceptum ab uno . . . in litus pervectum."

25. The story of Arion appears in *Fasti* II.79–118. James Frazer notes, "Manuscripts of the *Fasti* are very numerous; the British Museum alone possesses fifteen of them, of which the oldest is believed to date from the twelfth or early thirteenth century" (p. xxvii). Here and in subsequent citations in the text I use *Ovid's Fasti,* trans. Sir James G. Frazer, Loeb Classical Library (Cambridge: Harvard University Press, 1951).

26. The *Tristia* was certainly well known to Gower. As Andrew Galloway has shown, Gower identified himself as an intellectual with the exiled Ovid, constructing his self-portrait in *Vox Clamantis* out of "a dense cento of passages from Ovid's poems, especially his poems of exile." Andrew Galloway, "Gower in His Most Learned Role and the Peasants' Revolt of 1381," *Mediaevalia* 16 (1993): 330.

27. See, for example, the commentaries on the *Fasti* included in A. J. Minnis and A. B. Scott, eds., with the assistance of David Wallace, *Medieval Literary Theory and Criticism ca. 1100–ca. 1375: The Commentary Tradition,* rev. ed. (Oxford: Clarendon Press, 1988), pp. 28–30, 362–63.

28. See Fisher, *John Gower,* p. 123; *Complete Works of John Gower,* 3:347.

29. Fisher, *John Gower,* pp. 122–23.

30. Commenting on the "anomaly" of the dedication to Germanicus in a work ostensibly written for Augustus, Frazer declares that the "only reasonable explanation . . . appears to be that after the death of Augustus the author cancelled the original dedication and substituted a dedication to Germanicus in the hope that the clement and popular prince, himself a poet, would be moved by the compliment to intercede with the reigning Emperor Tiberius in order to procure the poet's pardon, or at least a mitigation of his sentence" (*Ovid's Fasti,* p. xix).

31. Macaulay preserves these lines in praise of Gower, written by "a certain philosopher," in *Complete Works of John Gower,* 3:479.

32. The harmonizing music of Arion makes him resemble Amphion, the mythic founder of Athens and the father of rhetoric. As Brunetto Latini describes him, he "made stones and wood appear by the sweetness of his song, that is, through his good words he brought men out of the wild rocks where they were living and led them to live in common in that city." Brunetto Latini, *The Book of the Treasure (Li Livres dou Tresor),* trans. Paul Barrette and Spurgeon Baldwin, Garland Library of Medieval Literature, series B, vol. 90 (New York: Garland, 1993), III.1, p. 280. As Russell Peck notes, Gower's Ovidian source "makes no mention of the music's effect on man's governance" (*Kingship and Common Profit,* p. 23).

33. Fisher, *John Gower,* p. 118. See Nigel Saul, *Richard II* (New Haven: Yale University Press, 1997), p. 259.

34. See Fisher, *John Gower,* pp. 27, 31, 289.

35. Nicholson, "Dedications," p. 174.

36. Yeager, *John Gower's Poetic,* p. 268.

37. James Murphy, "John Gower's *Confessio Amantis* and the First Discussion of Rhetoric in the English Language," *PQ* 41 (1962): 411.

38. Ibid., p. 408.

39. See Götz Schmitz, *The Middel Weie: Stil- und Aufbauformen in John Gower's "Confessio Amantis,"* Studien zur englischen Literatur 11 (Bonn: Bouvier, 1974).

40. See Murphy, "First Discussion of Rhetoric," p. 410.

41. In Chapter 19 of Book I of *Vox Clamantis,* he records approvingly the death of the "Jay," Wat Tyler, at the hands of Mayor William Walworth at Smithfield.

42. Dante Alighieri, *The Banquet,* trans. Christopher Ryan, Stanford French and Italian Studies (Saratoga, Calif: ANMA Libri, 1989), IV.v.19, p. 133.

43. On the power of the word, see Patrick J. Gallacher, *Love, the Word, and Mercury: A Reading of John Gower's "Confessio Amantis"* (Albuquerque: University of New Mexico Press, 1975), pp. 23, 149.

44. Gower's relationship as a poet to the figure of the eloquent and wily Ulysses is complex. In recording the frenzy of the Peasants' Revolt, Gower's own voice is lamentatious, like that of "the orator Ulysses," who "was then of no help with his words of well chosen speech, and blessed discourse was not his" (*Voice of One Crying* I.13, p. 71). For Gower's later use of Ulysses as a figure for the rhetorician, see Katharine S. Gittes, "Ulysses in Gower's *Confessio Amantis:* The Christian Soul as Silent Rhetorician," *ELN* 24.2 (1986): 7–14.

45. On this historical topic, see Lester Hutchinson, *The Conspiracy of Catiline* (New York: Barnes and Noble, 1967); Charles M. Odahl, *The Catilinarian Conspiracy* (New Haven, Conn.: College and University Press, 1971); Sallust, *Bellum Catilinae* (Chico, Calif.: Scholars Press, 1984).

46. On Richard's alleged plots, see Louisa D. Duls, *Richard II in the Early Chronicles,* Studies in English Literature 79 (The Hague: Mouton, 1975), pp. 32, 36, 40.

47. John Gower, *The Tripartite Chronicle,* in *The Major Latin Works of John Gower,* p. 290; *Cronica Tripertita,* in *The Complete Works of John Gower,* 4:315, I.23–24: "Tres sunt antiqui proceres, quos regis iniqui / Ira magis nouit, et eos occidere vouit."

48. See Anthony Tuck, *Richard II and the English Nobility* (London: Edward Arnold, 1973), pp. 117–18.

49. On the question of the threat of deposition, see Duls, *Early Chronicles,* pp. 37–38; regarding which army was raised first, see pp. 32–33, 62.

50. *John Capgrave's Abbreuiacion of Cronicles,* ed. Peter J. Lucas, EETS 285 (Oxford: Oxford University Press, 1983), p. 194.

51. *Cronica Tripertita* I.71–72: "Querit Aper latebras, fraudes mortisque tenebras, / Quo regnum periat regisque superbia fiat" (p. 316).

52. *Cronica Tripertita* I.75–76: "Ducit Aper gentes, quas concitat arma gerentes, / Liber vt hiis pergat proceresque per omnia spergat" (p. 316).

53. Brunetto Latini, *Li Livres dou Tresor,* ed. Francis J. Carmody (Berkeley: University of California Press, 1948), III.34, p. 344.

54. The Latin sidenote that is translated here reads, "Eciam episcopus Cicestrie, tunc regis confessor, conscius culpe extera loca petens propria fugiendo reliquit" (*Cronica Tripertita,* p. 317).

55. On the strategic revival of the "old tradition of conducting state trials in parliament," see Tuck, *Richard II and the English Nobility,* pp. 122–23.

56. The Latin sidenote reads, "Parliamentum gradatim processit precipue contra illos qui regis iniqui fautores iniqui fuerunt" (*Cronica Tripertita,* p. 318).

57. On the questions put to the justices, see Duls, *Early Chronicles,* pp. 31–32, 40–41; Tuck, *Richard II and the English Nobility,* pp. 116–17; *Historia Vitae et Regni Ricardi Secundi,* ed. George B. Stow, Jr. (Philadelphia: University of Pennsylvania Press, 1977), pp. 106–8.

58. *Cronica Tripertita* I.166–67: "Crimine presante super hoc quod fecerat ante, / Ad furcas tractus fit ibi pendendo subactus" (p. 318).

59. *Cronica Tripertita* I.174–77: "Non fuit hec pena, delictis que fore plena / Posset, et hoc certe vox plebis dixit aperte; / Set nimis ornate penam ficta pietate / Pontifices regis moderantur ab ordine legis" (p. 319). According to Anthony Goodman, "Archbishop Courtenay, speaking on behalf of the bishops, begged for commutation," as did

the queen. See Anthony Goodman, *The Loyal Conspiracy: The Lords Appellant under Richard II* (London: Routledge and Kegan Paul, 1971), p. 45.

60. Brunetto Latini, *Book of the Treasure* III.29, p. 301: "Catelline . . . noumoit ses ancestres et lor bones oevres devant les signatours quant il se voloit covrir de la conjurison de Rome, et quant il lor disoit que çou n'estoit mie por mal mais por aidier les febles et les nonpoissans, si comme il avoit acoustumé tousjours, ce disoit" (*Li Livres dou Tresor*, p. 340).

61. Brunetto Latini, *Book of the Treasure* III.35, p. 305: "ke la felonie et les forfés de ciaus ki sont pris ne sormonte nostre dignité ne noustre douçour, plus i devons regarder nostre bonne renomee que nostre courous" (*Li Livres dou Tresor*, p. 345).

62. Brunetto Latini, *Book of the Treasure* III.35, pp. 306–7: "Quant li lacedoniens orent pris Atenes, il establirent .xxx. homes ki estoient mestre del commun; cil ocioient au commencement les piesmes desloiaus homes tot sans jugement, li peules en estoit liés et disoient ke bien faisoient. Aprés crut la coustume et la licence petit a petit, si k'il ocioient bons et mauvais a lor volenté, tant que li autre en estoient espoenté, et fu la cités en tel servage . . . revertissoit . . . . Luce Sillaire fu mout loés de ce k'il juga et ocist Damacipe et autres ki avoient esté contre le commun de Rome; mais cele chose fu commencement de grant mal" (*Li Livres dou Tresor*, p. 346).

63. Duls, *Early Chronicles*, p. 29, n. 2.

64. Ibid., pp. 52–53, 61, 63–66; Tuck, *Richard II and the English Nobility*, pp. 124–26.

65. The innocence of Burley was supported not only by Richard and Anne, but also by the duke of York. See Duls, *Early Chronicles*, p. 65; Goodman, *Loyal Conspiracy*, p. 46.

66. *Cronica Tripertita* I.141: "Stat quia non recta, magis est culpanda senecta" (p. 318).

67. *Cronica Tripertita* I.202–3: "Transit adulator, sceleratus et insidiator, / Consilii fautor, inuentor et inuidus auctor" (p. 319).

68. *Cronica Tripertita* I.208–10: "Tempore quo stabant hii tres, regnum solidabant, / Legem firmabant victiataque iura fugabant: / Sic emendatum Regem faciunt renouatum" (p. 319).

69. George R. Coffman, "John Gower, Mentor for Royalty: Richard II," *PMLA* 69.4 (1954): 953–64.

70. Brunetto Latini, *Book of the Treasure* III.36, p. 307: "C'est Decius Sillanus, s'en passa briement a poi de paroles sans prologue et sans coverture nule, pour ce que sa matire estoit *de* honeste chose, si comme de livrer a mort les traitors dou commun de Rome" (*Li Livres dou Tresor*, p. 347).

71. On Gower's use of plain style, see Judith D. Shaw, "*Lust* and *Lore* in Gower and Chaucer," *Chaucer Review* 19.2 (1984): 110–22.

72. See the Latin verse inserted between VII.1710 and 1711 of *Confessio*, which introduces the treatment of Truth.

73. See John Gower, *Mirour de l'Omme*, in *Complete Works*, 1: 249–56, ll. 22225–23208. I use this edition for the French text.

74. John Gower, *Mirour de l'Omme (The Mirror of Mankind)*, trans. William B. Wilson, rev. Nancy Wilson Van Baak (East Lansing, Mich.: Colleagues Press, 1992), p. 295, hereafter cited parenthetically in the text. "Tiele est la dueté des Roys, / Amer et servir dieu ainçois, / Et sainte eglise maintenir." *Mirour*, ll. 22237–39, in *Complete Works of John Gower*, 1:249.

75. *Mirour*, l. 22359: "Fai ce q'a ta coronne appent," in *Complete Works of John Gower*, 1:250.

76. See *Mirour*, ll. 22285–91, in *Complete Works of John Gower*, 1:249–50.

77. See Duls, *Early Chronicles*, pp. 37–38.

78. Tuck, *Richard II and the English Nobility*, p. 119; Goodman, *Loyal Conspiracy*, pp. 32–33; Duls, *Early Chronicles*, p. 63. Apparently Richard was temporarily deposed,

and then restored to the throne, owing to internal division among the Appellants about who should succeed him. Gloucester's right was contested by Henry of Derby, who advanced his own claim.

79. Capgrave, *Abbreuiacion of Cronicles*, pp. 195–96.

80. On the Medusa as a common symbol for the carnal reader, see R. A. Shoaf, "*The Franklin's Tale:* Chaucer and Medusa," *Chaucer Review* 21 (1986): 274–90.

81. On the letter of poetry as a siren song, see my *Chaucer and the Universe of Learning* (Ithaca: Cornell University Press, 1996), pp. 192–95; Richard J. Schrader, "Chauntecleer, the Mermaid, and Daun Burnel," *Chaucer Review* 4.4 (1970): 284–90.

82. See Peter G. Biedler, "The Tale of Acteon (*CA*, I, 333–78)," in *John Gower's Literary Transformations in the Confessio Amantis*, ed. Peter G. Biedler (Washington, D.C.: University Press of America, 1982), pp. 7–10.

83. On the hart as Richard's device, see Dillian Gordon, "The White Hart of 'Richart,'" in *Making and Meaning: The Wilton Diptych* (London: National Gallery Publications, 1993), pp. 49–50.

84. Adam of Usk refers to Henry Bolingbroke as "the dog, because of his livery of linked collars of greyhounds, . . . and because he drove utterly from the kingdom countless numbers of harts—the hart being the livery of King Richard." *The Chronicle of Adam Usk, 1377–1421*, ed. and trans. C. Given-Wilson (Oxford: Clarendon Press, 1997), p. 53. The author of *Richard the Redeless* also refers to Bolingbroke as a "greehond" in the context of an allegorical woodland chase of Richard's "hertis." See *Richard the Redeless*, in *Mum and Sothsegger*, ed. Mabel Day and Robert Steele, EETS o.s. 199 (London: Humphrey Milford, Oxford University Press, 1936), II.113–15.

85. Cf. Peck, *Kingship and Common Profit*, p. 39.

4. Chaucer's Ricardian Allegoires

1. I use *The Complete Works of John Gower*, ed. G. C. Macaulay, 4 vols. (Oxford: Clarendon Press, 1899–1902), giving citations to individual works parenthetically (see Chapter 3, n5).

2. See Larry D. Benson, "The Occasion of the Parliament of Fowls," in *The Wisdom of Poetry: Essays in Early English Literature in Honor of Morton W. Bloomfield*, ed. Larry D. Benson and Siegfried Wenzel (Kalamazoo, Mich.: Medieval Institute Publications, 1982), pp. 123–44.

3. I use *The Riverside Chaucer*, ed. Larry D. Benson, 3rd ed. (Boston: Houghton Mifflin, 1987), giving citations parenthetically in the text.

4. For a useful review of scholarship on the question of historical allegory, see the notes in *The Riverside Chaucer*, p. 1061.

5. *Historia Vitae et Regni Ricardi Secundi*, ed. George B. Stow, Jr. (Philadelphia: University of Pennsylvania Press, 1977), p. 166.

6. *Chronicle of Adam Usk*, pp. 1–2.

7. For the sunburst on the monument, see Dillian Gordon, *Making and Meaning: The Wilton Diptych* (London: National Gallery Publications, 1993), p. 61.

8. John M. Bowers, "*Pearl* in Its Royal Setting: Ricardian Poetry Revisited," *SAC* 17 (1995): 139. See also John Cherry, *Medieval Craftsmen: Goldsmiths* (Toronto: University of Toronto Press, 1992), pp. 47–49; John Norton-Smith, *Geoffrey Chaucer* (London: Routledge and Kegan Paul, 1974), pp. 69–71.

9. See Robert B. Burlin, *Chaucerian Fiction* (Princeton: Princeton University Press, 1977), p. 43. According to Anthony Steele, "a considerable number of individual pardons" to participants in the Peasants' Revolt were "granted at the nominal request of the new queen, Anne of Bohemia, during 1382–83." Anthony Steele, *Richard II* (Cambridge: Cambridge University Press, 1962), p. 90.

10. *The Westminster Chronicle, 1381–1394*, ed. and trans. L. C. Hector and Barbara F. Harvey (Oxford: Clarendon Press, 1982), p. 503.

11. *Political Poems and Songs Relating to English History*, ed. Thomas Wright, 2 vols. (London: Longman, Green, Longman, and Roberts, 1859), 297.

12. Ibid., p. 298.

13. Quoted in Judson B. Allen, *The Ethical Poetic of the Later Middle Ages: A Decorum of Convenient Distinction* (Toronto: University of Toronto Press, 1982), p. 265. Allen argues that the Prologue praises Anne for her courageous intercession for Burley.

14. As we have seen, in 1390 Gower uses the phrase "latere age" to characterize Chaucer in *Confessio Amantis*, Book VIII. In the G Prologue to the *Legend*, which Chaucer composed after Anne's death in 1394, Chaucer refers to himself as being old (see ll. 262, 400–401).

15. David Wallace, *Chaucerian Polity: Absolutist Lineages and Associational Forms in England and Italy* (Stanford: Stanford University Press, 1997), p. 371.

16. Ibid., p. 370. For a directly counter argument about the (lack of) "occasionality" of the G Prologue, see John Fisher, "The Revision of the Prologue to the *Legend of Good Women:* An Occasional Explanation," *SAB* 43 (1978): 75–84.

17. Michael Hanrahan, "Seduction and Betrayal: Treason in the *Prologue* to the *Legend of Good Women*," *Chaucer Review* 30.3 (1996): 230.

18. Ibid., p. 239.

19. Ibid.

20. *John Capgrave's Abbreuiacion of Cronicles*, ed. Peter J. Lucas, EETS 285 (Oxford: Oxford University Press, 1983), p. 197.

21. Anthony Tuck, *Richard II and the English Nobility* (London: Edward Arnold, 1973), pp. 140, 155.

22. Hans-Jürgen Diller, "'For Engelondes sake': Richard II and Henry of Lancaster as Intended Readers of Gower's *Confessio Amantis*," in *Functions of Literature: Essays Presented to Erwin Wolff on his Sixtieth Birthday*, ed. Ulrich Broich, Theo Stemmler, and Gerd Stratmann (Tübingen: Max Niemeyer, 1984), p. 49.

23. The dating of the two Prologues has been the subject of scholarly debate. As M. C. E. Shaner and A. S. G. Edwards note in *The Riverside Chaucer*, however, "Most modern critics and editors, while admitting the matter is still open to debate, accept G as the later version and date it 1394 . . . or later, because of the deletion of all reference to Queen Anne" (p. 1060).

24. For an argument that the *Legend* is "complete and finished" (p. 122), see Donald W. Rowe, *Through Nature to Eternity: Chaucer's "Legend of Good Women"* (Lincoln: University of Nebraska Press, 1988).

25. Anthony Goodman, *The Loyal Conspiracy: The Lords Appellant under Richard II* (London: Routledge and Kegan Paul, 1971), p. 62; Louisa D. Duls, *Richard II in the Early Chronicles*, Studies in English Literature 79 (The Hague: Mouton, 1975), p. 73, n. 4; Thomas Walsingham, *Historia Anglicana (1381–1422)*, ed. Henry Thomas Riley, Rolls Series, 28, no. 1, pt. 2 (London: Her Majesty's Stationery Office, 1864; repr. 1965), p. 215; *Annales Ricardi Secundi et Henrici Quarti, Regum Angliae (1392–1406)*, in *Chronica Monasterii S. Albani*, ed. Henry Thomas Riley, Rolls Series 28, no. 3 (London: Longmans, Green, Reader, and Dyer, 1866; repr. 1965), pp. 168–69.

26. Wallace, *Chaucerian Polity*, p. 372.

27. See my *Chaucer and the Universe of Learning* (Ithaca: Cornell University Press, 1996), pp. 179–99; "Chaucer's 'Literature Group' and the Medieval Causes of Books," *ELH* 59 (1992): 269–87.

28. Lee W. Patterson, "'What Man Artow?': Authorial Self-Definition in *The Tale of Sir Thopas* and *The Tale of Melibee*," *SAC* 11 (1989): 117–75. See also C. David Benson, "Their Telling Difference: Chaucer the Pilgrim and His Two Contrasting Tales," *Chaucer Review* 18 (1983): 61–76.

29. On the political implications of the "Melibee," see Lynn Staley Johnson, "Inverse Counsel: Contexts for the *Melibee*," *SP* 87 (1990): 137–55; Gardiner Stillwell, "The Political Meaning of Chaucer's Tale of Melibee," *Speculum* 19 (1944): 433–44.

30. Judith Ferster, *Fictions of Advice: The Literature and Politics of Counsel in Late Medieval England* (Philadelphia: University of Pennsylvania Press, 1996), p. 92.

31. Helen Cooper, *Oxford Guides to Chaucer: The Canterbury Tales* (Oxford: Oxford University Press, 1989), p. 312.

32. Ferster, *Fictions of Advice*, p. 107.

33. [Cicero], *Rhetorica ad C. Herennium*, trans. Harry Caplan, Loeb Classical Library (Cambridge: Harvard University Press, 1954; repr. 1981), IV.xxx.41, pp. 330–31.

34. Ibid., IV.xxvii.37, pp. 320–21.

35. *Riverside Chaucer*, p. 929. For an introduction to Edward and his cult, see Lawrence E. Tanner, "Some Representations of St. Edward the Confessor in Westminster Abbey and Elsewhere," *Journal of the British Archaeological Association*, 3rd ser., 15 (1952): 1–12.

36. Gordon, *Making and Meaning*, p. 54.

37. *English Coronation Records*, ed. Leopold G. Wickham Legg (Westminster: Archibald Constable, 1901), p. 192.

38. Ibid. In his Introduction, Legg argues that, although the king did drink from Edward's chalice, the communion wine was actually consecrated in another chalice, and the presiding archbishop also used another paten (p. lxii).

39. Ibid., p. 166. For the Latin text, see p. 147.

40. Ibid., pp. lxii, 186–87.

41. *Westminster Chronicle*, pp. 414–17. On March 10, 1390, Richard sent, as a partial replacement for the lost shoe, "a pair of red velvet shoes, with fleurs-de-lis worked on them in pearls, which had been blessed by Pope Urban VI shortly before his death" (p. 414).

42. Ibid., p. 9.

43. Ibid.

44. Ibid., p. 11.

45. Ibid., p. 451.

46. Ibid., p. 511.

47. Ibid., p. 507.

48. See *The Life of King Edward*, ed. and trans. Frank Barlow (London: Thomas Nelson, 1984), pp. 14–15; *Lives of Edward the Confessor*, ed. Henry Richards Luard, Rolls Series 3 (London: Longman, Brown, Green, Longman, and Roberts, 1858), pp. 214–15.

49. Caroline M. Barron, "Richard II: Image and Reality," in Gordon, *Making and Meaning*, pp. 15, 18.

50. On the question of the diptych's date and commission, see Gordon, *Making and Meaning*, pp. 59–67.

51. Ibid., p. 60.

52. Barron, "Richard II," p. 18. On the question as to when Richard began to impale his arms with those of the Confessor, see Anthony Steele, *Richard II* (Cambridge: Cambridge University Press, 1962), p. 240.

53. Gordon, *Making and Meaning*, p. 55.

54. Goodman, *Loyal Conspiracy*, p. 25.

55. Tuck, *Richard II and the English Nobility*, p. 71.

56. Goodman, *Loyal Conspiracy*, p. 25.

57. Ibid., p. 103.

58. *Westminster Chronicle*, p. 201.

59. Edward II's cause for canonization was rivaled by that of his political opponent Thomas of Lancaster. See J. W. McKenna, "Popular Canonization as Political Propa-

ganda: The Cult of Archbishop Scrope," *Speculum* 45 (1970): 608–23; Josiah C. Russell, "The Canonization of Opposition to the King in Angevin England," in *Haskins Anniversary Essays in Mediaeval History*, ed. Charles H. Taylor and John L. LaMonte (Boston: Houghton Mifflin, 1929), pp. 279–90.

60. Wallace, *Chaucerian Polity*, p. 331.

61. Tuck, *Richard II and the English Nobility*, p. 71. See also G. P. Cuttino and T. W. Lyman, "Where Is Edward II?" *Speculum* 53 (1978): 522–43.

62. *The Diplomatic Correspondence of Richard II*, ed. Edouard Perroy, Camden 3rd Series, vol. 48 (London: Royal Historical Society, 1933), letter no. 95, p. 62.

63. *Westminster Chronicle*, p. 437. For evidence of the cult of Edward II, see *Adam Davy's Five Dreams about Edward II*, ed. F. J. Furnivall, EETS o.s. 69 (London: Trübner, 1878). The manuscript of Davy's *Dreams* suggests that Edward II, like Edward the Confessor, was associated with Saint Alexius, a prince who married against his will.

64. Steel, *Richard II*, p. 122; Tuck, *Richard II and the English Nobility*, p. 103.

65. Barron, "Richard II," p. 18.

66. *Westminster Chronicle*, p. 159.

67. *Riverside Chaucer*, p. 933.

68. Chaucer, unlike Dante in *Inferno* 33, does not charge Ugolino with cannibalism. According to Chaucer's Monk, Ugolino gnawed the arms of his dead child (or possibly his own arms) "for wo" and not "for hunger" (VII.2444–49).

69. Wallace, *Chaucerian Polity*, p. 331. See pp. 319–31 for a detailed discussion of the Bernabò stanza.

70. Donald K. Fry, "The Ending of the *Monk's Tale*," *JEGP* 71 (1972): 355–68, esp. 356–57.

71. In seven *Canterbury Tales* manuscripts, the Monk is interrupted by the Host rather than by the Knight.

72. See Charles S. Watson, "The Relationship of the 'Monk's Tale' and the 'Nun's Priest's Tale,'" *Studies in Short Fiction* 1 (1964): 277–88.

73. For recent attempts to probe the significance of Chaucer's historical allusions in this tale, see Richard W. Fehrenbacher, "'A Yeerd Enclosed Al Aboute': Literature and History in the 'Nun's Priest's Tale,'" *Chaucer Review* 29.2 (1994): 134–48; Peter W. Travis, "Chaucer's Trivial Fox Chase and the Peasants' Revolt of 1381," *Journal of Medieval and Renaissance Studies* 18 (1988): 195–220.

74. For a well-known but unconvincing attempt at an allegorical reading, see J. Leslie Hotson, "Colfox vs. Chaunticleer," *PMLA* 39 (1924): 762–81.

75. Robert A. Pratt, "Some Latin Sources of the Nonnes Preest on Dreams," *Speculum* 52.3 (1977): 538–70, esp. 547. Chauntecleer's examples of Croesus and Daniel echo "The Monk's Tale," and the example of Andromache appears in *Renart le Contrefait*, an analogue of the tale. The rest of Chauntecleer's examples, with the exception of Saint Kenelm, derive from Holcot's commentary.

76. *Chronicle of Adam Usk*, pp. 1–2.

77. Thomas Walsingham, *Historia Anglicana (1272–1381)*, ed. Henry Thomas Riley, Rolls Series 28, no. 1, pt. 1 (London: Her Majesty's Stationery Office, 1863, repr. 1965), p. 332.

78. *The Early South-English Legendary*, ed. Carl Horstmann, EETS o.s. 87 (London: N. Trübner, 1887; repr. 1973), pp. 348–49.

79. Pratt, "Some Latin Sources," p. 558, n. 49. See *Early South-English Legendary*, p. 348.

80. *Early South-English Legendary*, p. 349.

81. Ibid., p. 350.

82. Ibid., pp. 351–53.

83. Kate Oelzner Petersen, *On the Sources of the Nonne Preste Tale* (1898; New York: Haskell, 1966), pp. 9, 67–68.

84. *Early South-English Legendary,* p. 351.

85. Duls, *Early Chronicles,* p. 114.

86. John Gower, *Vox Clamantis,* in *Complete Works,* VI.vii.555, 4:246.

87. Hanrahan, "Seduction and Betrayal," p. 236.

88. The ancient coat of arms of the English kings displays three lions passant.

89. For a strong refutation of this view, see Douglas Kelly, "Theory of Composition in Medieval Narrative Poetry and Geoffrey of Vinsauf's *Poetria Nova,*" *Mediaeval Studies* 31 (1969): 117–48.

90. John Gower, "The Voice of One Crying," in *The Major Latin Works of John Gower,* trans. Eric W. Stockton (Seattle: University of Washington Press, 1962), pp. 53–54; hereafter cited parenthetically in the text.

91. This paragraph and the preceding one are taken from my essay "The Peasants' Revolt: Cock-crow in Gower and Chaucer," in *Four Last Things: Death, Judgment, Heaven, and Hell in the Middle Ages,* ed. Allen J. Frantzen, Essays in Medieval Studies 10, 1993 Proceedings of the Illinois Medieval Association (Chicago: Loyola University Press, 1994), pp. 53–64.

92. *Historia Vitae et Regni Ricardi Secundi,* ed. Stow, p. 65.

93. Charles Oman, *The Great Revolt of 1381,* ed. E. B. Fryde, 2nd ed. (1906; Oxford: Clarendon Press, 1969), p. 69.

94. Ibid., p. 76.

95. Translated in *The Peasants' Revolt of 1381,* ed. and trans. R. B. Dobson, 2nd ed. (London: Macmillan, 1983), p. 178. The Latin text reads: "Rex vero ultra aetatem mirabiliter ingenio praeventus, et audacia concitus, calcaribus urgens equum ad eos accessit, et in circuitu eorum equitans, dixit eis: 'Quid est hoc, homines mei? Quid agitis? Nunquid sagittare vultis Regem vestrum? Non causemini, nec sitis tristes de morte proditoris et ribaldi. Ego enim cro Rex vester, ego capitaneus et ductor vester; sequimini me in campum.'" Walsingham, *Historia Anglicana (1272–1381),* p. 465.

96. Ferster, *Fictions of Advice,* p. 33.

97. Ibid., p. 38.

98. See Dolores W. Frese, "The *Nun's Priest's Tale:* Chaucer's Identified Masterpiece?" *Chaucer Review* 16 (1982): 330–43.

5. Penitential Politics in *Sir Gawain and the Green Knight*

1. "Introduction" to *Sir Gawain and the Green Knight,* ed. J. R. R. Tolkien and E. V. Gordon, 2nd ed., ed. Norman Blake (Oxford: Clarendon Press, 1967; repr. 1984), p. xi. I use this edition throughout, citing line numbers parenthetically in the text.

2. W. G. Cooke, "*Sir Gawain and the Green Knight:* A Restored Dating," *Medium Aevum* 58.1 (1989): 34. Cooke argues, against what he acknowledges to be the "accepted commonplace" of a late fourteenth-century dating, for a midcentury composition, on the sole grounds that Gawain is armed in "cote-armure" instead of a breastplate (p. 42).

3. Angus McIntosh, "A New Approach to Middle English Dialectology," *English Studies* 44 (1963): 1–11, esp. 5. See also Angus McIntosh, M. L. Samuels, and Michael Benskin, *A Linguistic Atlas of Late Medieval English* (Aberdeen: Aberdeen University Press, 1986), 3:37–38.

4. See Ralph W. V. Elliott, "Hills and Valleys in the *Gawain*-Country," *Leeds Studies in English,* n. s. 10 (1978): 18–41; idem, "Woods and Forests in the *Gawain*-Country," *Neuphilologische Mitteilungen* 80 (1979): 48–64.

5. Michael J. Bennett, *Community, Class, and Careerism: Cheshire and Lancashire Society in the Age of Sir Gawain and the Green Knight,* Cambridge Studies in Medieval Life and Thought, 3rd ser., no. 18 (Cambridge: Cambridge University Press, 1983), p. 234. See

also his "*Sir Gawain and the Green Knight* and the Literary Achievement of the North-West Midlands," *Journal of Medieval History* 5 (1979): 63–89.

6. John M. Bowers, "*Pearl* in Its Royal Setting: Ricardian Poetry Revisited," *SAC* 17 (1995): 113.

7. For an early attempt, see J. R. Hulbert, "A Hypothesis Concerning the Alliterative Revival," *MP* 28 (1931): 405–22. For a more recent attempt, see William McColly, "*Sir Gawain and the Green Knight* as a Romance à Clef," *Chaucer Review* 23.1 (1988): 78–92.

8. Bowers ascribes a late date to *Pearl* and treats *Sir Gawain* as the earlier of the two poems, dating it in the "mid-1380s, when northern interests were braced against a royal court mostly concentrated in the southeast during Richard's minority" ("*Pearl* in Its Royal Setting," p. 119). My argument necessitates dating *Sir Gawain* after 1397, when Richard's situation was very different. Bowers's fine essay was called to my attention after I had drafted mine.

9. Larry D. Benson, *Art and Tradition in "Sir Gawain and the Green Knight"* (New Brunswick, N.J.: Rutgers University Press, 1965), p. 28.

10. See ibid., pp. 124–25, for a discussion of the poet's characteristic use of "variation" or *expolitio*.

11. Anthony Tuck, *Richard II and the English Nobility* (London: Edward Arnold, 1973), pp. 116–17; W. R. J. Barron, *Trawthe and Treason: The Sin of Gawain Reconsidered* (Manchester: Manchester University Press, 1980), pp. 36–37.

12. Tuck, *English Nobility,* pp. 121–26.

13. Ibid., pp. 187–90.

14. *Historia Vitae et Regni Ricardi Secundi,* ed. George B. Stow, Jr. (Philadelphia: University of Pennsylvania Press, 1977), p. 117.

15. See *The Major Latin Works of John Gower,* trans. Eric W. Stockton (Seattle: University of Washington Press, 1962), p. 481, n. 19.

16. Benson, *Art and Tradition,* p. 28.

17. William Langland, *Piers Plowman: The B Version,* ed. George Kane and E. Talbot Donaldson (London: Athlone Press, 1975), Prologue, l. 196.

18. *Chronicle of Adam Usk,* p. 140.

19. John Gower, *The Tripartite Chronicle,* in *Major Latin Works,* I.15–16, p. 290. For the Latin text, see John Gower, *Cronica Tripertita,* in *The Complete Works of John Gower,* ed. G. C. Macaulay, 4 vols. (Oxford: Clarendon Press, 1902), 4:314.

20. *Richard the Redeless,* in *Mum and the Sothsegger,* ed. Mabel Day and Robert Steele, EETS o.s. 199 (London: Humphrey Milford, Oxford University Press, 1936), I.87–88. Subsequent citations are given parenthetically in the text by Passus and line number.

21. Benson, *Art and Tradition,* pp. 3–55.

22. Ibid., p. 273, n. 33.

23. Louisa D. Duls, *Richard II in the Early Chronicles,* Studies in English Literature 79 (The Hague: Mouton, 1975), p. 87.

24. *John Capgrave's Abbreuiacion of Cronicles,* ed. Peter J. Lucas, EETS 285 (Oxford: Oxford University Press, 1983), p. 208.

25. *Annales Ricardi Secundi et Henrici Quarti, Regum Angliae (1392–1406),* in *Chronica Monasterii S. Albani,* ed. Henry Thomas Riley, Rolls Series, 28, no. 3 (London: Longmans, Green, Reader, and Dyer, 1866; repr. 1965), p. 216; translated in Duls, *Early Chronicles,* p. 79.

26. *Annales Ricardi,* p. 218; trans. Duls, *Early Chronicles,* p. 79. The syntax of the Latin text emphasizes the length of time that the trunk stood erect: "Corpus truncum se erexit in pedes, stetitque, nullo sustentante. per tantum spatium temporis quo Oratio Dominica posset dici."

27. See Thomas Walsingham, *Historia Anglicana,* ed. Henry Thomas Riley, Rolls Series, 28, no. 1, pt. 2 (London: Her Majesty's Stationery Office, 1864; repr. 1965), p. 226.

28. *Chronicle of Adam Usk*, p. 31.

29. Gower, *Tripartite Chronicle* II.147–48, p. 304; *Cronica Tripertita*, p. 324.

30. *Capgrave's Abbreuiacions*, p. 208; *Annales Ricardi*, pp. 218–19.

31. *Capgrave's Abbreuiacions*, pp. 208–9.

32. *Annales Ricardi*, p. 219. On the hidden grave of Arundel, see also Gower, *Tripartite Chronicle* II.156, trans. Stockton, p. 305; *Cronica Tripertita*, p. 324.

33. For Arundel's "notorious tactlessness," see Anthony Goodman, *The Loyal Conspiracy: The Lords Appellant under Richard II* (London: Routledge and Kegan Paul, 1971), pp. 62, 105. Arundel offended Richard by his apparent rudeness at Queen Anne's funeral on August 3, 1394—so much so that Richard struck him in the face, desecrating Westminster Abbey with his blood, and had him imprisoned in the Tower. See Duls, *Early Chronicles*, p. 73, n. 4; *Annales Ricardi*, p. 169.

34. *Chronicle of Adam Usk*, p. 29.

35. See Robert E. Kaske, "Gawain's Green Chapel and the Cave at Wetton Mill," in *Medieval Literature and Folklore Studies: Essays in Honor of Francis Lee Utley*, ed. Jerome Mandel and Bruce A. Rosenberg (New Brunswick, N.J.: Rutgers University Press, 1970), pp. 111–21.

36. Gower, *Tripartite Chronicle*, I.46, II.53–54, pp. 291, 301; *Cronica Tripertita*, pp. 315, 321.

37. *Annales Ricardi*, p. 206.

38. See "On the King's Ministers," in *Political Poems and Songs Relating to English History*, ed. Thomas Wright, 2 vols. (London, 1859–61), 1:363–66.

39. Benson, *Art and Tradition*, p. 90. For studies of these two types, see Richard Bernheimer, *Wild Men in the Middle Ages: A Study in Art, Sentiment, and Demonology* (New York: Octagon Books, 1970), and William Anderson, *Green Man* (London: HarperCollins, 1990).

40. Tuck, *English Nobility*, pp. 191, 199.

41. Benson, *Art and Tradition*, p. 30.

42. Duls, *Early Chronicles*, p. 33.

43. *Chronicle of Adam Usk*, p. 11.

44. Gower, *Tripartite Chronicle*, I.66, p. 292; *Cronica Tripertita*, p. 316.

45. Duls, *Early Chronicles*, p. 33.

46. Tuck, *English Nobility*, pp. 121, 138.

47. *Annales Ricardi*, pp. 184–85.

48. The occurrence of these events in December may have inspired the *Gawain*-poet to place the appearance of the Green Knight at Camelot at Christmastime rather than at Pentecost, the usual time in Arthurian romances for miraculous intrusions.

49. Tuck, *English Nobility*, p. 83.

50. Ibid., p. 84.

51. Ibid., p. 85. Cf. McColly, "Romance à Clef," p. 80.

52. Walsingham, *Historia Anglicana*, p. 227.

53. Sir Charles Oman, *Political History of England*, vol. 4, ed. William Hunt and Reginald L. Poole (London: Longmans, Green, 1930), 137.

54. Tuck, *English Nobility*, p. 192.

55. Ibid., p. 85. As Tuck notes, Richard II himself used the imagery of crown and gems to describe the king's relationship to the nobility.

56. Much has been written about the symbol. See, for example, Robert W. Ackerman, "Gawain's Shield: Penitential Doctrine in *Sir Gawain and the Green Knight*," *Anglia* 76 (1958): 254–65; Richard H. Green, "Gawain's Shield and the Quest for Perfection," *ELH* 29.2 (1962): 121–39; Gerald Morgan, "The Significance of the Pentangle Symbolism in *Sir Gawain and the Green Knight*," *MLR* 74 (1979): 769–90; A. D. Horgan, "Gawain's *Pure Pentaungle* and the Virtue of Faith," *Medium Aevum* 56 (1987): 310–16; Ross G.

Arthur, *Medieval Sign Theory and "Sir Gawain and the Green Knight"* (Toronto: University of Toronto Press, 1987), esp. pp. 18–46.

57. See *Sir Gawain and the Green Knight*, pp. 92–93.

58. Henry Lyttleton Savage, *The Gawain-Poet: Studies in His Personality and Background* (Chapel Hill: University of North Carolina Press, 1956), p. 168.

59. Ibid., p. 168. Savage himself proposed Enguerrand de Coucy, the father of Robert de Vere's wife, Philippa.

60. McColly, "Romance à Clef," p. 81. See Arthur Charles Fox-Davies, *A Complete Guide to Heraldry*, illustrated by Graham Johnston, rev. ed. (London: T. C. and E. C. Jack, 1929), p. 134. In keeping with the principle of variation, the poet may have given Gawain a gold, rather than an argent, mullet because Gawain (unlike de Vere) was of royal blood. See Savage, *Gawain-Poet*, p. 162.

61. Fox-Davies, *Guide to Heraldry*, pp. 295–96.

62. Tuck, *English Nobility*, p. 62.

63. Ibid., pp. 117–19; Goodman, *Loyal Conspiracy*, p. 27.

64. *Sir Gawain and the Green Knight*, p. 100. See McColly, "Romance à Clef," pp. 80–81.

65. *Sir Gawain and the Green Knight*, p. 129. See the conclusion of this chapter for a related hagiographic interpretation of "Bertilak de Hautdesert."

66. Goodman, *Loyal Conspiracy*, p. 113. Arundel's other properties in the northwest included Chirk Castle and Chirkland, Oswestry Castle and Lordship, Clun Castle and Clunsland, and Shrawardine Castle in Shropshire.

67. Ibid.

68. Ibid., p. 61.

69. Ibid., p. 121.

70. Tuck, *English Nobility*, p. 192.

71. Ibid. On Holt Castle, see also N. J. G. Pounds, *The Medieval Castle in England and Wales: A Social and Political History* (Cambridge: Cambridge University Press, 1990), pp. 170, 253.

72. According to Ralph Elliott, in the poet's dialect, "*holt* signified hilly as well as wooded terrain" ("Woods and Forests," p. 52).

73. See Donald R. Howard, "Structure and Symmetry in *Sir Gawain*," *Speculum* 39 (1964): 425–33; A. C. Spearing, *The Gawain-Poet* (Cambridge: Cambridge University Press, 1970), pp. 180–219; Gerald Morgan, "The Action of the Hunting and Bedroom Scenes in *Sir Gawain and the Green Knight*," *Medium Aevum* 56 (1987): 200–216.

74. Savage, *The Gawain-Poet*, p. 32.

75. Debra Hassig, *Medieval Bestiaries: Text, Image, Ideology*, RES Monographs on Anthropology and Aesthetics (Cambridge: Cambridge University Press, 1995), p. 210, n. 2. On the hart as Richard's device, see Dillian Gordon, "The White Hart of 'Richart,'" in *Making and Meaning: The Wilton Diptych* (London: National Gallery Publications, 1993), pp. 49–50.

76. *Chronicle of Adam Usk*, p. 53.

77. Gower, *Tripartite Chronicle* I.71–72, p. 292; *Cronica Tripertita*, p. 316.

78. Gower, *Tripartite Chronicle*, I.85, p. 293; *Cronica Tripertita*, p. 316. On the general significance of the boar, see Hassig, *Medieval Bestiary*, pp. 46, 88, 174.

79. John A. Burrow, *A Reading of "Sir Gawain and the Green Knight"* (London: Routledge and Kegan Paul, 1965), p. 97.

80. Savage, *The Gawain-Poet*, p. 46. See also Hassig, *Medieval Bestiaries*, pp. 62–71.

81. Mention of Gloucester's other cognizance, the badge of the Swan, appears in Gower's *Cronica Tripertita* and in *Richard the Redeless* (III.26–30).

82. Duls, *Early Chronicles*, p. 75; *Annales Ricardi*, p. 206: "semper ferebatur super hastam, in ejus praesentia, cauda vulpis."

83. Gower, *Tripartite Chronicle* I.87 and Latin sidenote, p. 293; *Cronica Tripertita*, p. 316.

84. Tuck, *English Nobility*, p. 78.

85. Ibid; Duls, *Early Chronicles*, p. 59.

86. Walsingham, *Historia Anglicana*, 2:160. Richard II supposedly approved the match between Lancecrona and de Vere because of a "maleficium" cast on him by a friar in de Vere's household.

87. Ibid., 2:156.

88. Previous approaches to *Sir Gawain* as a penitential romance have focused on the confession scenes. See John A. Burrow, "The Two Confession Scenes in *Sir Gawain and the Green Knight*," *MP* 57 (1959): 73–79; Michael M. Foley, "Gawain's Two Confessions Reconsidered," *Chaucer Review* 9.1 (1974): 73–79.

89. Quoted in Duls, *Early Chronicles*, p. 8.

90. Goodman, *Loyal Conspiracy*, p. 108.

91. Ibid., p. 106.

92. *Annales Ricardi*, p. 219.

93. Victoria Weiss, "Gawain's First Failure: The Beheading Game in *Sir Gawain and the Green Knight*," *Chaucer Review* 10 (1976): 361–66; Sheri Ann Strite, "*Sir Gawain and the Green Knight*: To Behead or Not to Behead—That *Is* a Question," *PQ* 70.1 (1991): 1–12.

94. Ronald Tamplin, "The Saints in *Sir Gawain and the Green Knight*," *Speculum* 44.3 (1969): 403. See also Robert J. Blanch, "The Game of Invoking Saints in *Sir Gawain and the Green Knight*," *American Benedictine Review* 31 (1980): 237–62.

95. See Gordon, *Wilton Diptych*, pp. 54–55; Arthur Penrhyn Stanley, *Historical Memorials of Westminster Abbey*, 8th ed. (London: John Murray, 1896), p. 124.

96. Stanley, *Historical Memorials*, pp. 14–20.

97. Ibid., p. 25.

98. Ibid., p. 27.

99. Ibid., p. 105. See Gordon, *Wilton Diptych*, p. 54. The story of the ring is recounted in "St. John the Evangelist," in *The South English Legendary*, ed. Charlotte D'Evelyn and Anna J. Mill, 2 vols., EETS 235 and 236 (London: Oxford University Press, 1956), 2:609–10.

100. Stanley, *Historical Memorials*, p. 26. Stanley notes that Queen Philippa of Hanault (d. 1369), the mother of Edward III's seven sons, used this Marian relic repeatedly to protect herself against the dangers of childbirth. On the Virgin's girdle, see Richard H. Green, "Sir Gawain and the *Sacra Cintola*," *English Studies in Canada* 11 (1985): 1–11.

101. Stanley, *Historical Memorials*, p. 125. See also Gordon, *Wilton Diptych*, pp. 55, 61; Bowers, "*Pearl* in Its Royal Setting," p. 126.

102. On the portrait of Richard, see Gordon, *Wilton Diptych*, p. 40; E. W. Tristram, *English Wall Painting of the Fourteenth Century* (London: Routledge and Kegan Paul, 1955), pp. 42–43.

103. Stanley, *Historical Memorials*, p. 124.

104. Gordon, *Wilton Diptych*, p. 62.

105. Ibid., pp. 55–57.

106. "St. Julian," in *South English Legendary*, 1:384–389. In this synopsis I quote directly ll. 11, 19, 21, 49, 82. See also Jacobus de Voragine, *The Golden Legend: Readings on the Saints*, trans. William Granger Ryan, 2 vols. (Princeton: Princeton University Press, 1993), 1:127–28.

107. The *Legenda Aurea* and the *South English Legendary* say only that Julian was away from home when his parents arrived. The Old French Prose Life, however, specifies that he was out hunting. See Benjamin F. Bart and Robert Francis Cook, *The Legendary Sources of Flaubert's "Saint Julien"* (Toronto: University of Toronto Press, 1977), p. 53; Eugène Vinaver, *The Rise of Romance* (New York: Oxford University Press, 1971), pp. 114–16.

108. Cf. Tamplin, "The Saints," p. 406. Ignoring the hagiographic intertexts leads

Andrea Hopkins to emphasize the unusualness of *Sir Gawain* as a penitential romance, in *The Sinful Knights: A Study of Middle English Penitential Romances* (Oxford: Clarendon Press, 1990), pp. 204–18.

109. Tamplin, "The Saints," p. 407.

110. "St. Giles," in *South English Legendary*, 2:384–89. In this synopsis I quote directly ll. 110, 129, 147. See also Jacobus de Voragine, *The Golden Legend*, 2:147–49.

111. For scriptural references to John the Baptist, see Matthew 3:1–17, 11:1–19, 14:1–12; Mark 1:1–11, 6:14–29; Luke 1:57–80, 3:1–22, 7:18–35, 9:7–9. I thank Thomas Ohlgren for pointing out to me that John also (albeit figuratively) wielded an ax.

112. As Tolkien and Gordon note (*Sir Gawain and the Green Knight*, p. 128), and as my learned colleague Thomas Kelly has instructed me, the name "Bertilak" appears in numerous Old French romances. See G. D. West, *An Index of Proper Names in French Arthurian Prose Romances* (Toronto: University of Toronto Press, 1978). "Lac" or "Lak" also appears in English surnames and placenames, however (O.E. *lacu* = lake, pool); and according to *The Middle English Dictionary*, by the fourteenth century the word "lak" was also used with the meaning "basin." "Berti" sounds sufficiently like "birthe" (from O.E. *byrþ*) to suggest the meaning of "birth." Thus "Berti" + "lak" could be decoded as a "birth basin" or baptismal font.

113. Gordon, *Wilton Diptych*, p. 55.

114. Ibid., p. 56.

115. *Annales Ricardi*, p. 238.

116. *Historia Vitae Ricardi Secundi*, p. 47. John's actual feast, observed with a vigil, is June 24.

117. See Bowers, "*Pearl* in Its Royal Setting," p. 124.

118. According to E. W. Tristram, "a very considerable increase in paintings of St. John the Baptist is noticeable" in the late fourteenth century (*English Wall Paintings*, p. 26).

119. Ibid., p. 184. The wall painting is described on pp. 184–85 and is reproduced in plates 42–45. I owe this reference to my colleague Thomas Ohlgren, who kindly pointed it out to me.

120. It is worth noting that another of Richard's favorite saints, Saint Edmund, who is pictured along with Saints Edward the Confessor and John the Baptist in the Wilton Diptych, also suffered beheading. His severed head spoke, and it was miraculously rejoined to his body in the grave. See *South English Legendary*, 2:511–15.

121. See Bowers, "*Pearl* in Its Royal Setting," p. 123.

122. *Annales Ricardi*, p. 201.

123. Ibid., p. 202.

124. Gordon, *Wilton Diptych*, p. 56.

125. *Annales Ricardi*, p. 232.

126. Ibid., p. 237.

127. See Tuck, *English Nobility*, pp. 192–93; Bowers, "*Pearl* in Its Royal Setting," pp. 136–37. On the emblematic use of the *planta genista* by Richard II as part of the king's livery, see Gordon, *Wilton Diptych*, pp. 51–53.

6. Joan of Arc, Margaret of Anjou, and Malory's Guenevere

1. W. T. Waugh, "Joan of Arc in English Sources of the Fifteenth Century," in *Historical Essays in Honour of James Tait*, ed. J. G. Edwards, V. H. Galbraith, and E. F. Jacob (Manchester: Butler and Tanner, 1933), p. 387. For a useful survey of Jehannine chronicle entries, see Nadia Margolis, *Joan of Arc in History, Literature, and Film: A Select, Annotated Bibliography* (New York: Garland, 1990).

2. Waugh, "Joan of Arc in English Sources," p. 392.

3. Ibid., p. 393; V. J. Scattergood, *Politics and Poetry in the Fifteenth Century* (London: Blandford, 1971), p. 80.

4. James Darmesteter, "Joan of Arc in England," in *English Studies*, trans. Mary Darmesteter (London: T. Fisher Unwin, 1896), p. 10.

5. Deborah Fraioli, "The Literary Image of Joan of Arc: Prior Influences," *Speculum* 56.4 (1981): 811.

6. Nellie Slayton Aurner, "Sir Thomas Malory—Historian?" *PMLA* 48.2 (1933): 383. Aurner notes, furthermore, that Sir Thomas Malory of Warwickshire served in the retinue of Richard Beauchamp, earl of Warwick, in France. As a result, "he would have witnessed the crowning of Henry VI in Paris and probably have been on duty in Rouen at the burning of Jeanne d'Arc" (p. 362). The identification of this Thomas Malory with the Malory who wrote the *Morte Darthur* is, however, highly dubious.

7. Richard R. Griffith, "The Authorship Question Reconsidered: A Case for Thomas Malory of Papworth St. Agnes, Cambridgeshire," in *Aspects of Malory*, ed. Toshiyuki Takamiya and Derek Brewer (Cambridge: D. S. Brewer, 1981), pp. 159–77. See also R. M. Lumiansky, "Sir Thomas Malory's *Le Morte Darthur*, 1947–1987: Author, Title, Text," *Speculum* 62.4 (1987): 878–97.

8. Richard R. Griffith, "The Political Bias of Malory's *Morte Darthur*," *Viator* 5 (1974): 365–86.

9. Thomas Malory, *Works*, ed. Eugène Vinaver, 2nd ed., 3 vols. (Oxford: Clarendon Press, 1967; repr. 1973), 3:1174; hereafter cited parenthetically by page in the text.

10. For a treatment of this episode, see E. Kay Harris, "Evidence against Lancelot and Guenevere in Malory's *Morte Darthur*: Treason by Imagination," *Exemplaria* 7.1 (1995): 179–208.

11. On the question of sources, see Edward D. Kennedy, "Malory and His English Sources," in Takamiya and Brewer, *Aspects of Malory*, pp. 27–55.

12. Ernest C. York, "Legal Punishment in Malory's *Le Morte Darthur*," *ELN* 11 (1973): 16.

13. J. R. Reinhard, "Burning at the Stake in Medieval Law and Literature," *Speculum* 16 (1941): 186.

14. York, "Legal Punishment," p. 20.

15. Barbara Hanawalt, "The Female Felon in Fourteenth-Century England," *Viator* 5 (1974): 265.

16. On the punishment for heresy, see Edward Peters, *Inquisition* (London: Collier Macmillan, 1988).

17. This letter was published for the first time in English translation in 1548 in Edward Hall's *Union of the Two Noble and Illustre Famelies of Lancastre and Yorke*. I quote from Hall's *Chronicle* (1809; New York: AMS Press, 1965), p. 157.

18. *The Retrial of Joan of Arc*, ed. Régine Pernoud, trans. J. M. Cohen (London: Methuen, 1955), p. 221.

19. Ralph Higden, *Polychronicon, Together with the English Translations of John Trevisa*, ed. Joseph R. Lumby, Rolls Series 8, no. 41 (London, 1882; Wiesbaden: Kraus Reprint, 1964), p. 561.

20. Ibid.

21. Waugh, "Joan of Arc in English Sources," p. 395.

22. Hanawalt, "Female Felon," p. 266.

23. *Procès de Condamnation et de Réhabilitation de Jeanne D'Arc Dite la Pucelle*, ed. Jules Quicherat, 5 vols. (1845; New York: Johnson Reprint, 1965), 3:140, 154.

24. *Procès*, 3:147–48; *Retrial*, p. 162.

25. *Procès*, 2:298–99; *Retrial*, p. 177.

26. *Procès*, 2:5, 8, 3:168; *Retrial*, pp. 183, 209, 211.

27. J. R. Lander, *Conflict and Stability in Fifteenth-Century England* (London: Hutchinson University Library, 1969), p. 67.

28. The English purchased Joan for ten thousand gold coins from the duke of Burgundy, whose liegeman Jean de Luxembourg had captured her at Compiègne. See Scattergood, *Politics and Poetry,* p. 80.

29. *From Camelot to Joyous Guard: The Old French "La Mort Le Roi Artu,"* trans. J. Neale Carman, ed. Norris J. Lacy (Lawrence: University Press of Kansas, 1974), p. 83; *La Mort Le Roi Artu,* ed. Jean Frappier (Paris: M. J. Minard, 1964), p. 123.

30. *Le Morte Arthur: A Romance in Stanzas of Eight Lines,* ed. J. Douglas Bruce, EETS e.s. 88 (London: Kegan Paul, Trench, Trübner, 1903), pp. 57–58.

31. I use the term "martyr" in a popular, rather than technical, sense. Joan of Arc was actually canonized in 1920 as a virgin, not a martyr, because she died as a political figure, not "for the faith," as the early Christian martyrs did. On the definition of martyrdom, see Kenneth L. Woodward, *Making Saints* (New York: Simon and Schuster, 1990), pp. 127–55.

32. *The Trial of Jeanne d'Arc,* trans. W. P. Barrett (London: Routledge, 1931), p. 115; "voces ei dixerunt quod ipsa liberabitur per magnam victoriam" (*Procès,* 1:155).

33. See G. L. Harriss, *Cardinal Beaufort: A Study of Lancastrian Ascendancy and Decline* (Oxford: Clarendon Press, 1988), pp. 209–10.

34. *Retrial,* p. 212; *Procès,* 2:352.

35. *Retrial,* p. 186; *Procès,* 2:19.

36. *Retrial,* p. 188; *Procès,* 3:53.

37. *Retrial,* p. 189; *Procès,* 3:182.

38. *Retrial,* p. 189; *Procès,* 3:182.

39. *Retrial,* pp. 189–90.

40. Hall, *Chronicle,* p. 158.

41. *From Camelot to Joyous Guard,* p. 82; *Mort Artu,* p. 122.

42. As Scattergood explains, Edward IV was "so called because his badge was the rose, and because he was born at Rouen" (*Politics and Poetry,* p. 190).

43. Phyllis Rackin, *Stages of History: Shakespeare's English Chronicles* (Ithaca: Cornell University Press, 1990), p. 157. On the differing attitudes of the French and the English toward royal adulterers, see Charles Wood, *Joan of Arc and Richard III: Sex, Saints, and Government in the Middle Ages* (New York: Oxford University Press, 1988).

44. William Shakespeare, *The First Part of King Henry VI,* Arden edition, ed. Andrew S. Cairncross (1962; London and New York: Routledge, 1969; repr. 1995), p. 114; hereafter cited parenthetically in the text.

45. Pius II, *Commentaries, Books VI–IX,* trans. Florence Alden Gragg, with historical notes by Leona C. Gabel, Smith College Studies in History 35 (Northampton, Mass.: Department of History of Smith College, 1951), p. 580. Quoted in Patricia-Ann Lee, "Reflections of Power: Margaret of Anjou and the Dark Side of Queenship," *Renaissance Quarterly* 39 (1986): 198–99.

46. Pius II, *Commentaries,* p. 580; Lee, "Reflections of Power," pp. 198–99. In Shakespeare's own time, Queen Elizabeth, a virgin and a battle leader, was inevitably associated with both Margaret of Anjou and Joan of Arc. See Leah S. Marcus, *Puzzling Shakespeare: Local Reading and Its Discontents* (Berkeley: University of California Press, 1988), esp. pp. 52–53, 89.

47. Lee, "Reflections of Power," p. 185.

48. Scattergood, *Politics and Poetry,* p. 104.

49. Lee, "Reflections of Power," p. 193.

50. Charles Ross, *Edward IV* (Berkeley: University of California Press, 1974), p. 107.

51. Ibid., p. 109.

52. Ibid., pp. 113–14.

53. Ibid., p. 122.

54. Ibid., p. 123.

55. Ibid., p. 126.

56. Nellie Slayton Aurner, ed. *Malory: An Introduction to the Morte Darthur* (New York: Thomas Nelson, 1938), p. xxvi.

57. Larry D. Benson, *Malory's "Morte Darthur"* (Cambridge: Harvard University Press, 1976), p. 180.

58. Ibid., p. 179.

59. Ibid., p. 180. Henry Beaufort, earl of Somerset, was another of Margaret's favorites.

60. Judson Boyce Allen, *The Ethical Poetic of the Late Middle Ages: A Decorum of Convenient Distinction* (Toronto: University of Toronto Press, 1982), p. 151.

61. Agnes Sorel became Charles's mistress in 1444.

62. Griffith, "Political Bias," p. 366. For a composite Lancastrian interpretation, see Aurner, "Sir Thomas Malory—Historian?"

63. Edward D. Kennedy, "Malory and the Marriage of Edward IV," *Texas Studies in Literature and Language* 12 (1970): 161–62.

64. Ibid., p. 161.

65. Griffith, "Political Bias," p. 385.

66. Ibid., p. 380.

67. Ibid., p. 377.

68. *Historical Poems of the XIVth and XVth Centuries*, ed. Rossell Hope Robbins (New York: Columbia University Press, 1959), p. 227.

69. Quoted in Scattergood, *Politics and Poetry*, p. 205.

70. Beverly Kennedy, *Knighthood in the Morte Darthur*, Arthurian Studies II (Cambridge: D. S. Brewer, 1985), p. 55.

71. Ibid., p. 345.

72. Griffith, "Political Bias," p. 380.

73. Sidney Anglo, "The *British History* in Early Tudor Propaganda," *Bulletin of the John Rylands Library* 44 (1961): 22.

74. Ibid.

75. Griffith, "Political Bias," p. 381.

76. Anglo, "The *British History*," pp. 43–45.

77. I use Angus J. Kennedy and Kenneth Varty's translation of Christine de Pisan, "Le Ditié de Jehanne d'Arc," *Nottingham Medieval Studies* 18 (1974): 29–55; 19 (1975): 53–76. For an excellent study of the prophetic elements in the poem, see Kevin Brownlee, "Structures of Authority in Christine de Pizan's *Ditié de Jehanne d'Arc*," in *The Selected Writings of Christine de Pizan*, trans. Renate Blumenfeld-Kosinski and Kevin Brownlee, ed. Renate Blumenfeld-Kosinski (New York: W. W. Norton, 1997), pp. 371–90.

78. *Trial*, p. 65; "quando ipsa venit versus regem suum, aliqui petebant sibi an in patria sua erat aliquod nemus quod vocaretur gallice *le Bois-chesnu*, quia erant prophetiae dicentes quod circa illud nemus debebat venire quaedam puella que faceret mirabilia" (*Procès*, 1:68).

79. Geoffrey of Monmouth, *History of the Kings of Britain*, trans. Sebastian Evans, rev. Charles W. Dunn (New York: E. P. Dutton, 1958), VII.4, pp. 144–45. Geoffrey of Monmouth, *Historia Regum Britanniae*, ed. Acton Griscom (1929; Geneva: Slatkine Reprints; 1977), pp. 390–91: "Que ut omnes sortes inierit. solo anelitu suo fontes nociuos siccabit. Exin ut sese salubri liquore refecerit. gestabit in dextera sua nemus colidonis. in sinistra uero. murorum lundonie propugnacula. Quacumque incedet passus sulphureos faciet. qui dupplici flamma fumabunt. Fumus ille excitabit rutenos. & cibum sub marinis conficiet."

80. Fraioli, "Literary Image of Joan of Arc," p. 811.

81. *Retrial*, p. 67; *Procès*, 2:444. See Fraioli, "Literary Image of Joan of Arc," p. 825, n. 58.

82. *Retrial,* p. 88; *Procès,* 3:83–84.

83. Geoffrey of Monmouth, *History,* p. 152; *Historia regum Britanniae,* p. 397. According to Pernoud, mounting the back of the "Sagittary" was taken to mean triumphing over the archers of England (*Retrial,* p. 5).

84. Fraioli, "Literary Image of Joan of Arc," p. 820.

85. Ibid., p. 829.

86. André Vauchez, "Joan of Arc and Female Prophecy in the Fourteenth and Fifteenth Centuries," in *The Laity in the Middle Ages: Religious Beliefs and Devotional Practices,* ed. Daniel E. Bornstein, trans. Margery J. Schneider (Notre Dame: University of Notre Dame Press, 1993), p. 261.

87. Anne Llewellyn Barstow, *Joan of Arc: Heretic, Mystic, Shaman,* Studies in Women and Religion 17 (Lewiston, N.Y.: Edwin Mellen, 1986), esp. pp. 45–79.

88. Vauchez, "Female Prophecy," p. 263.

89. On the subject of English deserters in 1430, see Darmesteter, "Joan of Arc in England," pp. 8–9; Waugh, "Joan of Arc in English Sources," p. 388.

90. *Retrial,* pp. 137–38, 143–45; *Procès,* 3:71–72, 106–10.

91. Geoffrey of Monmouth, *History,* p. 145; *Historia regum Britanniae,* p. 391.

92. See Fraioli, "Literary Image of Joan of Arc," p. 819.

93. Geoffrey of Monmouth, *History,* p. 145; "Interficiet eam ceruus .x. ramorum. quorum .iiij. aurea diademata gestabunt. Sex uero residui in cornua bubalorum uertentur. que nefando sonitu tres insulas britannie commouebunt. Excitabitur daneum nemus. & in humanam uocem erumpens clamabit. Accede kambria. & iunge lateri tuo cornubiam. & dic guintonie. . . .'Festinat namque dies qua ciues ob scelera periurii peribunt. . . . Ue genti periure. quia urbs inclita propter eam ruet'" (*Historia regum Britanniae,* p. 391).

94. *Retrial,* p. 216.

95. Darmesteter, "Joan of Arc in England," p. 11.

96. *Trial,* p. 94; *Procès,* 1:115–16.

97. *Retrial,* p. 188; *Procès,* 3:53.

98. *Historical Poems of the XIVth and XVth Centuries,* pp. 215–18.

99. Ibid., p. 225.

100. Mary Giffin, "'O Conqueror of Brutes Albyon,'" in *Studies on Chaucer and His Audience* (Quebec: Les Éditions L'Éclair, 1956), p. 102.

101. Ibid., p. 103.

102. Malory, *Works,* 1:44.

103. Bonnie Wheeler, "Joan of Arc's Sword in the Stone," in *Fresh Verdicts on Joan of Arc,* ed. Bonnie Wheeler and Charles T. Wood (New York: Garland, 1996), pp. xi–xvi.

104. *John Capgrave's Abbreuiacion of Cronicles,* ed. Peter J. Lucas, EETS 285 (Oxford: Oxford University Press, 1983), p. 164.

105. See Elizabeth T. Pochoda, *Arthurian Propaganda: "Le Morte Darthur" as an Historical Ideal of Life* (Chapel Hill: University of North Carolina Press, 1971).

106. Griffith, "Authorship Question," p. 172.

107. *Retrial,* p. 177; *Procès,* 3:162–63.

108. Quoted in Waugh, "Joan of Arc in English Sources," p. 390.

109. See my *Job, Boethius, and Epic Truth* (Ithaca: Cornell University Press, 1994), pp. 172–78.

110. *From Camelot to Joyous Guard,* p. 167; *Mort Artu,* p. 254.

111. On the close identification of penitent saints and romance heroes, see Andrea Hopkins, *Sinful Knights: A Study of Middle English Penitential Romance* (Oxford: Clarendon Press, 1990).

112. See Henry Ansgar Kelly, "Joan of Arc's Last Trial: The Attack of the Devil's Advocates," in Wheeler and Wood, *Fresh Verdicts,* pp. 205–36.

Conclusion

1. David Bevington, *Tudor Drama and Politics: A Critical Approach to Topical Meaning* (Cambridge: Harvard University Press, 1968), pp. 1, 59. For an example, see J. Leslie Hotson, "Colfox vs. Chaunticleer," *PMLA* 39 (1924): 762–81.

2. John M. Bowers, "*Pearl* in Its Royal Setting: Ricardian Poetry Revisited," *SAC* 17 (1995): 114.

3. Judith Ferster, *Fictions of Advice: The Literature and Politics of Counsel in Late Medieval England* (Philadelphia: University of Pennsylvania Press, 1996), p. 10.

4. Bevington, *Tudor Drama and Politics*, p. 3; hereafter cited parenthetically in the text.

5. Bowers, "*Pearl* in Its Royal Setting," p. 114.

6. Ferster, *Fictions of Advice*, p. 9. See Annabel Patterson, *Censorship and Interpretation: The Conditions of Writing and Reading in Early Modern England* (Madison: University of Wisconsin Press, 1984).

7. Ferster, *Fictions of Advice*, p. 9.

8. Ibid., pp. 10, 36. Ferster's use of the term "hidden transcript" is inspired by James C. Scott, *Weapons of the Weak: Everyday Forms of Peasant Resistance* (New Haven: Yale University Press, 1985), and *Domination and the Arts of Resistance: Hidden Transcripts* (New Haven: Yale University Press, 1990).

9. Ferster, *Fictions of Advice*, p. 104.

10. C. S. Lewis, *The Allegory of Love* (Oxford: Oxford University Press, 1936; repr. 1979), p. 321.

11. Thomas H. Bestul, *Texts of the Passion: Latin Devotional Literature and Medieval Society* (Philadelphia: University of Pennsylvania Press, 1996), pp. 19–20.

12. See David Aers and Lynn Staley, *The Powers of the Holy: Religion, Politics, and Gender in Late Medieval English Culture* (University Park: Pennsylvania State University Press, 1996), p. 160.

13. William M. Purcell, *Ars poetriae: Rhetorical and Grammatical Invention at the Margin of Literacy* (Columbia: University of South Carolina Press, 1996), p. 73. Purcell quotes from *An Early Commentary on the Poetria Nova of Geoffrey of Vinsauf,* ed. Marjorie Curry Woods (New York: Garland, 1985), pp. 3, 5.

14. John M. Manly, "Chaucer and the Rhetoricians," *Proceedings of the British Academy* 12 (1926): 95–113; repr. in *Chaucer Criticism,* ed. Richard Schoeck and Jerome Taylor (Notre Dame: University of Notre Dame Press, 1960), 1:268–90.

15. Robert O. Payne, "Chaucer's Realization of Himself as Rhetor," in *Medieval Eloquence: Studies in the Theory and Practice of Medieval Rhetoric,* ed. James J. Murphy (Berkeley: University of California Press, 1978), p. 270.

16. Paul Zumthor, *Toward a Medieval Poetics,* trans. Philip Bennett (Minneapolis: University of Minnesota Press, 1992), p. 31.

17. Robert M. Jordan, *Chaucer's Poetics and the Modern Reader* (Berkeley: University of California Press, 1987), p. 13.

18. Robert O. Payne, *The Key of Remembrance: A Study of Chaucer's Poetics* (New Haven: Yale University Press, 1963; repr. 1964); Mary J. Carruthers, *The Book of Memory: A Study of Memory in Medieval Culture* (Cambridge: Cambridge University Press, 1990); V. A. Kolve, *Chaucer and the Imagery of Narrative: The First Five Canterbury Tales* (Stanford: Stanford University Press, 1984); Martin Camargo, *The Middle English Verse Love Epistle* (Tübingen: Max Niemeyer, 1991).

19. Rita Copeland, *Rhetoric, Hermeneutics, and Translation in the Middle Ages: Academic Traditions and Vernacular Texts* (Cambridge: Cambridge University Press, 1991), p. 174.

Bibliography

Primary Sources

Accessus ad auctores. Ed. R. B. C. Huygens. Leiden: E. J. Brill, 1970.
Adam Davy's Five Dreams about Edward II. Ed. F. J. Furnivall. EETS o.s. 69. London: Trübner, 1878.
Adam of Usk. *The Chronicle of Adam Usk, 1377–1421.* Ed. and trans. C. Given-Wilson. Oxford: Clarendon Press, 1997.
Annales Ricardi Secundi et Henrici Quarti, Regum Angliae (1392–1406). In *Chronica Monasterii S. Albani.* Ed. Henry Thomas Riley. Rolls Series 28, no. 3. London: Longmans, Green, Reader, and Dyer, 1866; repr. 1965.
The Anonimalle Chronicle, 1333–1381. Ed. V. H. Galbraith. Manchester: Manchester University Press, 1970.
Aristotle. *Poetics.* Trans. Ingram Bywater. New York: Modern Library, 1954.
——. *Rhetoric.* Trans. W. Rhys Roberts. New York: Modern Library, 1954.
Augustine, Saint. *City of God against the Pagans.* Trans. William M. Green. Loeb Classical Library. 7 vols. Cambridge: Harvard University Press, 1972.
——. *Confessions.* Trans. William Watts. 2 vols. Loeb Classical Library. Cambridge: Harvard University Press, 1912, repr. 1977.
——. *On Christian Doctrine.* Trans. D. W. Robertson, Jr. New York: Macmillan, 1958.
Averroës. *Middle Commentary on Porphyry's Isagoge.* Trans. Herbert A. Davidson. Cambridge, Mass.: Medieval Academy of America, 1969.
Boccaccio. "Expository Lectures on Dante's *Comedy.*" In *Medieval Literary Theory and Criticism, ca. 1100–ca. 1375: The Commentary Tradition,* 503–19. Ed. A. J. Minnis and A. B. Scott, with the assistance of David Wallace. Rev. ed. Oxford: Clarendon Press, 1988.
——. "Short Treatise in Praise of Dante." In *Medieval Literary Theory and Criticism, ca. 1100–ca. 1375: The Commentary Tradition,* 492–503. Ed. A. J. Minnis and A. B. Scott, with the assistance of David Wallace. Rev. ed. Oxford: Clarendon Press, 1988.
Boethius's "In Ciceronis Topica." Trans. Eleonore Stump. Ithaca: Cornell University Press, 1988.
Brunetto Latini. *The Book of the Treasure (Li Livres dou Tresor).* Trans. Paul Barrette and Spurgeon Baldwin. Garland Library of Medieval Literature, ser. B, vol. 90. New York: Garland, 1993.
——. *Li Livres dou Tresor.* Ed. Francis J. Carmody. Berkeley: University of California Press, 1948.

Capgrave, John. *John Capgrave's Abbreuiacion of Cronicles.* Ed. Peter J. Lucas. EETS 285. Oxford: Oxford University Press, 1983.

Cassiodorus. *Explanation of the Psalms.* Trans. P. G. Walsh. Ancient Christian Writers, no. 51. 3 vols. New York: Paulist Press, 1990.

Chaucer, Geoffrey. *The Riverside Chaucer.* Ed. Larry D. Benson. 3rd ed. Boston: Houghton Mifflin, 1987.

Chaucer: Life-Records. Ed. Martin M. Crow and Clair C. Olson. Austin: University of Texas Press, 1966.

Christine de Pisan. "Le Ditié de Jehanne d'Arc." Ed. and trans. Angus J. Kennedy and Kenneth Varty. *Nottingham Medieval Studies* 18 (1974): 29–55; 19 (1975): 53–76.

Cicero, Marcus Tullius. *De inventione.* Trans. H. M. Hubbell. Loeb Classical Library. Cambridge: Harvard University Press, 1949; repr. 1960.

———. *De optimo genere oratorum.* Trans. H. M. Hubbell. Loeb Classical Library. Cambridge: Harvard University Press, 1949; repr. 1960.

———. *De re publica.* Trans. Clinton Walker Keyes. Loeb Classical Library. Cambridge: Harvard University Press, 1928; repr. 1952.

———. *The Speeches.* Trans. Louis E. Lord. Loeb Classical Library. Cambridge: Harvard University Press, 1937; repr. 1964.

[Cicero, Marcus Tullius]. *Rhetorica ad C. Herennium.* Trans. Harry Caplan. Loeb Classical Library. Cambridge: Harvard University Press, 1954; repr. 1981.

Conrad of Hirsau. "Dialogue on the Authors." In *Medieval Literary Theory and Criticism, ca. 1100–ca. 1375: The Commentary Tradition,* 39–64. Ed. A. J. Minnis and A. B. Scott, with the assistance of David Wallace. Rev. ed. Oxford: Clarendon Press, 1988.

Dante Alighieri. *The Banquet.* Trans. Christopher Ryan. Stanford French and Italian Studies. Saratoga, Calif.: ANMA Libri, 1989.

———. "Epistle to Can Grande della Scala." In *Medieval Literary Theory and Criticism, ca. 1100–ca. 1375: The Commentary Tradition,* 458–69. Ed. A. J. Minnis and A. B. Scott, with the assistance of David Wallace. Rev. ed. Oxford: Clarendon Press, 1988.

The Didascalicon of Hugh of St. Victor. Trans. Jerome Taylor. Records of Western Civilization. New York: Columbia University Press, 1961; repr. 1991.

The Diplomatic Correspondence of Richard II. Ed. Edouard Perroy. Camden 3rd series, vol. 48. London: Royal Historical Society, 1933.

An Early Commentary on the Poetria Nova of Geoffrey of Vinsauf. Ed. Marjorie Curry Woods. New York: Garland, 1985.

The Early English Versions of the "Gesta Romanorum." Ed. Sidney J. H. Herrtage. EETS e.s. 33. London: Oxford University Press, 1879; repr. 1962.

The Early South-English Legendary. Ed. Carl Horstmann. EETS o.s. 87. London: N. Trübner, 1887; repr. 1973.

English Coronation Records. Ed. Leopold G. Wickham Legg. Westminster: Archibald Constable, 1901.

From Camelot to Joyous Guard: The Old French "La Mort le Roi Artu." Trans. J. Neale Carman. Ed. Norris J. Lacy. Lawrence: University Press of Kansas, 1974.

Geoffrey of Monmouth. *Historia regum Britanniae.* Ed. Acton Griscom. 1929; Geneva: Slatkine Reprints, 1977.

———. *History of the Kings of Britain.* Trans. Sebastian Evans. Rev. Charles W. Dunn. New York: E. P. Dutton, 1958.

Geoffrey of Vinsauf. *The "Poetria Nova" and Its Sources in Early Rhetorical Doctrine.* Ed. and trans. Ernest Gallo. The Hague: Mouton, 1971.

Gower, John. *The Complete Works of John Gower.* Ed. G. C. Macaulay. 4 vols. Oxford: Clarendon Press, 1899–1902.

———. *The Major Latin Works of John Gower.* Trans. Eric W. Stockton. Seattle: University of Washington Press, 1962.

——. *Mirour de l'Omme (The Mirror of Mankind)*. Trans. William B. Wilson. Rev. Nancy Wilson Van Baak. East Lansing, Mich.: Colleagues Press, 1992.

Gregory the Great. "Ad Leandrum." In *Moralia in Job*. Ed. Mark Adriaen. CCSL 143. Turnhout: Brepols, 1979.

Hall, Edward. *Chronicle (The Union of the Two Noble and Illustre Famelies of Lancastre and Yorke)*. 1809; New York: AMS Press, 1965.

Higden, Ralph. *Polychronicon, Together with the English Translations of John Trevisa*. Ed. Joseph R. Lumby. Rolls Series 8, no. 41. London, 1882; Wiesbaden: Kraus Reprint, 1964.

Historia Vitae et Regni Ricardi Secundi. Ed. George B. Stow, Jr. Philadelphia: University of Pennsylvania Press, 1977.

Historical Poems of the XIVth and XVth Centuries. Ed. Rossell Hope Robbins. New York: Columbia University Press, 1959.

Honorius of Autun. *Expositio in Cantica Canticorum*. PL 172, c347–496.

Horace. *Art of Poetry*. In *The Works of Horace*. Trans. C. Smart. Rev. Theodore A. Buckley. London: Bell and Daldy, 1870.

"Introductions to the Authors." In *Medieval Literary Theory and Criticism, ca. 1100–ca. 1375: The Commentary Tradition*, 15–36. Ed. A. J. Minnis and A. B. Scott, with the assistance of David Wallace. Rev. ed. Oxford: Clarendon Press, 1988.

Jacobus de Voragine. *The Golden Legend: Readings on the Saints*. Trans. William Granger Ryan. 2 vols. Princeton: Princeton University Press, 1993.

Knighton, Henry. *Chronicon*. Ed. Joseph Rawson Lumby. Rolls Series 92, no. 2. 1895; London: Kraus Reprint, 1965.

Langland, William. *Piers Plowman: The A Version*. Ed. George Kane. London: Athlone Press, 1960.

——. *Piers Plowman: The B Version*. Ed. George Kane and E. Talbot Donaldson. London: Athlone Press, 1975.

——. *The Vision of William Concerning Piers Plowman*. Ed. Walter W. Skeat. EETS o.s. 81. London: N. Trübner, 1884; repr. 1973.

The Life of King Edward. Ed. and trans. Frank Barlow. London: Thomas Nelson, 1984.

Lives of Edward the Confessor. Ed. Henry Richards Luard. Rolls Series, Vol. 3. London: Longman, Brown, Green, Longman, and Roberts, 1853.

Malory, Thomas. *Works*. Ed. Eugène Vinaver. 2nd ed. 3 vols. Oxford: Clarendon Press, 1967; repr. 1973.

Medieval English Political Writings. Ed. James M. Dean. TEAMS Middle English Texts Series. Kalamazoo, Mich.: Medieval Institute Publications, 1996.

La Mort Le Roi Artu. Ed. Jean Frappier. Paris: M. J. Minard, 1964.

Le Morte Arthur: A Romance in Stanzas of Eight Lines. Ed. J. Douglas Bruce. EETS e.s. 88. London: Kegan Paul, Trench, Trübner, 1903.

Ovid. *Ovid's Fasti*. Trans. Sir James G. Frazer. Loeb Classical Library. Cambridge: Harvard University Press, 1951.

The Peasants' Revolt of 1381. Ed. and trans. R. B. Dobson. 2nd ed. London: Macmillan, 1983.

Pius II. *Commentaries, Books VI and IX*. Trans. Florence Alden Gragg, with historical notes by Leona C. Gabel. Smith College Studies in English 35. Northampton, Mass.: Department of History of Smith College, 1951.

Plato. *Gorgias*. Trans. Terence Irwin. Oxford: Clarendon Press, 1979.

——. *The Republic*. Trans. Paul Shorey. 2 vols. Loeb Classical Library. Cambridge: Harvard University Press, 1953.

Pliny. *Natural History*. Ed. and trans. H. Rackham. 10 Vols. Loeb Classical Library. 10 Vols. Cambridge: Harvard University Press, 1940; repr. 1947.

The Plowman's Tale: The ca. 1532 and 1606 Editions of a Spurious Canterbury Tale. Ed. Mary Rhinelander McCarl. New York: Garland, 1997.

Political Poems and Songs Relating to English History. Ed. Thomas Wright. 2 vols. London: Longman, Green, Longman, and Roberts, 1859–61.

Porphyry the Phoenician. *Isagogue.* Trans. Edward W. Warren. Mediaeval Sources in Translation, no. 16. Toronto: Pontifical Institute of Mediaeval Studies, 1975.

Procès de Condamnation et de Réhabilitation de Jeanne D'Arc Dite la Pucelle. Ed. Jules Quicherat. 5 Vols. 1845; New York: Johnson Reprint, 1965.

The Retrial of Joan of Arc. Ed. Régine Pernoud. Trans. J. M. Cohen. London: Methuen, 1955.

Richard the Redeless. In *Mum and Sothsegger.* Ed. Mabel Day and Robert Steele. EETS o.s. 199. London: Humphrey Milford, Oxford University Press, 1936.

Sallust. *Bellum Catilinae.* Chico, Calif.: Scholars Press, 1984.

Shakespeare, William. *The First Part of Henry VI.* Ed. Andrew S. Cairncross. Arden edition. 1962; London: Routledge, 1969; repr. 1995.

The Sibylline Oracles. Trans. Milton S. Terry. 1890; El Paso, Texas: Selene Books, 1991.

Sir Gawain and the Green Knight. Ed. J. R. R. Tolkien and E. V. Gordon. 2nd ed. Ed. Norman Blake. Oxford: Clarendon Press, 1967; repr. 1984.

The South English Legendary. Ed. Charlotte D'Evelyn and Anna J. Mill. 2 vols. EETS 235 and 236. London: Oxford University Press, 1956.

Speculum Christiani: A Middle English Religious Treatise of the Fourteenth Century. Ed. Gustaf Holmstedt. EETS o.s. 182. London: Humphrey Milford, Oxford University Press, 1933.

"The Testimony of William Thorpe." In *Two Wycliffite Texts,* 24–132. Ed. Anne Hudson. EETS o.s. 301. Oxford: Oxford University Press, 1993.

The Trial of Jeanne D'Arc. Trans. W. P. Barrett. London: Routledge, 1931.

Walsingham, Thomas. *Historia Anglicana.* Ed. Henry Thomas Riley. Rolls Series 28, no. 1, pts. 1 and 2. London: Her Majesty's Stationery Office, 1864; repr. 1965.

The Westminster Chronicle, 1381–1394. Ed. and trans. L. C. Hector and Barbara F. Harvey. Oxford: Clarendon Press, 1982.

Secondary Sources

Ackerman, Robert W. "Gawain's Shield: Penitential Doctrine in *Sir Gawain and the Green Knight.*" *Anglia* 76 (1958): 254–65.

Aers, David. *Chaucer, Langland, and the Creative Imagination.* London: Routledge and Kegan Paul, 1980.

Aers, David, and Lynn Staley. *The Powers of the Holy: Religion, Politics, and Gender in Late Medieval English Culture.* University Park: Pennsylvania State University Press, 1966.

Alford, John A., ed. *A Companion to "Piers Plowman."* Berkeley: University of California Press, 1988.

Allen, Judson B. *The Ethical Poetic of the Later Middle Ages: A Decorum of Convenient Distinction.* Toronto: University of Toronto Press, 1982.

———. "Langland's Reading and Writing: *Detractor* and the Pardon Passus." *Speculum* 59 (1984): 342–62.

Althusser, Louis. "Ideology and Ideological State Apparatuses (Notes toward an Investigation)." In *Lenin and Philosophy, and Other Essays,* 127–86. Trans. Ben Brewster. New York: Monthly Review Press, 1971.

Anderson, William. *Green Man.* London: HarperCollins, 1990.

Anglo, Sidney. "The *British History* in Early Tudor Propaganda." *Bulletin of the John Rylands Library* 44 (1961): 17–48.

Arthur, Ross G. *Medieval Sign Theory and "Sir Gawain and the Green Knight."* Toronto: University of Toronto Press, 1987.

Astell, Ann W. *Chaucer and the Universe of Learning*. Ithaca: Cornell University Press, 1996.
——. "Chaucer's 'Literature Group' and the Medieval Causes of Books." *ELH* 59 (1992): 269–87.
——. *Job, Boethius, and Epic Truth*. Ithaca: Cornell University Press, 1994.
——. "The Peasants' Revolt: Cock-crow in Gower and Chaucer." In *Four Last Things: Death, Judgment, Heaven, and Hell in the Middle Ages*, 53–64. Ed. Allen J. Frantzen. Essays in Medieval Studies 10. 1993 Proceedings of the Illinois Medieval Association. Chicago: Loyola University Press, 1994.
——. *The Song of Songs in the Middle Ages*. Ithaca: Cornell University Press, 1990; repr. 1994.
Aston, Margaret. *Lollards and Reformers: Images and Literacy in Late Medieval Religion*. London: Hambledon Press, 1984.
Atton, Henry, and Henry Hurst Holland. *The King's Customs*. 2 vols. London: Frank Cass, 1967.
Aurner, Nellie Slayton, ed. *Malory: An Introduction to the "Morte Darthur."* New York: Thomas Nelson, 1938.
——. "Sir Thomas Malory—Historian?" *PMLA* 48.2 (1933): 362–91.
Baker, Denise N. "From Plowing to Penitence: *Piers Plowman* and Fourteenth-Century Theology." *Speculum* 55.4 (1980): 715–25.
——. "The Pardons of *Piers Plowman*." *Neuphilologische Mitteilungen* 85.4 (1984): 462–72.
Baldwin, Anna P. "The Historical Context." In *A Companion to "Piers Plowman"*, 67–86. Ed. John A. Alford. Berkeley: University of California Press, 1988.
——. *The Theme of Government in "Piers Plowman."* Cambridge: D. S. Brewer, 1981.
Barron, Caroline M. "Richard II: Image and Reality." In Dillian Gordon, *Making and Meaning: The Wilton Diptych*, 13–19. London: National Gallery Publications, 1993.
Barron, W. R. J. *Trawthe and Treason: The Sin of Gawain Reconsidered*. Manchester: Manchester University Press, 1980.
Barstow, Anne Llewellyn. *Joan of Arc: Heretic, Mystic, Shaman*. Studies in Women and Religion 17. Lewiston, N.Y.: Edwin Mellen, 1986.
Bart, Benjamin F., and Robert Francis Cook. *The Legendary Sources of Flaubert's "Saint Julien."* Toronto: University of Toronto Press, 1977.
Bennett, J. A. W. "The Date of the A-Text of *Piers Plowman*." *PMLA* 58.2 (1943): 566–72.
Bennett, Michael J. *Community, Class, and Careerism: Cheshire and Lancashire Society in the Age of Sir Gawain and the Green Knight*. Cambridge Studies in Medieval Life and Thought. 3rd ser., no. 18. Cambridge: Cambridge University Press, 1983.
——. "*Sir Gawain and the Green Knight* and the Literary Achievement of the North-West Midlands." *Journal of Medieval History* 5 (1979): 63–89.
Benson, C. David. "Their Telling Difference: Chaucer the Pilgrim and His Two Contrasting Tales." *Chaucer Review* 18 (1983): 61–76.
Benson, Larry D. *Art and Tradition in "Sir Gawain and the Green Knight."* New Brunswick, N.J.: Rutgers University Press, 1965.
——. *Malory's "Morte Darthur."* Cambridge: Cambridge University Press, 1976.
——. "The Occasion of the Parliament of Fowls." In *The Wisdom of Poetry: Essays in Early English Literature in Honor of Morton W. Bloomfield*, 123–44. Ed. Larry D. Benson and Siegfried Wenzel. Kalamazoo, Mich.: Medieval Institute Publications, 1982.
Bernheimer, Richard. *Wild Men in the Middle Ages: A Study in Art, Sentiment, and Demonology*. New York: Octagon Books, 1970.
Bestul, Thomas H. *Texts of the Passion: Latin Devotional Literature and Medieval Society*. Philadelphia: University of Pennsylvania Press, 1996.
Bevington, David. *Tudor Drama and Politics: A Critical Approach to Topical Meaning*. Cambridge: Harvard University Press, 1968.

Biedler, Peter G. "The Tale of Acteon (*CA*, I, 333–78)." In *John Gower's Literary Trans-formations in the Confessio Amantis*, 7–10. Ed. Peter G. Biedler. Washington, D.C.: University Press of America, 1982.

Blanch, Robert J. "The Game of Invoking Saints in *Sir Gawain and the Green Knight*." *American Benedictine Review* 31 (1980): 237–62.

Bloomfield, Morton W. *Piers Plowman as a Fourteenth-Century Apocalypse*. New Brunswick, N.J.: Rutgers University Press, 1961.

Blythe, Joan Heiges. "Sins of the Tongue and Rhetorical Prudence in 'Piers Plowman.'" In *Literature and Religion in the Later Middle Ages: Philological Studies in Honor of Siegfried Wenzel*, 119–142. Ed. Richard G. Newhauser and John A. Alford. Medieval and Renaissance Texts and Studies 118. Binghamton: State University of New York Press, 1995.

Bowden, Muriel. *A Commentary on the General Prologue to the Canterbury Tales*. New York: Columbia University Press, 1948; repr. 1967.

Bowers, John M. "*Pearl* in Its Royal Setting: Ricardian Poetry Revisited." *SAC* 17 (1995): 111–55.

Brownlee, Kevin. "Structures of Authority in Christine de Pizan's *Ditié de Jehanne d'Arc*." In *The Selected Writings of Christine de Pizan*, 371–90. Trans. Renate Blumenfeld-Kosinski and Kevin Brownlee. Ed. Renate Blumenfeld-Kosinski. New York: W. W. Norton, 1997.

Burlin, Robert B. *Chaucerian Fiction*. Princeton: Princeton University Press, 1977.

Burrow, John A. "The Action of Langland's Second Vision." In *Style and Symbolism in "Piers Plowman": A Modern Critical Anthology*, 174–93. Ed. Robert J. Blanch. Knoxville: University of Tennessee Press, 1968.

——. *A Reading of "Sir Gawain and the Green Knight."* London: Routledge and Kegan Paul, 1965.

——. "The Two Confession Scenes in *Sir Gawain and the Green Knight*." *MP* 57 (1959): 73–79.

Camargo, Martin. *The Middle English Verse Love Epistle*. Tübingen: Max Neimeyer, 1991.

Caplan, Harry. "Memoria: Treasure-House of Eloquence." In *Of Eloquence: Studies in Ancient and Mediaeval Rhetoric*, 196–246. Ed. Anne King and Helen North. Ithaca: Cornell University Press, 1970.

Carlton, Susan Brown. "Poetics." In *Encyclopedia of Rhetoric and Composition: Communication from Ancient Times to the Information Age*, 528–37. Ed. Theresa Enos. New York: Garland, 1996.

Carruthers, Mary J. *The Book of Memory: A Study of Memory in Medieval Culture*. Cambridge: Cambridge University Press, 1990.

——. "*Piers Plowman*: The Tearing of the Pardon." *Philological Quarterly* 49.1 (1970): 8–18.

——. *The Search for St. Truth: A Study of Meaning in "Piers Plowman."* Evanston, Ill.: Northwestern University Press, 1973.

Cherry, John. *Medieval Craftsmen: Goldsmiths*. Toronto: University of Toronto Press, 1992.

Clanchy, M. T. *From Memory to Written Record: England, 1066–1307*. Cambridge: Harvard University Press, 1979.

Coffman, George R. "John Gower, Mentor for Royalty: Richard II." *PMLA* 69.4 (1954): 953–64.

Cohn, Norman. *The Pursuit of the Millenium*. Rev. ed. New York: Oxford University Press, 1970; repr. 1972.

Colaianne, A. J. *Piers Plowman: An Annotated Bibliography of Editions and Criticism, 1550–1977*. New York: Garland, 1978.

Coleman, Joyce. *Public Reading and the Reading Public in Late Medieval England and France*. Cambridge: Cambridge University Press, 1996.

Cooke, W. G. "*Sir Gawain and the Green Knight*: A Restored Dating." *Medium Aevum* 58.1 (1989): 34–48.

Cooper, Helen. *Oxford Guides to Chaucer: The Canterbury Tales.* Oxford: Oxford University Press, 1989.

Copeland, Rita. *Rhetoric, Hermeneutics, and Translation in the Middle Ages: Academic Traditions and Vernacular Texts.* Cambridge: Cambridge University Press, 1991.

Crane, Susan. "The Writing Lesson of 1381." In *Chaucer's England: Literature in Historical Context,* 201–21. Ed. Barbara Hanawalt. Medieval Studies at Minnesota 4. Minneapolis: University of Minnesota Press, 1992.

Cunliffe, Barry. *The City of Bath.* New Haven: Yale University Press, 1987.

Cuttino, G. P., and T. W. Lyman. "Where Is Edward II?" *Speculum* 53 (1978): 522–43.

Darmesteter, James. "Joan of Arc in England." In *English Studies,* 3–71. Trans. Mary Darmesteter. London: T. Fisher Unwin, 1896.

Delany, Sheila. "Substructure and Superstructure: The Politics of Allegory in the Fourteenth Century." *Science and Society* 38 (1974): 257–80.

——. "Undoing Substantial Connection: The Late Medieval Attack on Analogical Thought." *Mosaic* 5.4 (1972): 31–52.

Delhage, Philippe. "*Grammatica* et *ethica* au XIIe siècle." *Recherches de théologie ancienne et médiévale* 25 (1958): 59–110.

Diller, Hans-Jürgen. "'For Engelondes sake': Richard II and Henry of Lancaster as Intended Readers of Gower's *Confessio Amantis.*" In *Functions of Literature: Essays Presented to Erwin Wolff on His Sixtieth Birthday,* 39–53. Ed. Ulrich Broich, Theo Stemmler, and Gerd Stratmann. Tübingen: Max Niemeyer, 1984.

Doyle, A. I., and M. B. Parkes. "The Production of Copies of the *Canterbury Tales* and the *Confessio Amantis* in the Early Fifteenth Century." In *Medieval Scribes, Manuscripts, and Libraries: Essays Presented to N. R. Ker,* 163–210. Ed. M. B. Parkes and Andrew G. Watson. London: Scolar Press, 1978.

Duls, Louisa D. *Richard II in the Early Chronicles.* Studies in English Literature 79. The Hague: Mouton, 1975.

Dunning, T. P. *"Piers Plowman": An Interpretation of the A Text.* 2nd ed. Rev. T. P. Dolan. Oxford: Clarendon Press, 1980.

Eden, Kathy. *Poetic and Legal Fiction in the Aristotelian Tradition.* Princeton: Princeton University Press, 1986.

Elliott, Ralph W. V. "Hills and Valleys in the *Gawain*-Country." *Leeds Studies in English,* n.s. 10 (1978): 18–41.

——. "Woods and Forests in the *Gawain*-Country." *Neuphilologische Mitteilungen* 80 (1979):48–64.

Else, Gerald F. *Aristotle's Poetics: The Argument.* Cambridge: Harvard University Press, 1963.

Enders, Jody. *Rhetoric and the Origins of Medieval Drama.* Ithaca: Cornell University Press, 1992.

Faith, Rosamond. "The 'Great Rumour' of 1377 and Peasant Ideology." In *The English Rising of 1381,* 43–73. Ed. R. H. Hilton and T. H. Aston. Cambridge: Cambridge University Press, 1984.

Fehrenbacher, Richard W. "'A Yeerd Enclosed Al Aboute': Literature and History in the 'Nun's Priest's Tale.'" *Chaucer Review* 29.2 (1994): 134–48.

Ferster, Judith. *Fictions of Advice: The Literature and Politics of Counsel in Late Medieval England.* Philadelphia: University of Pennsylvania Press, 1996.

Fisher, John. *John Gower: Moral Philosopher and Friend of Chaucer.* New York: New York University Press, 1964.

——. "The Revision of the Prologue to the *Legend of Good Women:* An Occasional Explanation." *SAB* 43 (1978): 75–84.

Foley, Michael M. "Gawain's Two Confessions Reconsidered." *Chaucer Review* 9.1 (1974): 73–79.

Fox-Davies, Arthur Charles. *A Complete Guide to Heraldry.* Illustrated by Graham Johnston. Rev. ed. London: T. C. and E. C. Jack, 1929.

Fraioli, Deborah. "The Literary Image of Joan of Arc." *Speculum* 56.4 (1981): 811–30.

Frank, Robert W. "The Pardon Scene in *Piers Plowman.*" *Speculum* 26 (1951): 317–31.

Frese, Dolores W. "The *Nun's Priest's Tale:* Chaucer's Identified Masterpiece?" *Chaucer Review* 16 (1982): 330–43.

Fry, Donald K. "The Ending of the *Monk's Tale.*" *JEGP* 71 (1972): 355–68.

Gallacher, Patrick J. *Love, the Word, and Mercury: A Reading of John Gower's "Confessio Amantis."* Albuquerque: University of New Mexico Press, 1975.

Galloway, Andrew. "Gower in His Most Learned Role and the Peasants' Revolt of 1381." *Mediaevalia* 16 (1993): 329–47.

——. "The Rhetoric of Riddling in Late Medieval England: The 'Oxford' Riddles, the *Secretum Philosophorum,* and the Riddles in *Piers Plowman.*" *Speculum* 70 (1995): 68–105.

Giffin, Mary. "'O Conquerour of Brutes Albyon.'" In *Studies on Chaucer and His Audience,* 89–111. Quebec: Les Éditions L'Éclair, 1956.

Gillespie, Vincent. "The Evolution of the *Speculum Christiani.*" In *Latin and Vernacular: Studies in Late Medieval Texts and Manuscripts,* 39–60. Ed. A. J. Minnis. Cambridge: Boydell and Brewer, 1989.

Gittes, Katharine S. "Ulysses in Gower's *Confessio Amantis:* The Christian Soul as Silent Rhetorician." *ELN* 24.2 (1986): 7–14.

Goodman, Anthony. *John of Gaunt: The Exercise of Princely Power in Fourteenth-Century Europe.* New York: St. Martin's Press, 1992.

——. *The Loyal Conspiracy: The Lords Appellant under Richard II.* London: Routledge and Kegan Paul, 1971.

Gordon, Dillian. *Making and Meaning: The Wilton Diptych.* London: National Gallery Publications, 1993.

Green, Richard Firth. "Jack Philipot, John of Gaunt, and a Poem of 1380." *Speculum* 66 (1991): 330–41.

——. "John Ball's Letters: Literary History and Historical Literature." In *Chaucer's England: Literature in Historical Context,* 176–200. Ed. Barbara Hanawalt. Medieval Studies at Minnesota 4. Minneapolis: University of Minnesota Press, 1992.

Green, Richard H. "Gawain's Shield and the Quest for Perfection." *ELH* 29.2 (1962): 121–39.

——. "Sir Gawain and the *Sacra Cintola.*" *English Studies in Canada* 11 (1985): 1-11.

Griffith, Richard R. "The Authorship Question Reconsidered: A Case for Thomas Malory of Papworth St. Agnes, Cambridgeshire." In *Aspects of Malory,* 159–77. Ed. Toshiyuki Takamiya and Derek Brewer. Cambridge: D. S. Brewer, 1981.

——. "The Political Bias of Malory's *Morte Darthur.*" *Viator* 5 (1974): 365–86.

Griffiths, Lavinia. *Personification in "Piers Plowman."* Piers Plowman Studies 3. Cambridge: D. S. Brewer, 1985.

Hanawalt, Barbara. "The Female Felon in Fourteenth-Century England." *Viator* 5 (1974): 253–68.

Hanawalt, Barbara, ed. *Chaucer's England: Literature in Historical Context:* Medieval Studies at Minnesota, no. 4. Minneapolis: University of Minnesota Press, 1992.

Hanrahan, Michael. "Seduction and Betrayal: Treason in the *Prologue* to the *Legend of Good Women.*" *Chaucer Review* 30.3 (1996): 229–40.

Harris, E. Kay. "Evidence against Lancelot and Guinevere in Malory's *Morte Darthur:* Treason by Imagination." *Exemplaria* 7.1 (1995): 179–208.

Harriss, G. L. *Cardinal Beaufort: A Study of Lancastrian Ascendancy and Decline.* Oxford: Clarendon Press, 1988.

Hassig, Debra. *Medieval Bestiaries: Text, Image, Ideology.* RES Monographs on Anthropology and Aesthetics. Cambridge: Cambridge University Press, 1995.

Hilton, Rodney. *Bondmen Made Free: Medieval Peasant Movements and the English Rising of 1381.* London: Methuen, 1973; repr. 1980.

Hollander, Robert. *Dante's Epistle to Cangrande.* Ann Arbor: University of Michigan Press, 1993.

Hopkins, Andrea. *The Sinful Knights: A Study of Middle English Penitential Romances.* Oxford: Clarendon Press, 1990.

Horgan, A. D. "Gawain's *Pure Pentaungle* and the Virtue of Faith." *Medium Aevum* 56 (1987): 310–16.

Hotson, J. Leslie. "Colfox vs. Chaunticleer." *PMLA* 39 (1924): 762–81.

Howard, Donald R. "Structure and Symmetry in *Sir Gawain.*" *Speculum* 39 (1964): 425–33.

Hudson, Anne. "Epilogue: The Legacy of *Piers Plowman.*" In *A Companion to "Piers Plowman,"* 251–66. Ed. John A. Alford. Berkeley: University of California Press, 1988.

——. "'Laicus litteratus': The Paradox of Lollardy." In *Heresy and Literacy, 1000–1530,* 222–36. Ed. Peter Biller and Anne Hudson. Cambridge Studies in Medieval Literature 23. Cambridge: Cambridge University Press, 1994.

Hulbert, J. R. "A Hypothesis Concerning the Alliterative Revival." *MP* 28 (1931): 405–22.

Huppé, Bernard F. "The A-Text of *Piers Plowman* and the Norman Wars." *PMLA* 54.1 (1939): 37–64.

Hutchinson, Lester. *The Conspiracy of Catiline.* New York: Barnes and Noble, 1967.

Johnson, Lynn Staley. "Inverse Counsel: Contexts for the *Melibee.*" *SP* 87 (1990): 137–55.

Jordan, Mark. *Ordering Wisdom: The Hierarchy of Philosophical Discourses in Aquinas.* Notre Dame: University of Notre Dame Press, 1986.

Jordan, Robert M. *Chaucer's Poetics and the Modern Reader.* Berkeley: University of California Press, 1987.

Justice, Steven. *Writing and Rebellion: England in 1381.* New Historicism Series 27. Berkeley: University of California Press, 1994.

Kane, George B. "Some Fourteenth-Century 'Political' Poems." In *Medieval English Religious and Ethical Literature: Essays in Honor of G. H. Russell,* 82–91. Ed. Gregory Kratzmann and James Simpson. Cambridge: D. S. Brewer, 1986.

Kaske, Robert E. "Gawain's Green Chapel and the Cave at Wetton Mill." In *Medieval Literature and Folklore Studies: Essays in Honor of Francis Lee Utley,* 111–21. Ed. Jerome Mandel and Bruce A. Rosenberg. New Brunswick, N.J.: Rutgers University Press, 1970.

Kellogg, Eleanor H. "Bishop Brunton and the Fable of the Rats." *PMLA* 50.1 (1935): 57–69.

Kelly, Douglas. "The Scope of the Treatment of Composition in the Twelfth and Thirteenth-Century Arts of Poetry." *Speculum* 41 (1966): 261–78.

——. "Theory of Composition in Medieval Narrative Poetry and Geoffrey of Vinsauf's *Poetria Nova.*" *Mediaeval Studies* 31 (1969): 117–48.

——. "Topical Invention in Medieval French Literature." In *Medieval Eloquence: Studies in the Theory and Practice of Medieval Rhetoric,* 231–51. Ed. James J. Murphy. Berkeley: University of California Press, 1978.

Kelly, Henry Ansgar. "Joan of Arc's Last Trial: The Attack of the Devil's Advocates." In *Fresh Verdicts on Joan of Arc,* 205–36. Ed. Bonnie Wheeler an Charles T. Wood. New York: Garland, 1996.

Kennedy, Beverly. *Knighthood in the Morte Darthur.* Arthurian Studies II. Cambridge: D. S. Brewer, 1985.

Kennedy, Edward D. "Malory and His English Sources." In *Aspects of Malory,* 27–55. Ed. Toshiyuki Takamiya and Derek Brewer. Cambridge: D. S. Brewer, 1981.

——. "Malory and the Marriage of Edward IV." *Texas Studies in Literature and Language* 12 (1970): 155–62.

Kennedy, George A. *Classical Rhetoric and Its Christian and Secular Traditions from Ancient to Modern Times.* Chapel Hill: University of North Carolina Press, 1980.

Kermode, Frank. *The Genesis of Secrecy: On the Interpretation of Narrative.* Cambridge: Harvard University Press, 1979.

Kinney, Thomas L. "The Temper of Fourteenth-Century English Verse of Complaint." *Annuale Mediaevale* 7 (1966): 74–89.

Kirk, Elizabeth D. "Langland's Plowman and the Recreation of Fourteenth-Century Religious Metaphor." *YLS* 2 (1988): 1–21.

Kolve, V. A. *Chaucer and the Imagery of Narrative: The First Five Canterbury Tales.* Stanford: Stanford University Press, 1984.

Lander, J. R. *Conflict and Stability in Fifteenth-Century England.* London: Hutchinson University Library, 1969.

Lawlor, John. "*Piers Plowman:* The Pardon Reconsidered." *Modern Language Notes* 45.4 (1950): 449–58.

Lawton, David. "Dullness and the Fifteenth Century." *ELH* 54.4 (1978): 761–800.

Lea, Henry Charles. *A History of Auricular Confession and Indulgences in the Latin Church.* 3 vols. New York: Greenwood, 1968.

Lee, Patricia-Ann. "Reflections of Power: Margaret of Anjou and the Dark Side of Queenship." *Renaissance Quarterly* 39 (1986): 183–217.

Leff, Michael C. "The Topics of Argumentative Invention in Latin Rhetorical Theory from Cicero to Boethius." *Rhetorica* 1.1 (1983): 23–44.

Lerer, Seth. *Chaucer and His Readers: Imagining the Author in Late Medieval England.* Princeton: Princeton University Press, 1993.

Lewis, C. S. *The Allegory of Love.* Oxford: Oxford University Press, 1936; repr. 1971.

Lloyd, T. H. *The English Wool Trade in the Middle Ages.* Cambridge: Cambridge University Press, 1977.

Lumiansky, R. M. "Sir Thomas Malory's *Le Morte Darthur,* 1947–1987: Author, Title, Text," *Speculum* 62.4 (1987): 878–97.

Manly, John Matthews. *The Canterbury Tales.* New York: Henry Holt, 1928; repr. 1930.

—— "Chaucer and the Rhetoricians." *Proceedings of the British Academy* 12 (1926): 95–113; repr. in *Chaucer Criticism,* 1:268–90. Ed. Richard Schoeck and Jerome Taylor. Notre Dame: University of Notre Dame Press, 1960.

——. *Some New Light on Chaucer: Lectures Delivered at the Lowell Institute.* 1926; Gloucester, Mass.: Peter Smith, 1959.

Marcus, Leah S. *Puzzling Shakespeare: Local Reading and Its Discontents.* Berkeley: University of California Press, 1988.

Margolis, Nadia. *Joan of Arc in History, Literature, and Film: A Select, Annotated Bibliography.* New York: Garland, 1990.

McColly, William. "*Sir Gawain and the Green Knight* as a Romance à Clef." *Chaucer Review* 23.1 (1988): 78–92.

McIntosh, Angus. "A New Approach to Middle English Dialectology." *English Studies* 44 (1963): 1–11.

McIntosh, Angus, M. L. Samuels, and Michael Benskin. *A Linguistic Atlas of Late Medieval English.* Aberdeen: Aberdeen University Press, 1986.

McKenna, J. W. "Popular Canonization as Political Propaganda: The Cult of Archbishop Scrope." *Speculum* 45 (1970): 608–23.

McKeon, Richard. "Poetry and Philosophy in the Twelfth Century: The Renaissance of Rhetoric." *MP* 43.4 (1946): 217–34; repr. in *Rhetoric: Essays in Invention and Discovery,* 167–93. Ed. Mark Backman. Woodbridge, Conn.: Oxbow Press, 1987.

——. "Rhetoric in the Middle Ages." *Speculum* 17.1 (1942): 1-32; repr. in *Rhetoric: Essays in Invention and Discovery,* 121–66. Ed. Mark Backman. Woodbridge, Conn.: Oxbow Press, 1987.

McLeod, Susan H. "The Tearing of the Pardon in *Piers Plowman.*" *PQ* 56.1 (1977): 14–26.

Middleton, Anne. "The Audience and Public of *Piers Plowman.*" In *Middle English Allit-*

erative Poetry and Its Literary Background: Seven Essays, 101–23. Ed. David Lawton. Cambridge: D. S. Brewer, 1982.

——. "The Idea of Public Poetry in the Reign of Richard II." *Speculum* 53 (1978): 94–114.

Minnis, Alastair J. *Medieval Theory of Authorship: Scholastic Literary Attitudes in the Later Middle Ages.* 2nd ed. Philadelphia: University of Pennsylvania Press, 1988.

Minnis, Alastair J., and A. B. Scott, eds., with the assistance of David Wallace. *Medieval Literary Theory and Criticism, ca. 1100–ca. 1375: The Commentary Tradition.* Rev. ed. Oxford: Clarendon Press, 1988.

Mitchell, A. G. "Lady Meed and the Art of *Piers Plowman.*" In *Style and Symbolism in "Piers Plowman": A Modern Critical Anthology,* 174–93. Ed. Robert J. Blanch. Knoxville: University of Tennessee Press, 1968.

Morgan, Gerald. "The Action of the Hunting and Bedroom Scenes in *Sir Gawain and the Green Knight.*" *Medium Aevum* 56 (1987): 200–216.

——. "The Significance of the Pentangle Symbolism in *Sir Gawain and the Green Knight.*" *MLR* 74 (1979): 769–90.

Murphy, James J. "John Gower's *Confessio Amantis* and the First Discussion of Rhetoric in the English Language." *PQ* 41 (1962): 401–11.

——. *Rhetoric in the Middle Ages: A History of Rhetorical Theory from St. Augustine to the Renaissance.* Berkeley: University of California Press, 1974; rcpr. 1990.

Murphy, James J., ed. *Medieval Eloquence: Studies in the Theory and Practice of Medieval Rhetoric.* Berkeley: University of California Press, 1978.

Murrin, Michael. *The Veil of Allegory: Some Notes toward a Theory of Allegorical Rhetoric in the English Renaissance.* Chicago: University of Chicago Press, 1969.

Nicholas, David. *The Metamorphosis of a Medieval City: Ghent in the Age of the Arteveldes, 1302–1390.* Lincoln: University of Nebraska Press, 1987.

Nicholson, Peter. "The Dedications of Gower's *Confessio Amantis.*" *Mediaevalia* 10 (1984): 159–80.

Norton-Smith, John. *Geoffrey Chaucer.* London: Routledge and Kegan Paul, 1974.

Odahl, Charles M. *The Catilinarian Conspiracy.* New Haven, Conn.: College and University Press, 1971.

Oman, Sir Charles. *The Great Revolt of 1381.* Ed. E. B. Fryde. 2nd ed. Oxford: Clarendon Press, 1906; rcpr. 1969.

——. *Political History of England.* Ed. William Hunt and Reginald L. Poole. 12 vols. Vol. 4. London: Longmans, Green, and Co., 1930.

Ong, Walter J. "The Province of Rhetoric and Poetic." In *The Province of Rhetoric,* 48–56. Ed. Joseph Schwartz and John A. Rycenga. New York: Ronald Press, 1965.

Oram, William. "Elizabethan Fact and Spenserian Fiction." *Spenser Studies* 4 (1983): 33–47.

Orsten, Elisabeth M. "The Ambiguities in Langland's Rat Parliament." *Medieval Studies* 23 (1961): 216–39.

Owst, G. R. *Literature and Pulpit in Medieval England.* New York: Barnes and Noble, 1966.

Patterson, Annabel. *Censorship and Interpretation: The Conditions of Writing and Reading in Early Modern England.* Madison: University of Wisconsin Press, 1984.

Patterson, Lee W. *Chaucer and the Subject of History.* Madison: University of Wisconsin Press, 1991.

——. "'What Man Artow?': Authorial Self-Definition in *The Tale of Sir Thopas* and *The Tale of Melibee.*" *SAC* 11 (1989): 117–75.

Paulus, Nikolaus. *Indulgences as a Social Factor in the Middle Ages.* Trans. J. Elliot Ross. New York: Devin-Adair, 1922.

Payne, Robert O. "Chaucer's Realization of Himself as Rhetor." In *Medieval Eloquence: Studies in the Theory and Practice of Medieval Rhetoric,* 270–87. Ed. James J. Murphy. Berkeley: University of California Press, 1978.

――. *The Key of Remembrance: A Study of Chaucer's Poetics.* New Haven: Yale University Press, 1963; repr. 1964.

Pearsall, Derek. *An Annotated Critical Bibliography of Langland.* Ann Arbor: University of Michigan Press, 1990.

Peck, Russell A. *Kingship and Common Profit in Gower's "Confessio Amantis."* Carbondale: Southern Illinois University Press, 1978.

――. "Social Conscience and the Poets." In *Social Unrest in the Late Middle Ages,* 113–48. Ed. Francis X. Newman. Medieval and Renaissance Texts and Studies 39. Binghamton: State University of New York Press, 1986.

Peters, Edward. *Inquisition.* London: Collier Macmillan, 1988.

Petersen, Kate Oelzner. *On the Sources of the Nonne Preste Tale.* 1898; New York: Haskell, 1966.

Pochoda, Elizabeth T. *Arthurian Propaganda: "Le Morte Darthur" as an Historical Ideal of Life.* Chapel Hill: University of North Carolina Press, 1971.

Pounds, N. J. G. *The Medieval Castle in England and Wales: A Social and Political History.* Cambridge: Cambridge University Press, 1990.

Pratt, Robert A. "Some Latin Sources of the Nonnes Preest on Dreams." *Speculum* 52.3 (1977): 538–70.

Purcell, William. M. *Ars poetriae: Rhetorical and Grammatical Invention at the Margins of Literacy.* Columbia: University of South Carolina Press, 1996.

Quain, Edwin A. "The Medieval *Accessus ad Auctores.*" *Traditio* 3 (1945): 215–64.

Quilligan, Maureen. *The Language of Allegory: Defining the Genre.* Ithaca: Cornell University Press, 1979.

Rackin, Phyllis. *Stages of History: Shakespeare's English Chronicles.* Ithaca: Cornell University Press, 1990.

Reinhard, J. R. "Burning at the Stake in Medieval Law and Literature." *Speculum* 16 (1941): 186–209.

"Rhetoric and Poetry." In *The New Princeton Encyclopedia of Poetry and Poetics,* 1045–52. Ed. Alex Preminger and T. V. F. Brogan. Princeton: Princeton University Press, 1993.

Robbins, Rossell Hope. "Dissent in Middle English Literature: The Spirit of (Thirteen) Seventy-six." *Medievalia et Humanistica,* n.s. 9 (1979): 25–53.

Robertson, D. W., Jr. "'And For My Land Thus Hastow Mordred Me?': Land Tenure, the Cloth Industry, and the Wife of Bath." *Chaucer Review* 14 (1980): 403–20.

Ross, Charles. *Edward IV.* Berkeley: University of California Press, 1974.

Rowe, Donald W. *Through Nature to Eternity: Chaucer's "Legend of Good Women."* Lincoln: University of Nebraska Press, 1988.

Russell, Josiah C. "The Canonization of Opposition to the King in Angevin England." In *Haskins Anniversary Essay in Mediaeval History,* 279–90. Ed. Charles H. Taylor and John L. LaMonte. Boston: Houghton Mifflin, 1929.

Saul, Nigel. *Richard II.* New Haven: Yale University Press, 1997.

Savage, Henry Lyttleton. *The Gawain-Poet: Studies in His Personality and Background.* Chapel Hill: University of North Carolina Press, 1956.

Scanlon, Larry. *Narrative, Authority, and Power: The Medieval Exemplum and the Chaucerian Tradition.* Cambridge: Cambridge University Press, 1994.

Scattergood, V. J. "Political Context, Date, and Composition of 'The Sayings of the Four Philosophers.'" *Medium Aevum* 37 (1968): 157–65.

――. *Politics and Poetry in the Fifteenth Century.* London: Blandford, 1971.

Schmitz, Götz. *The Middel Weie: Stil- und Aufbauformen in John Gower's "Confessio Amantis."* Studien zur englischen Literatur 11. Bonn: Bouvier, 1974.

Schrader, Richard J. "Chauntecleer, the Mermaid, and Daun Burnel." *Chaucer Review* 4.4 (1970): 284–90.

Scott, James C. *Domination and the Arts of Resistance: Hidden Transcripts.* New Haven: Yale University Press, 1990.

———. *Weapons of the Weak: Everyday Forms of Peasant Resistance.* New Haven: Yale University Press, 1985.

Selzner, John L. "Topical Allegory in *Piers Plowman:* Lady Meed's B Text Debate with Conscience." *PQ* 59.3 (1980): 257–67.

Shaw, Judith D. "*Lust* and *Lore* in Gower and Chaucer." *Chaucer Review* 19.2 (1984): 110–22.

Shoaf, R. A. "*The Franklin's Tale:* Chaucer and Medusa." *Chaucer Review* 21 (1986): 274–90.

Simpson, James. "The Constraints of Satire in 'Piers Plowman' and 'Mum and the Soth-segger.'" In *Langland, the Mystics, and the Medieval English Religious Tradition: Essays in Honour of S. S. Hussey,* 11–30. Ed. Helen Phillips. Cambridge: D. S. Brewer, 1990.

Spearing, A. C. *The Gawain-Poet.* Cambridge: Cambridge University Press, 1970.

Specht, Henrik. "'Ethopoeia' or Impersonation: A Neglected Species of Medieval Characterization." *Chaucer Review* 21.1 (1986): 1–15.

Spitzer, Adele. "Self-Reference in the *Gorgias.*" *Philosophy and Rhetoric* 8 (1975): 1–22.

Stanley, Arthur Penrhyn. *Historical Memorials of Westminster Abbey.* 8th ed. London: John Murray, 1896.

Steele, Anthony. *Richard II.* Cambridge: Cambridge University Press, 1962.

Stillwell, Gardiner. "The Political Meaning of Chaucer's Tale of Melibee." *Speculum* 19 (1944): 433–44.

Strite, Sheri Ann. "*Sir Gawain and the Green Knight:* To Behead or Not to Behead—That *Is* a Question." *PQ* 70.1 (1991): 1–12.

Strohm, Paul. "Form and Social Statement in *Confessio Amantis* and *The Canterbury Tales.*" *SAC* 1 (1979): 17–40.

———. *Hochon's Arrow: The Social Imagination of Fourteenth-Century Texts.* Princeton: Princeton University Press, 1992.

———. *Social Chaucer.* Cambridge: Harvard University Press, 1989.

Tamplin, Ronald. "The Saints in *Sir Gawain and the Green Knight.*" *Speculum* 44.3 (1969): 403–20.

Tanner, Lawrence E. "Some Representations of St. Edward the Confessor in Westminster Abbey and Elsewhere." *Journal of the British Archaeological Association,* 3rd ser., 15 (1952): 1–12.

Travis, Peter W. "Chaucer's Trivial Fox Chase and the Peasants' Revolt of 1381." *Journal of Medieval and Renaissance Studies* 18 (1988): 195–220.

Tristram, E. W. *English Wall Painting of the Fourteenth Century.* London: Routledge and Kegan Paul, 1955.

Tuck, Anthony. *Richard II and the English Nobility.* London: Edward Arnold, 1973.

Vance, Eugene. *From Topic to Tale: Logic and Narrativity in the Middle Ages.* Theory and History of Literature 47. Minneapolis: University of Minnesota Press, 1987.

Vauchez, André. "Joan of Arc and Female Prophecy in the Fourteenth and Fifteenth Centuries." In *The Laity in the Middle Ages: Religious Beliefs and Devotional Practices.* Ed. Daniel E. Bornstein. Trans. Marjery J. Schneider. Notre Dame: University of Notre Dame Press, 1993.

Vinaver, Eugène. *The Rise of Romance.* New York: Oxford University Press, 1971.

Wallace, David. *Chaucerian Polity: Absolutist Lineages and Associational Forms in England and Italy.* Stanford: Stanford University Press, 1997.

Watson, Charles S. "The Relationship of the 'Monk's Tale' and 'The Nun's Priest's Tale.'" *Studies in Short Fiction* 1 (1964): 277–88.

Waugh, W. T. "Joan of Arc in English Sources of the Fifteenth Century." In *Historical Essays in Honour of James Tait,* 387–98. Ed. J. G. Edwards, V. H. Galbraith, and E. F. Jacob. Manchester: Butler and Tanner, 1933.

Weiss, Victoria. "Gawain's First Failure: The Beheading Game in *Sir Gawain and the Green Knight.*" *Chaucer Review* 10 (1976): 361–66.

Wenzel, Siegfried. "Medieval Sermons." In *A Companion to "Piers Plowman,"* 155–72. Ed. John A. Alford. Berkeley: University of California Press, 1988.

——. *Preachers, Poets, and the Early English Lyric.* Princeton: Princeton University Press, 1986.

West, G. D. *An Index of Proper Names in French Arthurian Prose Romances.* Toronto: University of Toronto Press, 1978.

Wheeler, Bonnie. "Joan of Arc's Sword in the Stone." In *Fresh Verdicts on Joan of Arc,* xi–xvi. Ed. Bonnie Wheeler and Charles T. Wood. New York: Garland, 1996.

Whitman, Jon. *Allegory: The Dynamics of an Ancient and Medieval Technique.* Cambridge, Mass.: Harvard University Press, 1987.

Wood, Charles. *Joan of Arc and Richard III: Sex, Saints, and Government in the Middle Ages.* New York: Oxford University Press, 1988.

Woods, Marjorie Curry. "In a Nutshell: *Verba* and *Sententia* and Matter and Form in Medieval Composition Theory." In *The Uses of Manuscripts in Literary Studies: Essays in Memory of Judson Boyce Allen,* 19–39. Ed. Charlotte Cook Morse, Penelope Reed Doob, and Marjorie Curry Woods. Studies in Medieval Culture 31. Kalamazoo, Mich.: Medieval Institute Publications, 1992.

Woodward, Kenneth. *Making Saints.* New York: Simon and Schuster, 1990.

Woolf, Rosemary. "The Tearing of the Pardon." In *"Piers Plowman": Critical Approaches,* 50–75. Ed. S. S. Hussey. London: Methuen, 1969.

Yeager, R. F. *John Gower's Poetic: The Search for a New Arion.* Cambridge: D. S. Brewer, 1990.

York, Ernest C. "Legal Punishment in Malory's *Le Morte Darthur.*" *ELN* 11 (1973): 14–21.

Yunck, John A. *The Lineage of Lady Meed: The Development of Mediaeval Venality Satire.* Notre Dame: University of Notre Dame Press, 1963.

Zumthor, Paul. *Toward a Medieval Poetics.* Trans. Philip Bennett. Minneapolis: University of Minnesota Press, 1992.

Index